TEAM CANADA TRADE MISSIONS (1994-2005):
A Popular Prime Minister's Passion Project

Everett Nana Kwame Ofori

Master of Business Administration (MBA)

(Heriot-Watt University, Scotland, UK)

Master of Science, Finance (MSF)

(College For Financial Planning, Colorado, USA)

Post-Graduate Diploma in Business Research

(Southern Cross University, NSW, Australia)

Acknowledgments

Thanks to Associate Professor Stewart Hase of the then Graduate College of Management, Southern Cross University, who reviewed my initial efforts.

Dr. Wayne Dreyer, of Manukau Institute of Technology, New Zealand, also did much to point me in the right direction. Many thanks.

Friends Emory Georges, Dr. Tomoya Oe, Mr. Takeshi Futami, Mr. David Akagi, and Dr. Francis Adu-Febiri gave me much needed encouragement.

Many thanks to Dr. Diane Roy of the Southern Cross University School of Business and Tourism, for giving me the full benefit of her insights.

Associate Professor Michael Charles turned my attention to my numerous blind spots and helped me to see with greater clarity what it takes to be a scholar.

Associate Professor Michelle Wallace guided me through what seemed like very treacherous research terrain in my choice of subject and methodology. I am most grateful for Associate Professor Wallace's efforts in helping me think along fresh new lines.

© Everett Ofori, 2022

All rights reserved. No part of this publication may be reproduced, stored in a retrieval system, or transmitted, in any form or by any means, without the prior permission in writing of Everett Ofori (everettoforijapan@gmail.com), or as expressly permitted by law, or under terms agreed with the appropriate reprographics rights organization.

ISBN: 1-894221-24-9 ISBN 13: 978-1-894221-24-5

OTHER BOOKS BY EVERETT OFORI

1. Succeeding From the Margins of Canadian Society: A Strategic Resource for New Immigrants, Refugees and International Students. Written by Dr. Francis Adu-Febiri and Everett Ofori, 2009 – ISBN 978-1-926585-27-7
2. Read Assure: Guaranteed Formula for Reading Success with Phonics, 2010 – ISBN 978-1894221054
3. Guaranteed Formula for Public Speaking Success, 2011 – ISBN 978-1894221078
4. 3,570 Real-world English Phrases for Speaking & Writing Practice (Vol. 1), 2011 – ISBN 978-1894221125
5. 3,570 Real-world English Phrases for Speaking & Writing Practice (Vol. 2), 2011 – ISBN 978-1894221139
6. Prepare for Greatness: How to Make Your Success Inevitable, 2013 – ISBN 13: 978-0921143000
7. The Changing Japanese Woman: From *Yamatonadeshiko* to *YamatonadeGucci*, 2013 – ISBN 13: 978-1894221047
8. The Global Student's Companion: 10,001 Timeless Themes & Topics for Dialogue, Discussion & Debate Practice. Compiled by Everett Ofori, 2015 – ISBN 13: 978-1-894221-02-3
9. Guaranteed Formula for Effective Business Writing, 2017 – ISBN 978-1894221108
10. English Language Mastermind: From Confident Communication to Higher Test Scores, 2018 – ISBN 978-1894221160
11. Guaranteed Formula for Writing Success, 2019 – ISBN 978-1-926918-22-8 12.
12. Guaranteed Formula for Writing Effective Business Emails & Letters, 2019 – ISBN 978-1894221061
13. Guaranteed Formula for Effective Meeting Facilitation and Participation, 2020 – ISBN 978-1894221085
14. Success Tips from Successful African Americans, ISBN 13: 978-1-894221-14-6

Abstract

This book takes a discourse and thematic analysis approach to examine the Team Canada Trade Missions, which were a prominent feature under the leadership of Prime Minister Jean Chrétien and the Liberal Party of Canada (1993-2006). Between 1994 and 2005, Team Canada Trade Missions, were organised under the auspices of the Department of Foreign Affairs and International Trade (DFAIT), which was a merger that signalled the 'growing importance of trade on the diplomatic agenda' (Pigman 2010, p. 44). The program involved sending businesspeople to selected countries in search of new business opportunities or to strengthen existing ties. A retrospective study such as this not only helps to preserve key aspects of events in national and business life, but also offers the opportunity for future business and government leaders to learn from past successes and failures.

This research contributes to the literature on trade missions. The discourse and thematic analyses approaches add methodological diversity to the existing crop of research studies in this field. From reports in the media and the Canadian government's pronouncements, the TCTM appeared to be highly successful. However, discordant voices emerged over time, which challenged the claims of government and participants of the trade missions regarding the contribution of the program to the Canadian economy. The study explored the wide differences in perceptions of the value of the TCTM between the government and business participants, and that diverse critics. The Scheurich (1997) and O'Connor (2005) discourse analysis framework, based on Foucault's (1972) *Archaeology of Knowledge*, served as the basis for analysis of two Canadian government policy documents. Thematic analysis (Castleberry & Nolen 2018) was used to explore documents relating to TCTM, including newspaper articles, websites, broadcasts, and critical commentaries, to identify major themes, similarities, and divergences.

A purposive sample of an expert panel of Canadian academics in the fields of international trade, international management, policy, and international marketing, were asked to contribute their perspectives on the subject through email interviews. The insights from the panel supplemented and complemented the information gathered on the trade missions from a variety of published sources. The criteria for success of the TCTM's highlighted by the government and the business community were broad, encompassing both financial and non-financial elements, including preparation, publicity, profit, partnership, and prestige. By contrast, those of the critics, including ordinary citizens, political opposition leaders, think tanks, anti-poverty activists and academics, focused on the fundamental question of whether the government should be involved in the trade missions in the first place, and why the government was willing to jettison Canada's cherished values such as the protection of workers' rights, anti-child labour and human rights for the sake of profit. Further, some critics' comments focused on the narrow criterion of whether there was a direct financial contribution to the economy as a result of the trade missions. The government found no common ground with those who claimed that the trade missions were of no use. On the importance of considering human rights in Canada's relationship with its partners, the government eventually came to agree. The power in the critics' discourse was experienced by the Liberal government because they were repeatedly forced to respond to the criticisms. However, there is no indication of a linear relationship between the criticisms levelled at the government and subsequent changes that have been observed in how contemporary Canadian trade missions are run.

Keywords

Discourse analysis; Globalisation; Internationalisation; Marketing Communications; Michel Foucault; Policy analysis; Policy archaeology; Public relations; Trade missions

Contents

Acknowledgments ii

Abstract v

Keywords vi

Contents vii

List of Tables xi

List of Figures xi

Key Dates—Canadian Political Leadership xii

List of Abbreviations xii

Chapter 1: Introduction to the Study 13

    1.1 Purpose of the Research 13

    1.2 Background to the Research 15

    1.3 Research Objective and Questions 20

    1.4 Research Working Model 21

    1.5 Justification for the Research 23

    1.6 Research Gap 24

    1.7 Contribution of the Research 26

    1.8 Methodology 27

    1.9 Definitions 28

    1.10 Delimitations, Scope and Key Assumptions 30

    1.11 Outline of the Thesis 30

    1.12 Concluding Remarks 31

Chapter 2: Literature Review 32

    A. Globalisation and Internationalisation 32

2.1 Introduction 32

2.2 Globalisation 36

2.3 The Reality of Globalisation 38

2.4 The Drive Towards Internationalisation 39

2.5 Government/Private Export Promotion Programmes 42

2.6 Initial Internationalisation Efforts 45

2.7 Challenges of International Marketing 47

2.8 Conditions for Success in International Markets 51

2.9 Trade Fairs 72

B. Trade Missions 73

2.10 Trade Missions 73

2.11 Trade Mission History in Canada Prior to Team Canada Trade Missions CTM operated under the ambit of the Criteria for TCTM 80

2.12 Criteria for TCTM 82

2.13 Selection Paradigm 82

2.14 Before a Trade Mission Takes Place 82

2.15 The Canadian Government's Marketing Communications Efforts 84

2.16 Government Targets for Marketing Communications 84

2.17 Message Strategy 87

2.18 Hierarchy of Effects 88

2.19 Evaluation of Integrated Marketing Communications 88

2.20 Canada: A Nation's Image 90

2.21 Summary 93

C. Conclusion 94

2.22 The Gap: Discourse Analysis and Thematic Analysis 94

Chapter 3: Methodology 95

3.1 Introduction 95

3.2 Justification for the Paradigm and Methodologies *97*

3.3 Discourse Analysis: Reaching Back to Foucault *99*

    3.3.1 Power/Knowledge 103

    3.3.2 Governmentality 103

3.4 Policy Archaeology: From Foucault to Scheurich–O'Connor *104*

3.5 Thematic Analysis *107*

3.6 Research Procedures *108*

3.7 Method I: Setting the Context—Using Scheurich–O'Connor Framework *110*

3.8 Method II: Thematic Analysis *115*

    3.8.1 Data Collection 115

    3.8.2 Thematic Analysis: Process 116

3.9 Method III: Email Survey of Expert Panel *117*

3.10 Ethical Considerations *118*

3.11 Conclusion *119*

Chapter 4: Data Analysis **120**

4.1 Introduction *120*

4.2 Part I: Analysis of Policy Documents using Scheurich-O'Connor Framework *120*

    4.2.1 Arena I: Problematising Globalisation 120

    4.2.2 Arena II: Network of Social Regularities 131

    4.2.3 Arena III: Assumptions—Range of Policy Solutions 137

    4.2.4 Arena IV: The Social Functions of Policy Studies 145

    4.2.5 Concluding Remarks 147

4.3 Part II: Thematic Analysis *148*

    4.3.1 Part IIa: Analysis of the Canadian Government's Marketing Communications and Other Prevailing Discourses Surrounding the TCTMs 148

    4.3.2 Part IIb: Analysis of Critical Discourses Against the TCTM 164

4.4 Breakdown of Critical Voices *171*

4.5 PROPONENTS: TCTM Participants, Government, Media *171*

4.6 CRITICS: Media, Think Tanks, NPOs/Activists, Citizens and Political Opposition *172*

    4.6.1 Media 172

  4.6.2 Think Tanks 173

  4.6.3 NPOs/Activists 174

  4.6.4 Citizens 174

  4.6.5 Political Opposition 175

  4.6.6 Others: Business Groups/Academics/US Ambassador 175

 4.7 Email Survey of Expert Panel 175

Chapter 5: Findings 179

 5.1 Introduction 179

 5.2 Research Overview 179

 5.3 Qualitative Research: In Search of Meaning 179

 5.4 Main Research Findings: Power Relations and Discourses Surrounding the TCTMs 180

 5.5 Ancillary Questions: Criteria for Success -- Government and TCTM Participants 190

 5.6 Ancillary Questions: Criteria for Success -- Critics 193

 5.7 Ancillary Questions: Divergences and Convergences 195

 5.8 Results of Email Survey of Expert Panel 199

 5.9 Conclusions 199

 5.10 Implications of the Research 203

  5.10.1 From a Policy Perspective 203

  5.10.2 From a Business Perspective 205

 5.11 Strengths of the Research 206

 5.12 Contributions to Knowledge 207

 5.13 Limitations of the Research 209

 5.14 Suggestions for Future Research 210

References 213

Appendix 1: Newspaper Articles & Team Canada Trade Missions Archive Sources for Thematic Analysis 267

Appendix 2: Thematic Analysis (Primary Codes) 279

Appendix 3: Email Survey Letter to Expert Panel of Canadian Business/Management/Economics Academics 305

Appendix 4: Raw Responses from Expert Panel involved in Email Interview 307

About the Author 315

List of Tables

Table 1. Timeline of Team Canada Trade Missions 19
Table 2. Concepts Covered in the Literature Review 32
Table 3. Data Sources 109
Table 4. Four Dimensions of Policy Archaeology 112
Table 5. Contrasting Discourses: Government and Business v. Critics 168
Table 6. Proponents versus Critics: A Closer Look 171

List of Figures

Figure 1. Research Working Model 21
Figure 2. Overarching Breakdown of Literature Review 35
Figure 3. Concept Map of Literature Review 37
Figure 4. Trade Missions Concept Map: Tapping into International Markets 77
Figure 5. Traditional View of History 99
Figure 6. History as a Field of Multiple Discourses 101
Figure 7. Proponents 172
Figure 8. Critics 173
Figure 9. The Five Ps of Trade Mission Benefits 191
Figure 10. Major Points of Divergence 195
Figure 11. Points of Convergence 198

Key Dates—Canadian Political Leadership

1994–2005	Team Canada Trade Missions		
1993–2003	Prime Minister of Canada	Jean Chrétien	Liberal Party
2003–2006	Prime Minister of Canada	Paul Martin	Liberal Party
2006–2015	Prime Minister of Canada	Stephen Harper	Conservative Party
2015–	Prime Minister of Canada	Justin Trudeau	Liberal Party

List of Abbreviations

DFAIT	Department of Foreign Affairs and International Trade
NAFTA	North American Free Trade Agreement
NGO	Non-Governmental Organisation
NPO	Non-Profit Organisation
SME	Small- and Medium-Sized Enterprises
TCTM	Team Canada Trade Missions

Chapter 1: Introduction to the Study

1.1 Purpose of the Research

Between 1994 and 2005, the Canadian government ran a series of 'Team Canada Trade Missions' (TCTM) to various parts of the world. While these were meant to improve Canada's export profile, there were criticisms during the program that the government's direct involvement was unnecessary, since the governmental apparatus was not meant to only serve the business community. Therefore, the purpose of this research was to examine how the trade missions were perceived differently in the community through the analysis of a wide variety of discourses present in documents, including policy statements, newspaper reports, marketing communications, news releases and speech transcripts. From such a retrospective study, the findings might potentially offer lessons for the future regarding whether there is a need for government to be closely involved with trade missions.

This research explored theoretical elements of discourse and how discursive intersections and clashes potentially contributed to change and subjectivity. From a discursive point of view, the issue of power and who wields it is important. Thus, an examination of the interplay of divergent strands of discourse within a society can enrich understanding of the theoretical underpinnings of knowledge, power and the possibilities for change.

Trade missions usually involve a group of businesspeople who travel to another locale to explore business opportunities and to make contacts. Wolf (2013, p. 24) defined a trade mission as a group of people who travel to a foreign country with the intent of promoting trade opportunities or meeting with potential customers at the destination to introduce their business, their products or services. Seringhaus and Rosson (1990, p. 244) argued that trade missions can serve to 'consummate a sale that had been some time in the making'. Likewise, Dana (2012, p. 244) highlighted the use of trade missions 'to provide domestic firms with the opportunity to acquire experiential knowledge about foreign countries,' while Etemad and Wright (2003) cited 'information' as the essence of trade missions, including introductions to influential people in the host country. According to Freixanet (2012), trade missions are one of many export-assistance programs governments offer to their business community. Seringhaus (1989), whose research laid the foundation for others in the field, distinguished between incoming and outgoing missions, which may be organised or sponsored by a government export promotion entity. Trade missions with heavy government involvement are worth researching because they consume national resources that could have gone towards other worthwhile activities or causes.

When globalisation emerged as a subject of discussion in the 1980s and early 1990s, the Canadian government attempted to craft a response that would allow Canada to maintain a position of strength and leadership rather than become a victim of the fast-moving globalisation process (Broad 1995). This determination was affirmed in Prime Minister Chrétien's 2001 speech at the Summit of the Americas, in which he declared that although many considered globalisation to be the source of 'profound problems' (Chrétien 2001, p. 14), he saw the potential to create 'untold opportunities and shared prosperity from Tierra del Fuego to Baffin Island' (Chrétien 2001, p. 14).

In the 1990s, the Canadian business community and government realised that there was heightened competition in the international marketplace (Dunning 2014). One of the responses to globalisation, which appeared to be simultaneously a threat and opportunity, was the government's institution of the TCTM, of which Hale (2006, p. 247) noted:

> During the 1980s, most Canadian governments and businesses came to recognise that relatively small countries like Canada could not stand aside from aspects of economic globalisation such as global trends towards the liberalisation of trade and investment flows, the effects of technological change on production systems and distribution networks, and the resulting pressures of international competition on domestic industries.

Among the responses was the 1994 establishment of the TCTM program. Its purpose was to 'capture markets in newly industrialised countries and the world's populous countries' (Phillips 2002, p. 1). The program sought to promote Canada's expertise in various fields, including technology, agriculture and education. The government emphasised a team approach and brought together government leaders and Canadian businesspeople to form trade mission delegations, which were considered important 'to promote the home country in a host country' (Ruel 2019, p. 2). Chrétien took a visible role in these missions. While Chrétien was in office, trade missions were supported by provincial premiers, territorial leaders and the Minister of Foreign Affairs and International Trade (DFAIT), all of whom acknowledged the importance of exports to the Canadian economy. Halabisky et al. (2005, p. 4) explained that, 'in 2002, exports accounted for 41 percent of Canada's Gross Domestic Product (GDP) and for one in every three jobs in Canada. Exports are strongly correlated with real GDP growth, with changes in exports driving changes in real GDP in Canada.'

Newspaper accounts and marketing communications created in support of the program suggested that the missions were successful, with billions of dollars in trade deals often cited as proof (e.g., Alberts 1999; Clarke 1998). Without challenges to this narrative, it is easy to understand why it might have been accepted as fact. However, the government's discourse regarding the success of TCTM was eventually challenged, disparaged and dismissed. For example, the apparent failure of the Chrétien government to criticise China on its human rights record while eagerly pursuing trade opportunities, 'provided critics with plenty of cause' (Leyton-Brown 2000, p. 88) to criticise the program.

1.2 Background to the Research

Czinkota et al. (2011) argued that governments consider exports to be a special domain with the potential to generate significant macroeconomic benefits. Therefore, an array of programs have been developed to help companies to export, particularly small- and medium-sized businesses (SMEs), which 'sometimes tend to be reluctant to commit themselves to international markets due to lack of knowledge and the perception of risk' (Ruel 2019, pp. 1, 31).

Most developed and developing countries recognise the importance of exports to their economy (Belloc & Di Maio 2011). As a result, rather than leaving businesses to fend for themselves, some governments take steps to provide services that facilitate the process for companies already involved in exporting, or for those wishing to do so. These efforts have been defined as export promotion policies, which denote the measures that a government takes to bear some of the private costs related to exports. Belloc and Di Maio (2011, p. 3) explained that export promotion policies involve efforts used to assist 'current and potential exporters in foreign market penetration and, for instance, export subsidies, reduced tax rates to exporting firms' earnings, favourable insurance rates, advantageous financial conditions, or variations in the exchange rates'.

The government plays the role of facilitator for export-oriented companies in some countries, whereas it is the private sector that plays a supportive role in others. For example, Seringhaus and Botschen (1991) conducted a cross-national study on Canada and Austria to explore the relationship between governments and the private sector in the area of exporting. They found that export promotion has been available since the beginning of the 20th century in industrialised countries.

Among the goals for export is the creation of awareness about opportunities and the provision of assistance, which can come in many forms. According to Seringhaus and Botschen (1991), governments often engage internationally minded businesses to become involved in export marketing and provide them with assistance to prepare, plan and develop expertise. However, governments around the world continue to support export efforts without clearly articulated reasons and these interventions stem from the perception that there are market barriers and a need to bridge trade gaps and deal with the often urgent need to cut down or eliminate a nation's trade deficit (Czinkota 2002). While some governments focus on increasing the competence of firms by providing counselling seminars or exporting handbooks, in other cases, direct or indirect subsidy programs are established. Low-cost financing or upfront payments from governments are sometimes made to the domestic company while it waits for its overseas payments for exports to come through. Such payments for exports are practically guaranteed, although the time for receipt can involve delays that domestic companies might not survive. Czinkota (2002, p. 317) explained that the main purpose of these subsidies 'is to increase the profitability of exporting to the firm, either by reducing the risks or by increasing the rewards.' Additional efforts by governments to reduce impediments for exporters include the elimination of 'multiple export licenses or permits issued by various government agencies' (Czinkota 2002, p. 317).

In practically all cases, Chrétien and later Paul Martin, accompanied TCTM participants to the target countries. Chrétien's 1994 trip to China angered human rights activists but delighted the businesspeople who participated in the trade mission because 'Canadian executives and Chinese officials signed 54 contracts and agreements in principle valued by Canadian officials at $8.6 billion (US $6.3 billion)' (Clayton 1994, p. 1). Between 1994 and 2005, the trade missions visited more than 25 countries in Asia, Europe, Latin America and the Caribbean. Some countries, such as China, received multiple trade missions.

TCTM-related newspaper reports often mentioned millions of dollars in contracts signed by participating entrepreneurs and businesses. Contrary to the belief that the business participants were sponsored by the government, they paid their own way. As reported in Team Canada (1997, p. 1), Ann Gingras, who was an art dealer from Aylmer, Quebec, 'was just one of the more than 500 participants who paid their full share—about $10,000—to take part in what is considered to be the most successful and comprehensive trade mission in Canadian history.' Gingras ('Team Canada' 1997, p. 1) argued that 'people are interested in Team Canada ... With it, they aren't just looking at a little art company on its own. It's a whole package.' Being part of the delegation made her more than a lone traveller in search of opportunities; it made her count as someone that businesspeople in the host country could take seriously.

From the above, it would seem that trade missions are positive and should attract the attention and support of the citizens of a nation. However, this was not the case with TCTM. A host of critics challenged the government's involvement in the program and sought to have it curtailed. As such, this study sought to examine the diverging narratives regarding the TCTM.

Nimijean (2014, p. 182) argued that 'Chrétien's economic policy response to globalisation was a series of neoliberal measures reducing the size of the Canadian welfare state'. On the surface, the establishment of the TCTM program might have appeared to be one of the success stories of Canada's ruling Liberal Party between 1993 and 2006. However, the focus on business might have meant neglect of the needs of other groups in society. The Department of Foreign Affairs and International Trade (DFAIT), which administered the trade missions, collected invaluable information from participants regarding the benefits of their experiences. Marketing communications involved in promoting the trade missions highlighted the successes of some of the participants and the challenges they faced.[1]

---

[1] https://works.bepress.com/everettofori/58/

Table 1. Timeline of Team Canada Trade Missions

Year	Target countries	Dollar volume of trade deals[2]	Special notes
Nov 1994	China/Hong Kong	Cdn$ 8,929 million	PM Chrétien attended / 12 days / 300 participants / 7 premiers
Jan 1995	Brazil, Argentina, Chile, Trinidad, and Uruguay	Cdn$ 2,760 million	PM Chrétien attended
Jan 1996	India, Pakistan, Indonesia, Malaysia	Cdn$ 11,175 million	PM Chrétien attended
Jan 1997	South Korea, Philippines, Thailand	Cdn $2.1 billion[3]	PM Chrétien attended
Jan 1998	Mexico, Brazil, Argentina, Chile	Cdn $1.78 billion / 117 contracts signed / 306 deals	PM Chrétien attended
1998-1999	Poland/Ukraine	-114 business representatives (Poland) / 38 signed deals valued at Cdn$132m /140 business representatives (Ukraine)[4]	PM Chrétien attended
Sep. 1999	Japan	Cdn$ 409 million	PM Chrétien attended; delegation of 350 Canadian businesses,, government and academic officials
Feb. 2001	Beijing and Shanghai, China/Hong Kong	Cdn$ 5,700 million	PM Chrétien attended 9 days
Feb. 2002	Russia and Germany	Cdn$ 584 million	PM Chrétien attended
2003	Europe: Netherlands, UK, Italy (March 25-April 14)	Deals worth more than Cdn$30 billion	PM Chrétien attended
2005	China	80 trade and bilateral deals made/Discussion of Canada as approved destination for Chinese tourists	PM Martin attended

---

[2] DFAIT – Department of Foreign Affairs and International Trade
[3] Team Canada 1997: Taking on the world. Canadian Business. March 1, 1997.
[4] Innovation, Science … 1998-99 Government of Canada.

It is evident from Table 1 that the Canadian government did not confine itself to doing business in only one part of the world but, in fact, saw a big portion of the world as a potential market for Canadian products.

1.3 Research Objective and Questions

Throughout history, there have been many private sector sponsorships of outward trade missions in Canada. There have also been provincial trade missions. These kinds of trade missions appear to be accepted as a given. The much-higher profile of Team Canada Trade missions, which involved the Prime Minister directly, seems to have attracted so much more attention and criticism. This research explores the discourses surrounding a particular set of trade missions in a way that other researchers in the export promotion field have not attempted. The main question that this research attempts to answer is the following:

What power relations and discourses surrounded the Team Canada Trade Missions?

Three ancillary questions following from the above will also be considered:
i) How did the Government and the Trade Mission Participants define criteria for success of the Team Canada trade missions (TCTM)?
ii) How did critics of TCTM define criteria for success of the Team Canada trade missions (TCTM)?
iii) Where, how, and why do these a) diverge and b) converge?

In Yazdannik, Yousefy, and Mohammadi (2017), the researchers show that 'how' questions are at the centre of Foucauldian research: 'Foucault's focus is on questions of how some discourses have shaped and created meaning systems that have gained the status and currency of "truth," and dominate how we define and organize both ourselves and our social world while other alternative discourses are marginalised and subjugated, yet potentially "offer" sites where hegemonic practices can be contested, challenged, and "resisted".

Also, Fiona Longmuir, who uses Foucault and Scott (1990) as a theoretical basis for her research, states: 'The question this paper seeks to consider is this: in leading radical change, how did this principal resist cultural, political and systemic forces that confined most other schools to more common improvement processes?' Finally, in Kevin Gormley's thesis, The Discursive Construction of the Concept of Creativity in Australian Education Policy and Practice, he asks the following research questions:

- How are discourses of creativity constructed in educational policy?
- How do practices of a school institution sustain particular discourses of creativity?
- What discourses of creativity are ignored or omitted in policy and practice?
- How does an individual accept or resist normalised assumptions about creativity constructed in policy and practice?

1.4 Research Working Model

Figure 1. Research Working Model

	Apparent Alliance between Government & Exporting Companies	
Pre-TCTM (Before 1994)	TCTM (1994-2005)	Post-TCTM (After 2005)
	Disparate Assortment of Critics of TCTMs: Individual Citizens, Anti-poverty advocates, Human rights advocates, Opposition party members, Media, NPOs	

Developed for this research by Everett Ofori

The research model presented in Figure 1 is the genesis of the research in that the Team Canada trade missions (1994-2005) gave the impression that the government was in an alliance with export-oriented companies. The working model highlights the environment prior to the Team Canada Trade Missions, focuses on activities within the eleven-year period of the trade missions, and touches on the immediate aftermath. It is not unlike the working model used by Ihlstrom and Nilsson (2011), which illustrated the 'stages of maturity for taking an enterprise toward e-business' (2011, p. 211) or that of Galunic (2018), which highlighted important 'checkpoints on the digital journey.'

The emphasis on timelines and time-marks in this research provide an appropriate context for understanding how the intense period of the Team Canada trade missions fit into Canadian business history. By the time Jean Chrétien came to power in 1993, there seemed to be a national consensus that Canada needed to adapt itself to the forces of globalisation and that this could be done by going beyond the North American Free Trade Agreement (NAFTA) and taking a proactive role in promoting Canadian businesses in a world trading system governed by rules. Despite the appearance of a consensus, once the trade missions began, various oppositional discourses opened up as the nation sought to reconcile the need for international trade revenues and adherence to its long-held values such as respect for human rights. Thus, by looking at the years before the Team Canada trade missions and what forces were at play, then, studying the government's response to globalisation with the trade missions, as well as a brief review of the years following the Team Canada Trade Missions, one gets a better picture of the whole trajectory of the trade missions, including their possible impact. The major forces of opposition (on the political side), included conservative and libertarian partisans, and the libertarian forces were represented by the Reform Party under Preston Manning, who straddled the conservative and libertarian viewpoints (Cody 1998). As CTV's Jim Munson states:

> Both the Reform and Conservative parties have criticised these Team Canada trips as being a waste of time. They argue that more attention should be paid to tax cuts and the economy at home. They also point out that after previous missions, Canadian exports have actually dropped. But don't tell that to the three-hundred businesspeople who are here. They believe the politicians have

actually opened doors and will do more in future Team Canada missions. (The Team Canada trade mission to Japan 1999)

This tension is at the heart of the research.

1.5 Justification for the Research

Research on trade missions has been slowly growing. Where a trade mission involves government entities such as the DFAIT, government ministers and financial support, other stakeholders such as labour, non-governmental organisations (NGOs), the academic community and general public, might be concerned that government largesse is being expended on the business community to the exclusion of other groups. This appears to have been the case with TCTM. The reason for the central question involving the power relations between the government and critics of the TCTM program was to explore the attempts by citizens to have a measure of influence over their government, in which they believed that the interests of the two parties might not coincide. Perhaps it was with this in mind that Menzies (1996, p. 41) complained that Chrétien, following a series of trade missions in the 1990s, had become a 'compliant international corporate cheerleader,' ostensibly to the exclusion of other important entities in society. In a discussion of trade missions, Lazar (1998, p. 72) highlighted the importance of government accountability so that citizens would know the 'tax cost of social programs.' Few studies have been conducted on Canadian trade missions, with only one major study undertaken on the TCTM. Head and Ries (2010, p. 772) performed a quantitative study that sought to gauge the impact of Canadian government policy on international trade, concluding that:

> While the lagged dependent variable specification suggests that Team Canada missions expanded exports by about 14 percent, we argue that the approximately zero effects found in the country-pair fixed-effects specification are more trustworthy.

1.6 Research Gap

Despite the global ubiquity of trade missions, they do not appear to hold much attraction for researchers. Seringhaus (1989, p. 5) claimed that 'trade missions as an export marketing tool are not widely publicised and discussed in texts on international marketing or exporting ... Research on trade missions is equally scarce.' Concerning the scarcity of research on trade missions, Spence (2003, p. 84) maintained that, 'in spite of the popularity of trade missions as well as their cost effectiveness, there have been few empirical studies demonstrating the influence of overseas trade missions on export performance.' In 2015, a literature search yielded hundreds of items regarding trade missions around the world, but very little in the way of scholarly research centred on this topic. While there has been ample research on internationalisation and globalisation and the role that trade missions, trade fairs and trade commissioners play in the process, there is limited research on the discourses surrounding trade missions from different constituencies. In Canada, highly contested multiple discourses among constituencies such as labour, SME and large businesses, NGOs, the academic community and the general public have not been analysed to extract lessons that might guide future policymaking.

The paucity of discourse analysis in business and marketing was acknowledged by Skalen (2010), who proposed a discourse analytical perspective that might serve the field of business research. Drawing from the work of Foucault, discourse analysis hinges upon the identification of key turning points and the raising of questions prior to these turning points. There are moments when discourse that has appeared to be dominant, unquestioned and taken for granted comes under scrutiny and is subject to questioning. The use of Foucauldian discourse analysis enables researchers to be wary of accepting dogma and theories and to consider the broader sweep of the environment or context of an event.

Understanding the nature of discourse is to understand that armed with a questioning mind, one can interrogate how 'conventional wisdom' comes to be. Heller (2016) problematised public relations in Britain and discovered in the process that the business of public relations, which is taken for granted today, has its roots in wartime propaganda from World War I. Such knowledge can enable better understanding of how to navigate a complex world and not be content with surface appearances. Institutions often have the means to magnify and spread their language to a broader cross-section of the population and with that, to wield the forms and techniques 'involved in the production of the subject' (Kärreman & Alvesson 2009, p. 1119). In this case, through repeated projection of discourse in the form of pronouncements regarding the success of trade missions and the inclusion of supporting images, citizens are programmed to accept the government's view of reality, regardless of whether it is accurate.

In the contemporary globalised economy, how individuals deploy words and language can affect the perception of power and cachet they hold. In one study focused on a multinational company based in Switzerland, it was found that the English language was connected to greater 'individual power and influence' (Gaibrois & Steyaert 2017, p. 70). Whether in a local community, business or in the wider world, which transcends national boundaries, one cannot operate successfully without understanding the effects of power and discourse. Kärreman and Levay (2017, p. 74) argued that discourses 'are expressions of power or knowledge relations,' which are related to 'historically developed systems of ideas.' Institutions and loci of power such as governments use 'talk, text and discourse' (Kärreman & Levay 2017, p.74) to shape the ways in which people talk about a particular subject.

An example of the power of discourse to lend credibility and support for practice is found in the efforts by Thai Oil Group and Bangkok Petroleum. Over a period of 15 years, the two companies released statements indicating that it was acceptable to focus on fossil fuels to make investments in renewable energy. Since oil and gas companies and other businesses communicate their practices and intentions through annual reports, these can be used as a basis for discourse analysis to reveal how the use of language in a political context 'has the power to shape one's view of the world and reality' (Chaiyapa et al. 2018, p. 449). It was found that through the discourse deployed by these oil companies over 15 years, there was increased 'public awareness and acceptance of biofuels' (Chaiyapa et al. 2018, p. 457).

1.7 Contribution of the Research

Trade missions attract global publicity but are not often the subject of scholarly study (Seringhaus 1989, p. 5). However, the situation has gradually changed, with scholars considering trade missions and government support of various export programs as being worthy subjects of analysis. For a program that ran for 11 years and had high-level government involvement, the contribution of the TCTM to the national economy and society should be one of public interest. Research on it can offer lessons for policymaking decisions, business and economics and contribute to the understanding and advancement of the theoretical aspects of international marketing. Further, the TCTM program consumed government resources, including the time of government officials. Government resources are limited, so the question of whether the program was worthwhile is an important matter for analysis. Although Head and Ries (2010) conducted a quantitative study to determine whether the program was financially beneficial to Canada, the scope was too narrow and focused on measuring possible net financial gain, which ignored much of the associated discourse from the government and participants.

The importance of the TCTM in business and social history is twofold. First, the government's partnership with the business sector for 11 years had lasting implications for society. Second, there was the issue of financial cost in addition to time expended by the prime minister and other government ministers. These two elements justify studying the program to extract lessons for posterity.

Although technology has made it easier to contact international companies, cultural differences, along with differences in business styles, expectations and cultural environments, are factors that make international trade and marketing major challenges for businesses considering expansion abroad. Trade missions must also be seen to fit into the reality of a nation that has long recognised the importance of international commerce to its wealth (Hart 2002). Trade missions are one way by which companies can learn about foreign markets and familiarise themselves with foreign territories, while remaining under the government's safe ambit or that of a recognised trade organisation. Such support lends legitimacy to the participants and provides a rise in status, which a solitary trade journey might not easily confer.

The combination of policy archaeology and conventional content analysis has the potential to contribute to a more comprehensive view of the TCTM program. To date, there is no evidence that discourse analysis has been used to examine the differential impact of discourse connected with trade missions in Canada. Any lessons learned from the experience could become part of the historical legacy of the Canadian business and political sectors. The implications of this research extend to government, business and other stakeholders in society, who may seek to effect change in policies or the direction of government. It is anticipated that this research will raise interest among researchers to focus on trade missions and perhaps invite other methods of analysis.

1.8 Methodology

Questions regarding the nature of reality and knowledge continue to be part of the discourse of academic research, encapsulated in the four main paradigms of positivism, postpositivism, critical theory and constructivism. Constructivism—under which the policy archaeology used for this study falls—accepts the possibility of a multiplicity of realities (Keengwe 2018; Lincoln & Guba 2013). There are divisions within this worldview, although there is a common thread: knowledge is not simply discovered or received from an authority; it is also constructed (Bazeley 2013). Discourse analysis involves the analysis of text, talk or action (Powers 2013, p. 6). The methodological approach taken in this study had two interrelated parts:

> 1) Discourse analysis of policy and practice, focused on Canadian government policy documents — *A Dialogue on Foreign Policy: Report to Canadians* (2003)[5] and *Canada in the World* (1995)[6] — published during the period of the

---

[5] *A dialogue on foreign policy: Report to Canadians 2003*, Minister of Foreign Affairs, Ottawa, Ontario.
[6] *Canada in the World* 1995, Ministry of Foreign Affairs, Ottawa, Ontario, viewed 1 December 2006, http://gac.canadiana.ca/view/ooe.b2644952E/1?r=0&s=3

trade missions, along with Chrétien-era speeches by the prime minister and his trade ministers, to uncover the reasons given by the government for the program prior to its inception and throughout its active implementation, to understand how the government considered the practice of trade missions to be in the national interest.

2) Thematic analysis involving coding, categorisation and interpretation of marketing communications, promotional materials, speeches and op-eds by leading Canadian business executives, labour and NGO representatives, editors and columnists from local and major national dailies, including The Toronto Star, Maclean's, National Post, Globe and Mail (see Appendix 1) to unearth how the government's narrative on criteria for success of the TCTM program was supported and challenged.

In this research, policy archaeology and thematic analysis were complemented by email interviews with an expert panel of Canadian academics. The rationale for selecting this group was to obtain a sample of Canadians who were broadly informed and 'articulate and introspective enough to provide rich descriptions' (Padgett 2008, p. 53). While there were insufficient responses to attain statistical significance, the responses provided an insightful backdrop to the overall analysis. Members of the expert panel were drawn from faculties of business management, policy, economics, international marketing and international business departments in Canadian universities from all provinces and territories. The researcher expected that responses from observers of the Canadian business and political scene would provide insights that would enrich those gleaned from the literature analysis.

1.9 Definitions

Globalisation

Globalisation is a contested term that some link with advanced western societies, but it has also been described as 'a process that encompasses the causes, course, and consequences of transnational and transcultural integration of human and non-human activities' (Al-Rodhan and Stoudman 2006, p. 13).

Internationalisation

Internationalisation involves the efforts of companies to extend their markets, increase their contacts and influence or to advance other profit-making endeavours beyond the domestic market. The internationalisation process involves multiple steps. The pre-export phase includes efforts to acquire information, the quest for counselling from pertinent sources, training, undertaking of feasibility studies and embarking on trade missions. The next step might include engaging representation overseas through foreign offices or obtaining assistance in placing a bid or putting in an application for export financing (Seringhaus 1987). For businesses, internationalisation efforts might include seeking access to information through making contacts or setting up overseas offices, whereas for governments, the motivation might be economic development (Manly 2016) to 'promote the creation and retention of high value-added jobs … and promote exports of goods and services' (Pigman 2010, p. 74). Geographical or cultural proximity often makes a difference in easing the roadblocks that companies know they must face. As Aliber and Click (1993, p. 217) point out, 'entry into some foreign markets may cost less than entry into others because of geographic proximity…or economic proximity. U.S. firms find it natural (i.e. easy) to first expand into Canada, and then into Great Britain and Australia – these foreign countries aren't very foreign.' Australia and New Zealand, as well as Norway and Sweden, are examples of cases where physical and cultural proximity have facilitated foreign market entry. As Welch, Benito and Petersen (2008, p. 347) state, 'physical proximity aids inter-personal, face-to-face communication, facilitating the lowering of uncertainty.' But other factors can trump geographical or cultural proximity. For example, 'American investors were attracted by the size of the Chinese market and the remarkable opening up of the country to trade and foreign investment' (Sengupta 2007, p. 103) in the late 1970s and early 1980s.

Trade Missions

A trade mission is a journey made by a group of people to a foreign country with the specific intention of seeking trade opportunities, finding potential customers, introducing products and services or doing business with 'a new or existing customer' (Wolf 2013, p. 24). Trade fairs are usually preceded by trade missions. Ruel (2019) emphasised the importance of knowledge acquisition in trade missions. While the need to boost exports is often highlighted, the 'intangible resources' (Ruel 2019, p. 17) of learning to 'cope with the rules of international markets' (Ruel 2019, p. 19) are significant.

Trade Fairs

Trade shows serve to provide a forum for introducing products to potential buyers and to generate initial indications of interest through direct sales to distributors or retailers. Companies usually send representatives to trade fairs, exhibitions or product release forums, where their latest products and offerings are put on display:

> To be evaluated by customers and suppliers, as well as by peers and competitors. Participation in events like these helps firms to identify the current market frontier, take stock of relative competitive positions and form future plans. (Maskell et al. 2006, p. 997)

1.10 Delimitations, Scope and Key Assumptions

Although it was assumed that a literature survey of export promotion would be instructive, this research purposely excluded regional trade missions offered under provincial umbrellas in Canada. In addition, although the trade missions of other countries are referred to, this research focused on a particular program that occurred from 1994 to 2005. In addition, although there were dozens of government documents that could have been examined, the researcher focused on two government publications that were released within the period under consideration, which focused directly on policies related to trade and export.

1.11 Outline of the Thesis

Chapter 1 has provided the background to the research, presented the research questions and an explanation for the choice of methodology. Justification for the choice of research topic was established, definitions were given for keywords and the study delimitations were outlined. Subsequent chapters extend and develop the research problem, data analysis, findings and implications.

Chapter 2 provides a literature review, which includes a discussion of globalisation and internationalisation as a prelude to examining the trade missions, including where they fit in the broader picture.

Chapter 3 provides the ontological and epistemological backdrop to this research and justifies the use of what is referred to as the Scheurich–O'Connor policy archaeology framework—combining the work of Scheurich (1997) and O'Connor (2005)—and conventional thematic analysis (e.g., Castleberry & Nolen 2018). To further examine the positions of the different camps connected to the TCTM program, an email interview asking four questions (see Appendix 3) was sent to academics across Canada who were working in fields such as business management, policy studies, international marketing and international management, to provide a broader perspective on the data.

Chapter 4 presents a stepped data analysis. First, the analysis of two policy documents and other Chrétien-era policy statements using the Scheurich–O'Connor policy archaeology framework is presented. Second, thematic analysis is used to study archival data, policy documents, op-eds, newspaper columns, speeches by Chrétien and his ministers, alongside other textual data. Third, email interviews with an expert panel of Canadian academics were conducted. This multi-pronged approach helped to capture a broad and deep understanding of the forces and power dynamics that drove and impinged upon the TCTM. Finally, Chapter 5 presents the findings from this research.

1.12 Concluding Remarks

This chapter has provided the background to the research on the TCTM program under the Liberal government, which was in power between 1993 and 2006. Motivations for the research and an outline of the chapters have been presented. The methodology, comprising the Scheurich–O'Connor discourse analysis framework and thematic analysis, involved an exploration of the pronouncements, assertions, data, hopes and policy prescriptions presented by government and TCTM business participants, alongside the opposition, challenges, differences, divergences and breaks in regular discourse presented by a multiplicity of critics. Further, Chapter 1 set the parameters and limitations of the study.

Chapter 2: Literature Review

A. Globalisation and Internationalisation
2.1 Introduction

This chapter provides a review of the literature concerning globalisation and internationalisation, including the challenges and opportunities presented to exporters and how government export promotion programs and trade missions fit into the process. The literature review enables the assessment of research on trade missions, identifies the foci of foregoing research, considers methodologies and identifies the research gap that was addressed by this study. Table 1 highlights the key concepts covered in the literature review, along with their sources. The use of sources from the 1990s and 2000s was essential to understand the prevailing context within which the TCTM unfolded.

Table 2. Concepts Covered in the Literature Review

Concept	Explanation	Source/Date
Globalisation	The world is not only interconnected but also interdependent.	Weiss 2006
	Globalisation is seen by some as of universal benefit and by others as exploitative of developing countries.	Hampden-Turner & Trompenaars 2006
	Globalisation has not only benefited advanced nations; it has also benefited developing countries.	Stiglitz 2002
Barriers to internationalisation	In the 1990s, the barriers to international trade were numerous.	Guiltinan & Paul 1991
Export promotion programs	Many countries established export promotion programs.	2012
	Benefits of export promotion programs are mostly indirect.	Durmusoglu et al. 2012
	Canadian exporters saw value in using export promotion programs.	Castaldi, De Noble & Cantor 1992
Exporting	Some companies without international marketing expertise thought exporting a waste of time.	McMahon 1989
Challenge of exporting is real	Despite proximity and cultural similarity, US and Canadian companies have often failed in trying to export to each other's domain.	Bolen 2013; Levinson 2013; O'Grady & Lane 1997; Petersen et al. 2002

Cultural variation	Cultural variation might explain in part the difficulty that some companies find doing business abroad.	Schwartz 1991
	The GLOBE study confirmed the existence of differences that can impact cultural competency.	Bertsch 2012
Commercial Diplomacy	Focuses on policymaking and business support; uses government and non-government channels.	Pigman 2016; Ruel 2019
Impact of cross-cultural barriers	Managers in different countries have to cope with different day-to-day concerns, making it a challenge to transpose managers or ideas smoothly.	McNeil & Pedigo 2001
	Americans found it difficult to overcome cultural barriers in China.	Rondinelli 1993
	Many Sino–foreign projects have failed because of the difficulty of overcoming cultural differences.	Fan & Zigang 2004
	Failure ensues when Western businesspeople are unable to bridge the communication and cultural gaps.	Goh & Sullivan 2010
	Companies that do not adapt to the foreign environment usually fail.	Abramson & Ai 1999
	Misunderstandings and misinterpretations are minefields, which can lead to failure.	Chua 2012
	Companies can succeed abroad if they take the time to educate themselves about their target market.	Fletcher & Melewar 2001
Government support	In some markets, government endorsement or testimonials can help a business to become accepted.	Georgevitch & Davis 2004; McCullough 2011
Market knowledge	It is important to know the customer and understand market needs.	Kotler & Armstrong 2011
	Understanding the marketing concept can be a boon to success.	Boone & Kurtz 2013
SMEs	SMEs are particularly in need of export assistance, such as government support.	Nummela et al. 2004
Success factors for export	Companies that understand success factors for exporting have a better chance of success.	Alvarez 2004; Ogunmokun & Ng 2004; Spence 2003
Role of government	Governments that build good relationships with their counterparts abroad pave the way for their companies to potentially succeed in other markets.	Katsikeas et al. 1997; Ruel et al. 2013

Trade fairs	Trade fairs are one way that companies attempt to get a toehold in foreign markets or to promote their products without a heavy commitment.	Seringhaus & Rosson 2001
Trade missions	Given the riskiness of initial international trade forays, trade missions can be useful as a market exploration measure.	Seringhaus 1989
	Trade missions are not only useful for beginning exporters but can be beneficial to experienced exporters.	Oudalov 2013
	TCTM did not make a positive return when considered against normal export trends.	Head & Ries 2010
	Australian firms that participated in trade missions between 2010 and 2013 experienced up to 172 per cent increase in exports.	Milic et al. 2017
	Trade missions alone are not enough to help companies, but in conjunction with trade fairs and counselling, could be useful to exporters.	Martincus & Carballo 2010
Marketing communications	Promotion of government export assistance programs such as trade missions require concerted marketing communications.	Kotler & Keller 2012
	Canada sought to promote a new image of itself through its marketing communications and trade missions.	Szondi 2005
	TCTM program was used as a part of Canada's international business development efforts.	Potter 2004
	Through the TCTM program, the government sought to rebrand Canada.	Anholt 2007
	It is a challenge to measure the effects of marketing communications because there are so many interlocking factors.	Kotler & Lee 2007
	The complex business environment makes it difficult to measure the effects of marketing communications.	Schultz & Block 2003

Much of the material recovered from databases such as EBSCOhost, ProQuest and SCOPUS demonstrated that researchers included trade missions within the export promotion and internationalisation literature. For this reason, the literature review begins by examining aspects of globalisation and internationalisation before considering trade missions, including what they entail in the way of preparation, host country experience and post-trade mission activities and effects.

Figure 2. Overarching Breakdown of Literature Review

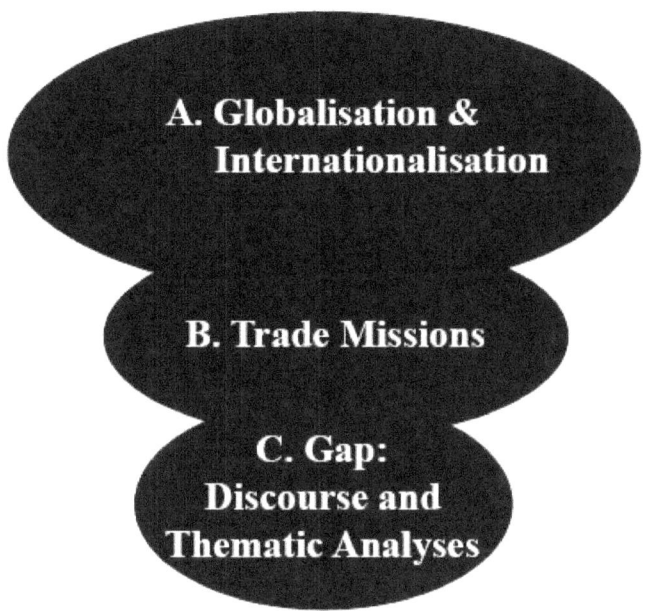

A. Efforts made by governments towards supporting export-oriented businesses are not borne of charity. Governments are concerned with the need to create jobs. Since increased exports betoken increased production and potentially higher revenues from which to draw taxes, the alliance between government and business with respect to export promotion is logical. However, trade missions are just one of a large array of export promotion tools available to governments, including trade offices, trade fairs, publications, information websites, seminars and training courses.

B. The period before a trade mission is characterised by several activities, including promotion, selection, and preparation of potential trip participants. Once the trade mission is underway, there are specific activities that occur, including introducing participants to potential partners, visiting prospective businesses, applying knowledge acquired such as those involving etiquette and, in some cases, signing contracts. The period following a trade mission may involve the initiation of export activities for some companies, whereas for others, limited or no further activity might result. Encouraged by their experience of a trade mission, some participants might elect to repeat the experience.

C.   The literature on trade missions focuses on results that the programs might garner. However, there is limited research on the 'specifics of trade missions' (Ruel 2019, p. 23) or the discourse surrounding the programs. While there are comments as to whether trade missions serve the egos of government officials or are used as fundraising tools, there has been limited examination of such discourses, which opened the way for the current research to fill a gap.

2.2 Globalisation

Globalisation has permeated society at multiple levels (De Wit 2009). Not only has it enabled countries to 'augment their GDPs but has also benefitted the consumers around the globe' (Maleek 2018). However, globalisation was a field of uncertainty during the early 1990s, which presented potential opportunities and the possibility of peril for companies and nations alike. To this point, Cordrey (1994, p. 55) claimed that 'almost every community can benefit from international business.' While the domestic market may have advantages, including proximity to potential customers or common language and understanding of the culture, proximity does not always translate into profits.

Figure 3 provides a concept map of the literature review, in which globalisation is presented as a possible starting point for internationalisation. The real or perceived barriers for companies that seek to extend themselves beyond the domestic sphere are considered, along with success factors and how trade missions might emerge as a method by which governments might support export-oriented companies.

Figure 3. Concept Map of Literature Review

GLOBALISATION: VISIONS OF MASSIVE SUCCESS

GLOBALISATION, defined by ease of communication, including the near-ubiquity of the Internet, faster air travel, expedited delivery systems, ease of funds transfer, has made the world economy more integrated, giving rise to hopes for expanded business and profits from abroad.

DRIVE TOWARDS INTERNATIONALISATION

INTERNATIONALISATION refers to the process of getting more involved in international markets. While some companies embark on this quest on their own, others seek assistance from the private sector or from government resources such as information, introductions, networking opportunities, seminars, trade commissioner services, trade missions, etc. Businesses, particularly, small and medium-sized businesses realise that their lack of knowledge, or lack of familiarity with foreign markets, creates a potential barrier to success.

REAL AND PERCEIVED COMPLEXITIES

Companies entering the international marketplace begin to perceive complexities for which they may not be equipped: lack of understanding of the foreign culture and market, lack of marketing expertise in the foreign market, language differences, whether to follow mass marketing or glocalisation, whether to form a wholly owned foreign setup, use licensing, set up a branch office, get in a joint-venture, or use a foreign agent.

KEY SUCCESS FACTORS FOR INTERNATIONALISATION

A number of factors are identified as being of potential advantage: Managers' positive attitude, Global orientation, Knowledge and skills related to international markets, Willingness to learn, Marketing expertise, Differentiation, and Commercial diplomacy.

OPTIONS

In seeking to enter the international marketplace, a businessperson might decide to rely on his/her own efforts, do research in the library or on the Internet; make use of consultants who might save a company time by providing more direct information, either from pre-existing reports or based on custom research conducted by experts; participate in trade fairs or trade missions.

THE CHOICE OF TRADE MISSIONS

Trade missions offer a comprehensive approach, providing information on markets, culture, as well as introducing a company to counterparts abroad while also conferring a measure of credibility on the company, even a fledgling one. In addition, for companies that are unsure of their capabilities, the assistance of an experienced organisation or the chance to benefit from the vast resources of the government, including respect, connections, information, knowledge, and advice, is very attractive.

ANALYSIS: POWER RELATIONS SURROUNDING TEAM CANADA TRADE MISSIONS

Different stakeholders in Canada, including labour, small and large businesses, non-governmental agencies, the academic community, and the general public raise questions about Team Canada Trade Missions.

Source: Developed for this research

2.3 The Reality of Globalisation

This chapter focuses on an overview of globalisation, the internationalisation process and how trade missions—one strand in government export assistance programs—might help export-oriented companies. Weiss (2006) claimed that globalisation refers to an interconnected and interdependent world, in which the accelerated increase in the volume of cross-trading in the areas of finance, investment and trade have occurred partly due to the convergence of several technologies. According to Weiss (2006, p. 438), globalisation:

> is about our global environment ... new opportunities for workers in all countries to develop their potential and to support their families through jobs created by greater economic integration.

Globalisation can be polarising, with some viewing it as being of universal benefit, while others see it as another means through which advanced Western economies exploit their less-developed counterparts (e.g., Hampden-Turner & Trompenaars 2006, p. 31). The view of globalisation as a Western-led form of exploitation is supported by Noumoff (2001, p. 51), who stated that, 'globalisation is a mere euphemism for the totalisation of capitalism on a global scale.' Conversely, Stiglitz (2002) claimed that international trade has been responsible for accelerating the economies of many countries, with growth in exports serving as the catalyst for the success of several Asian countries. Stiglitz (2002, p. 7) argued:

> Because of globalisation many people in the world now live longer than before and their standard of living is far better. People in the West may regard low-paying jobs at Nike as exploitation, but for many people in the developing world, working in a factory is a far better option than staying down on the farm and growing rice.

For others, it is not so much that the West is overshadowing the rest of the world, but that 'globalisation is spreading too quickly' (Korenovska 2008, p. 15). Another perspective on globalisation is that it is not a matter of broad wins or losses for countries because the impact is not just 'across traditional sectoral lines, but may also have strong effects within particular industries, with winners and losers in each industry' (van Bergeijk et al. 2011, p. 381). Even within a country, the effects on different companies might vary considerably.

In 1993, when the Liberal government of Chrétien came to power, there was a measure of uncertainty regarding how Canadian companies would fare in this newly emerging economic regime. For example, Canadian workers were concerned because globalisation had made workers vulnerable in the marketplace due to the expansion of non-union jobs and the greater leverage employers had with the proliferation of part-time jobs (Peters 2002).

2.4 The Drive Towards Internationalisation

International trade is considered to be a 'primary driver of global economic growth' (Pigman 2016, p. 1). However, while entering a foreign market may offer potential benefits, there are many factors that can confound the entry process. Among the barriers to international trade identified by Guiltinan and Paul (1991, p. 92) were the following:

1. Tariffs and duties paid as fees to import products.
2. Voluntary or involuntary quotas on the amount or types of products that can be imported.
3. Product requirements regarding health and safety, product standards and testing, packaging and labelling.
4. Customs and entry procedures, including inspection and licensing.
5. Government participation through subsidies, procurement policies favouring domestic firms and the level of intervention in competition.
6. National attitudes towards domestic versus foreign products.
7. Access to distribution channels may be limited by a preference for established local suppliers or shortages of space for new products.

It is insufficient to hope for increased business outside the domestic market. Knowledge of business operations in the target country or region is necessary, along with the requirement for a plan to address potential barriers.

The Canadian government provided a plethora of information to help organisations aiming to export. In fact, the Canadian government had a strong hand in the first five elements cited by Guiltinan & Paul (1991). In the first case, the Canadian government makes available to trade mission participants and exporters information on tariffs that various countries apply to Canadian products. This information is available at https://www.tariffinder.ca/en. By selecting a particular product and a target country, the would-be exporter can compare 'rates for multiple products or countries to identify…best options' (Canada Tariff Finder www.tariffinder.ca/en). Also, through the World Trade Organisation, the Canadian government has been active in negotiating reduced tariffs on some Canadian exports. In fact, following China's accession to the World Trade Organisation on January 1, 1995, Canada is said to have benefited 'from China's reduction in trade barriers which resulted in efficiency increases in the Chinese economic system, rendering it a superior supplier of products as well as a larger importer of products from Canada, the EU, Japan and the US' (Das 2008, p. 144).

In the case of the second, quotas, the Canadian government also assists exporters with information that would help them comply with expectations from the target countries. The government uses 'a secure WEB Interface and Electronic Data Interchange (EDI) interface to support the application, approval, and processing of import/export permits' (Global Affairs Canada www.international.gc/ca/). The Canadian government has been consistent in resisting taxes that the United States government wants the Canadian government to impose on its own exports to lessen their attractiveness in the American market against American produced lumber. As Kinnucan & Zhang (2004, p. 84) point out, 'if the choice is between acceding to U.S. demands for an export limit and an import duty imposed unilaterally by the United States, the export limit is clearly preferred, as an import duty harms Canada's producers, with no offset to the Canadian treasury or overall economy.'

In the case of the third, which has to do with health and safety, product standards and testing, packing and labelling, the Canadian government makes available the relevant information to exporters. One such area is the Food Exports requirements library that the government maintains, which details 'conditions the Canadian government has accepted for issuing export certificates. Their purpose is to facilitate access to overseas markets for Canadian exporters' (Food Export requirements library www.inspection.gc.ca/). In this connection, Canadian federal government standards for exporting meat products to the United States includes 'ante- and post-mortem inspection of slaughter animals managed by veterinary surgeons; monitoring for microbial contaminants' (Spriggs & Isaac 2001, p. 58) and adhering to a whole host of other standards.

In the fourth case, customs and entry procedures, The Canadian government provides a border information service, which provides telephone assistance to deal with border and customs regulations compliance. The Canadian Trade Commissioner Service provides market- and sector-specific information to exporters and resources specifically geared towards small and medium-sized businesses aiming to export, such as tariffs and trade incentive programs, marketing support for agri-food exporters, accelerated programs for technology companies such as access to free office space, connection to strategic partners and customers, help with raising venture capital, up-to-date information on trade, export, and investment opportunities around the world. Other services include key contacts and trade events tailored towards Canadian women, and assistance for companies that are dealing with foreign government buyers through the Canadian Commercial Corporation (Organisations that can help you export www.canadabusiness.ca). In addition, the government furnishes to would-be exporters information on reporting requirements, including those pertaining to restricted goods, because, the federal government 'has a responsibility to ensure that goods entering the international market from Canada do not pose a security threat to those countries' (Canada Border Services Agency n/a, p. 5). The government also makes the publication, Export Controls Handbook, available to would-be exporters. This publication provides information on 'how to obtain the necessary permits for the export or transfer of controlled items and how to comply with the requirements of the Export and Import Permits Act and its related regulations' (Export Controls Handbook 2017, p. 1).

Finally, in the fifth case, which is about government subsidies, procurement policies favouring domestic firms, CanExport, an arm of the federal government provides funds for exporters, innovators, associations and communities that are export oriented, with particular emphasis on small and medium-sized businesses and enterprises run by Indigenous persons or women (Funding and support programs www.tradecommissioner.gc.ca).

2.5 Government/Private Export Promotion Programmes

Many businesses, particularly small and medium-sized businesses do not consider themselves equipped to handle international business. Governments often recognise that firms are not living up to their potential when these firms make no attempt to access potentially lucrative foreign markets. As Brooks and Biesenroeck (2017) point out, 'Most countries operate an export promotion agency to help domestic firms succeed in export markets ... These programs help firms to lower variable or fixed costs of trading, e.g., by assisting firms to find a distributor, navigate foreign customs and product regulations, or adapt to foreign tastes.' While these export promotion programs have increased around the world, according to Freixanet (2012), their benefits lie in the provision of indirect benefits such as sales leads, rather than direct benefits such as the number of orders. Durmusoglu et al. (2012, p. 680), in examining the impact of export promotion programs among small and medium-sized enterprises in Turkey, found a positive impact in four areas, including 'financial, stakeholder relationship, strategic, and organisational learning goal achievements.' It is suggested by Ahmed et al. (2002) that government assistance of export-oriented companies could have the added benefit of expanding production and thus helping companies gain the advantage of economies of scale.

In Canada, private export programmes have run side-by-side with government programmes dating back several decades, with some trade groups organising trade missions by themselves, while also, at times, doing so in conjunction with the government. Even when the trade missions have been organised privately, they have often recognised the importance of taking advantage of government resources overseas or the importance of reporting back to the government about what their findings might have been on the trade mission. While the range of organisations that have participated in trade missions over the years varies widely, umbrella groups such as the Canadian Chamber of Commerce, the Canadian Manufacturing Association, and the Canola Growers Association, have been quite prominent. For example, in 1930, the Canadian Chamber of Commerce, headquartered in Montreal, organised a trade mission to Japan and China, with the full blessing of the Minister of Trade and Commerce, as they hoped to take advantage of the services of 'Canadian trade commissioners in the Far East' (Commerce Reports, 1930, p. 198). With the focus on a particular province, in 1962, the then Economics Minister, upon return from a six-week trip to Europe declared that the government had a special programme to 'organise a group of sales managers and 'order takers' from Ontario industry to go to Europe, 'not to visit and holiday, but to get some orders'' (Must export more and import less 1962, p. 15). In that same year, Manitoba province organised a trade mission to Europe that was judged highly successful (Trade mission is 'off to good start' 1962). In 1965, the suggestion by a Canadian senator to Chinese officials regarding the possibility of reciprocal trade missions, however, was rebuffed by the Chinese side 'on the ground that the idea was impossible as long as Canada maintains its present 'hostile' attitude towards [China]' (Chinese trade 1965).

In 1970, the Canadian Grains Council sent a fact-finding trade mission to 'the Caribbean, South America, and Southeast Asia to lay groundwork for markets that haven't yet been developed for Canadian feed grains' (Canadian Farmers Promote Grain Sales in South America 1970, p. 43). Besides trade organisations and industry groups, Canadian municipalities have sometimes taken on the responsibility of embarking on their own trade missions. Such, for example, was the case for Michael Harcourt, who, as mayor of Vancouver in 1973, 'led an 'Economic Mission' to Kuala Lumpur, Singapore and Hong Kong' (Ley, 2010, p. 38).

As reported in the Winnipeg Free Press, in 1965, as many as 27 specialised trade missions were planned by the Canadian trade department:

> It compares with three such missions in 1960 and five the following year. Last year there were 25 of which 15 were Canadians going abroad. With very impressive results from earlier missions, a department official said that hand-picked groups will spread all over the world during 1965, exploring marketing possibilities for everything from agricultural seeds to consulting engineering. (Trade missions swap, to boost Canada sales 1965, p. 31)

In the 1970s, the Alberta Export Agency sponsored a series of trade missions 'to and from Europe, South America, the Pacific Rim, the Middle East and Africa' (Kennedy 1975, p. 16). The year before, in 1974, the Canadian Association for Latin America (CALA), in connection with the Ontario Industry and Tourism minister, planned five trade missions to Latin America (Kennedy 1975, p. 16). The agency also maintained permanent offices in cities such as 'London, Tokyo, Los Angeles, Ottawa, and Ontario' (Kennedy 1975, p. 16). In 1982, the Alberta Canola Growers Association sent two of their members to Japan on a product promotion mission (Canola growers seek quota to maintain markets 1982, p. 25).

In recent years, Université Laval, has been organising and leading trade missions for businesses in Quebec. These trade missions are 'generally to help the businesses penetrate new international markets (market studies, export assistance) or to internationalise their value chain (import assistance, sub-contracting) (Audet & Marcotte 2018, p. 3). While the students are not paid, the $7,500 fee charged to each participating business helps to defray the cost for the participating students, who get academic credit for their efforts. The range of Canadian associations that organise their own trade missions is wide indeed and include PBB Global Logistics and Alliance of Manufacturers and Exporters, who went on a trade mission to China in the year 2000 (Trade mission to scale the Great Wall 2000), the Canadian Manufacturers and Exporters (CME), who joined the government in a trade mission to Jamaica and Barbados in 2008 (Canadian trade mission heads to Ja, B'dos 2008).

While there have always been trade missions independent of the government, many organisations recognise the importance of keeping the government apprised of their efforts or coordinating with the government so as to extract the best possible benefit from their trade missions.

2.6 Initial Internationalisation Efforts

Following initial concerns about globalisation in the early 1990s, the Canadian government led the charge to view the globe as an opportunity that could be tapped by Canadian businesses. For businesses without export experience, the following were a range of options they could consider.

Personal effort: Reading, networking and the internet

In Canada and the US, there has been access to computers and the internet since the early 1990s, enabling access to export-oriented information. Unfortunately, it can be difficult to determine which information on the internet is valid. For someone with limited experience in international exports, access to large amounts of information could be overwhelming. Books and trade directories offer the opportunity to learn about foreign companies, which may be country or industry specific. For some businesspeople, taking the time to acquire the relevant knowledge may not appear to be cost-effective. They may begrudge spending time conducting research when one could pay a consultant to provide the required information.

International business consultants

International business consultants search for information on potential international partners, where best to set up a branch office and other critical information such as the cultural characteristics of people in the target market. While the use of consultants potentially saves time, it may just provide information rather than lead the businessperson by the hand to the target markets. For a business that wants information, such consultants can be useful, although for someone with little experience of international markets, more is required to develop the confidence to operate in international markets. Furthermore, there is the issue of cost, which has to be balanced against the potential value of information. Consultants who are willing to do more than just provide information may come at a cost that a fledgling business cannot afford.

Castaldi et al. (1992) contended that previous studies of intermediaries in the US demonstrated an almost inverse relationship between perceptions of the importance of such services and the intermediaries' actual level of performance, whereas Canadian exporters felt that their intermediaries more effectively met their export needs. It would be unconscionable for a government to lead its businesspeople into a host country only to have the businesses lose through lack of proper institutional guardrails. This may explain why governments eagerly take an interest in supporting their export-oriented companies. Additionally, companies venturing into foreign markets know that they are weak on their own and that companies 'with privileged access to domestic political actors and close ties to the state enjoy private advantages' (Gertz 2017, p. 1). Like Canadian firms, US companies have not been averse to using the levers of commercial diplomacy to 'facilitate dispute resolution … and by pressuring host states to address investors' complaints by linking individual disputes to the broader bilateral relationship' (Gertz 2017, p. 2). When viewed in this light, it is clear that the attachment that businesspeople have to being led by government leaders is based in pragmatism. For their part, the array of senior diplomats, trade commissioners, trade attachés and other government functionaries and their networks (A Guide to Commercial Diplomacy, 2019, p. 49) make a difference because one of the key reasons many companies hold back is lack of intelligence on the world beyond their own shores:

> Research confirms that when governments have access to a good international network of support offering effective trade promotion and investment attraction services, export sales grow, with significant spillover benefits to the economy as a whole. (A Guide to Commercial Diplomacy, 2019, p. v)

Fraser (2001) points out that successes garnered from trade missions, such as the one taken to China in 2001 were not a matter of accident, and that, 'those contacts and those relationships were made possible by Canadian diplomats who have a solid understanding of one of the most inaccessible countries in the world' (p. A02).

The US Department of Commerce (1984) identified several factors that hampered the international market efforts of most small firms, including a lack of knowledge about how to sell abroad, the idea that exporting is too difficult and the belief that it is not easy to handle the cost of the product and the cost of the transaction. Further, most companies did not have international marketing expertise and considered exporting to be too risky. Some also thought that exporting might be a waste of time (McMahon 1989). Despite misgivings about exporting, many companies have been motivated by the pressure of economic necessity to seek ways to access foreign markets. Even though Canada and the US are neighbours and share a common language, the varying laws and potentially different responses to marketing communications from one region to the other have sometimes posed a challenge to companies. Having to cope with new markets that may have a completely different culture or language could be problematic for companies without the necessary expertise. The next section focuses on some of the complexities that might have made companies receptive to the idea of government assistance in the form of trade missions.

2.7 Challenges of International Marketing

Culture

Differences in values around the world mean that companies often employ different approaches to appeal to customers and would-be business partners. Cultural norms, which can place a wall around consumers, need to be understood if one is to operate successfully around the world. American companies trying to expand their services to Canada have occasionally failed (Bolen 2013), as have Canadian companies seeking to make inroads into the American market (Levinson 2013). Lack of cross-cultural competence has often been cited as the reason for many 'international business failures' (Ruel 2019, p. 32). In fact, in a study of Canadian retailers that attempted to break into the American market, Petersen et al. (2002, p. 207), reported that 'managers' false confidence about similarity between the two markets led to poor financial performance.'

An earlier study by O'Grady and Lane (1997, p. 159) found that of thirty-two Canadian retailers that had entered the United States with the intention of setting up operations, only seven had been successful, and subsequent research indicated that 'there is less cultural similarity in some important areas than previously assumed.' As Suarez (2015, p. 1) suggests, 'How well companies understand and manage culture now can make the difference between success and failure.'

Steenkamp (2001) saw a correspondence between Hofstede's research, which defines four dimensions of cultural variation, namely individualism/collectivism, power/distance, masculinity/femininity, and uncertainty avoidance, and societal problems such as the relationship between the individual and the group, social inequality, social implications of gender, and the handling of uncertainty that comes with economic and social practices (Steenkamp 2001, p. 30).

One criticism of Hofstede's research was that of equating nation-states with cultures and that Hofstede did not adequately address issues of classification, definition and sampling (Baskerville 2003). Hofstede did respond to these criticisms, noting that nations may not be the only units for cross-cultural comparisons, and that they are 'better than nothing' (Hofstede 2002, p. 2). Though country and culture are not necessarily synonymous, there seems to be a meaningful degree of within-country commonality and inter-country differences in culture, which cannot be ignored. Beyond the national level, however, there are other layers of culture, which are better not ignored. Canadian companies seeking to internationalise their operations need to be aware of these differences. Oversimplification of the issue of culture, in fact, may result in mistakes. Any criticism against Hofstede, however, does not erase the fact that there are national, cultural and regional differences that affect how people or businesses relate to one another.

One of the most comprehensive contributions to the study of cross-cultural values is GLOBE (gender egalitarianism, assertiveness, performance orientation and humane orientation), a quantitative study that spanned 10 years and involved 170 investigators, with a sample of 173,000 respondents from 951 organisations spread across 62 different cultural groups (Bertsch 2012). This study built on earlier studies such as that of Hofstede, but focused on managers rather than employees, as had been the case in Hofstede's study of IBM workers from 53 regions (Shi and Wang 2011). The GLOBE study did not negate what Hofstede and other researchers had found but showed that there are indeed differences that can affect outcomes. As Sokoll (2011, p. 141) states, 'Understanding cultural nuances, practices, and dimensions in today's ever globalising world is a key competency for today's organisational leaders and those of the future.'

Ethical dilemmas

Different cultures often have different attitudes towards ethical standards, and, as suggested by McNeil and Pedigo (2001), managers have to cope with ethical dilemmas in day-to-day business life. While the importance of upholding ethical standards is frequently emphasised in the literature, the importance of being culturally sensitive and cultivating mutual respect are also frequently mentioned. With respect to American companies doing business in China, for example, it has been reported that 'Americans have not quite learned to appreciate Chinese ways of doing business and have not always made an adequate effort to adapt to China's business environment' (Rondinelli 1993, p. 68). Canadian companies have also had difficulties operating successfully within the Chinese business environment. This has included issues of how best to present themselves and their products. This difficulty with handling cross-cultural barriers is also highlighted by Fan and Zigang (2004, p. 81), who state that, 'the great barriers caused by cultural differences like difficulty of communication, higher potential transaction costs, different objectives and means of cooperation and operating methods, have led to the failure of many Sino-foreign cooperation projects.'
According to Abramson and Ai (1999), companies that continue to do business in the same way they have in their home markets may fail to win in their new markets. Their research suggests that the size of an organisation did have a bearing on whether or not *guanxi*, a concept that involves exchange of favours and strength of personal

relationships, was important, while the length of time and experience of an individual expatriate also affected perceptions. If *guanxi* is important for small companies and for those newly set up in China, it would mean that Canadian companies considering entering the Chinese market would need a plan that includes how they would enter into the social and business networks known as *guanxi*. As McNeil and Pedigo (2001, p. 305) put it, 'The difficulty of understanding these relationship complexities and the challenge of navigating through this environment for an untried newcomer seems enormous.' The researchers go on to emphasise the necessity for managers of international businesses to create a formal corporate policy to forestall a continuous stream of ethical problems.

Communicating with customers in a foreign market

A Canadian company that can establish a presence in one of the emerging markets in the form of a branch office has to consider how to communicate effectively with the customers. Fletcher and Melewar (2001) observe that while it might be less of a problem for companies to communicate with overseas customers who resemble those in their own home country in terms of education, access to communications infrastructure, culture and position at the higher echelons of the socio-economic scale, and who perhaps possess a measure of westernisation, most of the world's population does not fall within these categories. It is telling that the class of customers that have been of interest to marketers for so long, namely the highly educated, are also experiencing declining birth rates. Fletcher and Melewar (2001) advise businesses to learn to communicate with the bulk of the world's people and to realise the profit potential of emerging economies. Companies that have invested in these new markets have seen their profits rise considerably, as with Coca-Cola, which is doubling its rates of growth in markets such as China, India and Indonesia every three years (Fletcher & Melewar 2001). To the extent that differences exist between developed and emerging markets, a Canadian company that rushes into such a market without adequate knowledge of the extent to which culture influences receptivity to marketing communications could end up losing its investment.

Whereas education levels in countries such as Japan, Canada, Sweden and the United States approach 100 per cent, in some emerging markets literacy rates may be as low as 20 per cent (Fletcher and Melewar 2001). This means that written communications cannot always be counted upon as the means of reaching the population. One example of creative communications methods used is theatre-based product demonstrations in Papua New Guinea (Fletcher and Melewar 2001). Canadian companies interested in such markets would need to be aware of such elements.

Small companies, in particular, need to consider if they have the necessary resources to reach potential customers in a new market (Broek 2017). It is also worth considering if it is even possible to profit in these new markets in light of how much effort the company has to put in. It is hardly surprising, from the foregoing, why there is a debate as to whether larger companies have a much better chance of success in international markets compared to their smaller counterparts.

2.8 Conditions for Success in International Markets

Customer satisfaction

Customer satisfaction is a key consideration for companies seeking success in international marketplaces. The importance of customer satisfaction, the core of marketing, has permeated the world of business and involves ensuring an understanding of customers and the ability to satisfy their needs. Kotler and Armstrong (2011, pp. 4–5) claimed that it is not just a matter of making a sale but, 'if the marketer does a good job of understanding customer needs; develops products that provide superior value; and prices, distributes and promotes them effectively, these products will sell very easily.'

The marketing concept has been empirically linked with higher sales, profitability and new product success. Boone and Kurtz (2013, p. 11) explained that the extent to which a company embraces the marketing concept has a direct bearing on market success and overall success, in that, 'companies that implement market-driven strategies are better able to understand their customers' experiences, buying habits and needs'.

Nakata and Sivakumar (2001) studied how multinational organisations instituted the marketing concept. Additionally, they wanted to determine how national culture could impact that process, which was information vital to Canadian companies looking abroad for greater profits. Among the implications cited by Nakata and Sivakumar (2001) were the need for organisations to be aware of the complexity of deploying the marketing concept and understanding and satisfying customers from different cultural backgrounds.

It is important for the would-be exporter to understand that customer satisfaction can help maintain long-term relationships (Helgesen 2007). While surveys are frequently used to gauge customer satisfaction, in the initial phases of entry, the trade mission participant would probably have to rely on resources in the target country such as trade commissioners to extract as much information as possible about potential customers. Since trade missions sometimes offer the opportunity for participants to meet their counterparts abroad, they could use the opportunity to ascertain directly what the potential customer's needs are. Research also indicates that the two main determinants of customer satisfaction are quality of products and handling of deliveries. As Helgesen (2007, p. 83) writes, 'Consequently, managers of the exporting company should provide quality products and focus on service quality in order to obtain a high level of customer service.'

Managers' positive attitude

Nummela et al. (2004) focused on SMEs which, in the face of increasing competition, might feel at a loss because of lack of adequate resources, experience, skills or the knowledge required to operate in international markets. An orientation towards exporting, learning, and the pursuit of innovation are key hallmarks of an organisation's operations (Fernández-Mesa & Alegre 2015, p. 148). The concept of global orientation underpins the research of Nummela et al. (2004) into the characteristics of Finnish managers in the information and communications technology field. Regardless of which strategy one chooses, there is a measure of commitment required to effectively compete in a broader marketplace. Nummela et al. (2004) concluded that in the information and communications technology business, internationalisation is a prerequisite for success, which may mean travelling to other countries or engaging in research of markets abroad. However, even the most globally minded manager might face other roadblocks such as lack of adequate financing for which the backing of a powerful entity such as the government might help to resolve.

A manager's positive attitude should be reflected in the preparation they make before embarking on the trade mission. A cursory attitude towards the trade mission might mean not paying attention to pre-travel seminars, briefings, or the vast array of resources provided by the trade mission organisers. On the other hand, managers who maintain a positive attitude will ensure that they absorb as much information as possible, follow advice provided by experts on the ground, and do any follow-ups that are necessary following the trade mission.

Global orientation

Nummela et al. (2004) pointed out that the concept of global orientation includes entrepreneurial orientation, which embraces dimensions such as risk-taking, innovativeness and proactiveness. All things being equal, the manager with a global orientation will make a greater effort to overcome obstacles and achieve the goal of accessing the target foreign markets.

When it comes to going on trade missions, it may not be enough to just send anyone who happens to be in a seniority position. People who have a global orientation have a predilection for taking an interest in acquiring new cultures 'such as learning and using languages other than one's mother tongue, obtaining cultural knowledge and multicultural experiences, learning the customs, traditions, and norms of other cultures' (Chen et al. 2015, p. 304). A person with such an orientation is likely to feel more comfortable on a trade mission and to seek to extract information that could be of use to a company. So, care ought to be taken in the choice of who is designated to represent a company on a trade mission.

Knowledge and skills

Nummela et al. (2004) claimed that it is not enough to have a global orientation; one also needs to possess knowledge and skills such as foreign language ability to engender successful penetration into foreign markets. On the subject of global orientation, Nummela et al. (2004, p. 51) suggested that not all SME managers have the ability to enter into global operations and that the most important criterion for distinguishing successful companies from less successful ones in the future is 'in-house human-resource capital.' This raises the question whether global orientation is something that can easily be acquired. Nummela et al. (2004) argued that global orientation relates to international experience and international education. Therefore, companies that have staff with international experience and international education have a better chance of success in breaking into the international market and should be prioritised by governments or organisations offering export assistance.

Just signing up for a trade mission without taking the time to build background knowledge is bound to lead to frustration. 'Preparation, patience, and persistence' (Deng, Verma, & Lendsey 1995, p. 56) have been cited as being important when dealing with Malaysian businessmen; it may apply to more than just Malaysian businessmen, however. Having the requisite knowledge to prepare one's company's 'product's competitive features and the promotional literature' (Deng, Verma, & Lendsey 1995, p. 56) are some of the key elements would-be trade mission participants have to consider. The frustrations of small exporters quite often stem from 'a lack of planning and preparation. Either the exporters do not know what to do or, if they know what to do, do not think it is actually necessary' (Deng, Verma, & Lendsey 1995, p. 56).

Willingness to learn

In considering export performance, Nummela et al. (2004) posited that willingness to learn is a key driver of global orientation even for managers who do not have international experience. Having worked in a foreign country or obtained an education in a foreign country could signal that one can adapt to a foreign environment, although it says nothing about one's attitude towards the foreign countries in question.

Nummela et al. (2004) apprised managers of the need to be aware of people in their ranks with a background in dealing across national and cultural lines. Participating in a trade mission offers an opportunity for experiential learning that can complement what one might glean from books or from talking to people who have prior experience of trade missions. Students at the University of Laval, Quebec, Canada, who participated in trade missions as international development officers and coordinators, for their part, learned about 'sales: knowing how to sell a product or service, communicating convincingly, knowing how to negotiate and properly representing the interests of a client' (Audet & Marcotte 2018, p. 5). For participants in trade missions, whether at the preparatory stage, the mission proper, or the aftermath, the trade mission is essentially a 'learning event' (Ruel 2018, p. 71).

Marketing expertise

Ogunmokun and Ng (2004) examined additional factors besides global orientation. The primary thrust of their research was to determine why some Australian companies performed better on the exporting front. Factors that signalled success included motivation to export, firm characteristics, marketing expertise, managers' attitude towards exporting, marketing strategies and exporting problems. Marketing expertise accounted for as much as 27 per cent of success in exports compared with companies that performed poorly in exports. Companies with a lack of knowledge of overseas markets had a significantly lower probability for success (Ogunmokun & Ng 2004). For companies that lacked overseas marketing expertise, matchmaking—putting the Canadian Trade Commissioners at the service of Canadian exporters—was a big part of the TCTM.

Trade mission participants will initially benefit from taking advantage of existing resources about marketing expertise from the organiser, government brochures or from their own research. But it must be understood that the marketplace is not static. It is continually evolving. Thus, the would-be exporter would have to 'respond to changing needs and expectations of the marketplace, including moves by their competition (Boso, Adeola, Danso, and Assadinia 2019, 138). In order to properly do so, the trade mission participant should take advantage of the trade mission to gather information that would help develop a marketing edge. This could also mean understanding more than just the superficial aspects of the culture.

Differentiation

Another major factor in successful internationalisation was the extent to which companies were able to benefit from market skimming and pricing or to differentiate their products in the foreign marketplace, which accounted for approximately 23 per cent of success in conducting international business (Ogunmokun & Ng 2004, p. 172). Additionally, the extent to which managers believed that exporting was more profitable than focusing on the domestic venture was important. Ogunmokun and Ng (2004, p. 172) concluded that:

> The managers of successful firms studied had a more positive perception and attitude towards exporting compared to the managers of unsuccessful firms. This could mean that the attainment of good performance in exporting requires having a positive perception towards exporting.

Organisations that prepare prior to making forays into the international market have a good chance of success. Spence (2003) found that acquiring specific knowledge about target markets before embarking on missions, and prior communication with potential business partners, boosted the chances of success. This was corroborated by Alvarez's (2004) research in Chile, which demonstrated that participants involved in preparatory activities before embarking on trade missions made significant commercial gains from the marketing events. This has implications for understanding the TCTM strategy. It could be argued that the high level of publicity that attended the trade missions, during the pre- and post-mission phases, may have contributed to raising awareness among non-exporting companies regarding the benefits of accessing foreign markets. Attending a trade mission sometimes allows a participant to meet a potential match. As it is likely that the product that is being marketed might have competition from the target market and elsewhere, being able to articulate what makes one's products different from others could be highly useful in not just getting a toehold in the new market, but also being able to penetrate the target market more deeply. One area where differentiation has proven particularly important is in 'service differentiation capabilities' (Durmaz & Eren 2018, p. 191).

Marketing policy elements

Marketing policy elements relate to export market selection and competitive pricing, as well as to payment terms, packaging characteristics, new product development and promotional efforts. In this connection, the exporting firm cannot ignore the importance of possible foreign distributor competencies, which might be sought to facilitate the process. Knight and Cavusgill (2004, p. 133) argued that 'this is because quality products are easier for foreign distributors to sell and foreign distributors can also enhance product quality by providing superior after-sales service, [and] intensive distribution.'

Burton and Schlegelmilch (1987) focused on background and attitudinal factors within exporting and non-exporting firms and found that exporting firms were more likely to have a higher level of formal education among staff and the possibility that managers spoke a foreign language. Exporters also appeared to be more committed to the development of new products and were more flexible and willing to seek new information. Conversely, non-exporters were more complacent and focused on short-term rather than long-term goals. Understanding what the competition offers when it comes to payment terms, packaging, and range of products, can all help a would-be exporter to craft terms that will find resonance in the target market. Tapping into the whole range of resources available through the trade mission and its ancillary services such as the trade commissioner program can help an exporter avoid unnecessary mistakes in entering a new market.

Commercial, Economic, Business and Cultural diplomacy

Commercial diplomacy, unlike economic diplomacy which focuses on 'policy issues and trade agreements' (Ruel 2019, p. 9) settles on 'policy making and business support' (Ruel 2019, p. 9), and makes use of both government and non-government channels to seek out 'new markets and investment opportunities' (Ruel 2019, p. 10; Pigman 2016, p. 1). It has also been described as a service that the government performs for the benefit of the business community (Kostecki & Naray 2007). Most governments, including that of Canada, maintain as part of their diplomatic functions a division that focuses on trade and has as part of its goal the promotion of the nation's commercial activities in the country or region in which the embassy is located. While there is not much that can be done about such external factors as the state of the economy in a target market, it seems that, for many other factors, governments can play a role. It is for this reason that one Australian industrialist said that 'Business is conducted by companies, but governments may open doors' (Kostecki & Naray 2007). In this regard, Canadian companies have a distinct advantage in having a government willing to ensure that its diplomatic relations with potential partners are largely favourable. In fact, trade missions, as Ruel (2019, p. xi, 8) avers, take pride of place as the most prominent instrument in the range of commercial diplomacy options open to governments. Pigman (2016, p. 16) also echoes the idea that the trade mission is 'one of the oldest forms of diplomacy.'

What is referred to in the literature as economic diplomacy, makes use of a wide variety of diplomatic tools such as lobbying, negotiation, and intelligence gathering on the part of public officials, particularly those from diplomatic missions to support 'the promotion of certain types of trade and foreign direct investments that advance the country's economic interest' (Assche & Warin, 2019, p. 16). Trade missions are cited, along with export promotion services and investment promotion centres as part of the nation's efforts to win through economic diplomacy. Business diplomacy centres more on the relationship between a company and various non-business counterparts. For instance, 'global companies are expected to abide by multiple sets of national laws and multilateral agreements set down by international organisations such as the World

Trade Organisation (WTO) and the International Labour Organisation (ILO)' (Saner, Liu & Sondergaard, 2001, p. 85).

Whether it's a matter of commercial diplomacy, cultural diplomacy, economic diplomacy, or business diplomacy, governments such as that of Canada do not see any reason why they should hold back on using government resources to facilitate external trade, considering that, at worst, it would have little or no effect, and at best, it might contribute significantly towards helping Canadian companies to extract significant revenues from their operations in foreign markets.

Business diplomacy involves executives and their representatives establishing and keeping positive relationships with foreign government leaders and non-governmental stakeholders as a way to build credibility and sustain a sense of legitimacy in the eyes of their international counterparts (Saner et al. 2000). It has become increasingly evident that the quality of a company's products alone is not enough to garner success in foreign markets. Thus, the would-be exporter or international business player is almost compelled to enter into interactions or negotiations with local and international non-governmental organisations that keep an eye on how global companies handle their business dealings (Betlem 2012). Other elements that require the attention of those engaged in business diplomacy are the need to keep an eye on 'working conditions, environmental standards and employment practices' (Betlem 2012, p. 1). Success at business diplomacy also means being aware of the workings of international trade bodies and organisations and taking steps to avoid possible conflicts.

In dealing with companies, customers, and governments with a different set of cultural values, exporters can deploy their diplomatic skills, which simply means taking strategic steps to get what they want 'without arousing hostility' (London 1999, p. 11). This also means that those engaged in business diplomacy have to be adept at negotiating, mediating and convincing others in a manner that is respectful and takes consideration of the needs of their counterparts (London 1999).

Saner (2009) suggests that governments can be most effective in supporting their trade agenda if there is a high level of coordination among different ministers.

After all, products that may be up for export may come from a wide variety of sectors, requiring leaders from all those varied sectors to work together.

In addition, the increasing need for firms to operate outside their domestic sphere has meant that many firms with little or no experience dealing with governments now have to seek a way to do so. For some, the most obvious way is to tag along with government leaders from their own country who may have credibility with their foreign counterparts, allowing the unknown businesses to operate under the glow of their own government in the eyes of the foreign businesses and potential prospects. Though governments, such as that of Canada, have been willing to take on this role, companies can themselves make use of the strategies of business diplomacy, 'which seeks to transfer and adapt the techniques and mindset of the diplomat to the needs of the firm' (Riordan 2014, p. 1). Rather than blithely entering foreign markets without preparation, would-be international traders need to take into consideration the geopolitical risks to which they could be exposed in any given market. This also means coming to an understanding of the key actors, governmental and otherwise, 'who shape those risks' (Riordan 2014, p. 1). In addition, success could mean expanding a company's networks so that when confronting new challenges, the responsibility does not fall on a singular entity but on the group. Through business diplomacy, firms can form coalitions that would exert pressure on 'governments or other key actors to change regulatory frameworks, change the law or modify their behaviour' (Riordan 2014, p. 5).

The other side of business diplomacy, of course, is public diplomacy, which relates more to how governments, through various programmes aimed at foreign audiences, seek to shape perceptions in order to 'protect a country's national interests' (Ordeix-Rigo & Duarte 2009, p. 550). But executors of public diplomacy need not necessarily be confined to official government representatives. This is because public diplomacy cuts across trade and culture to encompass other areas of life such as tourism, entertainment, and the economy as a whole. Ordeix-Rigo and Duarte (2009) suggest that companies take a more proactive role in public diplomacy to 'draft and implement their own programs, independent from the government's initiatives' (p. 555).

If done properly, a company might end up getting the all-important sense of power and legitimacy it needs to operate successfully in another country.

Companies seeking to export have to confront the reality of going into uncharted waters in terms of disparities in market culture, everyday business practices, channels of distribution, legal structures and communication networks (Morgan et al. 2012). While a company can use external resources such as trade missions to prepare for foreign market entry, there are other prerequisites that may straddle the internal and the external. For example, Morgan et al. (2012) identified some antecedents to exporting: marketing planning, which involves the deployment of planning skills and the setting of marketing goals; market information acquisition, which involves identifying how competitors have accessed the target market and learning from multiple sources about customers, competitors and modes of distribution in the market of interest; information interpretation, which involves integrating acquired information to arrive at some insights regarding the possibility of success; and finally, market information dissemination, which involves sharing key insights with decision-makers in the organisation.

The research was based on thousands of raw data in the form of bulletins, press releases, success stories, produced by the Department of Foreign Affairs, journal and newspaper articles spanning the breadth and width of Canada, along with speeches by government officials and government reports. Information on some of the participating companies can be found in one portion of the data used for this research.[7]

Regarding the antecedents, prior to the trade missions, potential participants were advised to analyse the extent to which they were ready to engage in export. They were also advised to undertake market research in order to ascertain that the target country really did offer potential benefits to them. In addition, rather than going blindly, potential participants were encouraged to identify their potential customers in the target market and to 'understand your competition in the market and how you can best compete' (How to Prepare for your Trade Mission http://www.tradecommissioner.gc.ca/). In

---

[7] Team Canada Trade Missions – Database: https://works.bepress.com/everettofori/58/

addition, would-be participants were advised to send senior decision-makers on the trip and to ensure that these representatives had their market research and training materials at hand. Finally, participants were asked to 'arrange matchmaking meetings in advance' (How to Prepare for your Trade Mission http://www.tradecommissioner.gc.ca/) and to prepare and review their marketing and promotional materials before departure. Finally, advice on post-mission follow-up was also offered. The trade commissioners who assist would-be trade mission participants also provide information on country and sector information, tariff, sanctions and export controls, funding and support, and a wealth of export guides and statistics.

In the course of gathering information on their own, some companies might conclude that the learning curve could be shortened through participation in a trade mission, since trade mission organisers, whether private or government-affiliated, provide much of the information that serve as prerequisites for foreign market entry. Some companies might conclude that having the guidance of knowledgeable people such as those associated with a trade mission would increase their chances of success. Kostecki and Naray (2007) maintained that the value-creating activities of commercial diplomacy include support activities, such as ascertaining whether there is a market for a product, potential business matches in the target market and answering basic questions on the legal and political status of the target market. If companies were to undertake the market intelligence necessary to determine whether to enter a market, it might be too costly in terms of money and time. The government's facilitation of business by undertaking background work does not mean that the government takes over the functions of a company. Rather, governments introduce companies but do not do the business for them (Kosteki & Naray 2007).

The importance of trade to the Canadian government and the perception of the government regarding its role are reflected in the large number (more than 160) of trade commission offices maintained around the world (Our Trade Offices n.d.). These offices have experts with business and host country expertise and experience, and these professionals can offer Canadian companies in-depth information to facilitate business dealings. The trade commission offices continually conduct research and can locate potential business partners. In 1945, Canada had 38 missions. By 1981, there were 110 missions in 78 countries and by 2003, there were 164 missions abroad with more than 500 trade commissioners (Potter 2004). There are costs involved in participating in trade missions, so companies must consider carefully whether it is worth the investment. In addition to paying for the cost of participation, there is also a temporary loss of the services of participating personnel.

The use of overseas trade offices is part of economic diplomacy, which encompasses the activities that governments undertake through their international networks, 'to enable international trade and investment' (Moons & van Bergeijk 2016, p. 1). While some literature has cast doubt on the efficacy of such government assistance (e.g., Seringhaus & Botschen 1991), governments nevertheless continue to provide such assistance. They recognise that it is costly for individual businesses to gather relevant information from countries with which they are wholly unfamiliar and that government establishments in foreign locales can, with proper staffing and expertise, unearth and compile information useful to many businesses. If individual companies were to invest these resources they would be less inclined to share such information with their competitors (Moons & van Bergeijk 2016, p. 1). However, government provision of such information can benefit a large swathe of the business community and save time and money, which allows these companies to invest their resources in other areas.

The literature suggests that government is very much at the centre when it comes to some of the most successful trade missions around the world. This was the case during the Clinton administration in the 1990s, when the US Commerce Secretary, Ron Brown, led numerous businesspeople to several countries around the world. Brown's successor, William Daley, made the point that commercial diplomacy continued to be important, stating that 'our commercial officers and our ambassadors are totally engaged in trying to help American business' (Dunne 1998, p. 14). In the US, senior government officials have played an active role in the promotion of US-made telecommunications systems as well as power plants and other goods. For example, the Clinton administration won a $6 billion order from Saudi Arabia in 1994 for commercial jets owing to pressure from the president and vice-president, secretary of state and ministers for commerce and transportation (Dunne 1998). The issue of interdependence between the government and businesses is not unique to TCTM. The Canadian government, realising that the success of businesses means more revenues from taxes, chose to use its clout to open doors of opportunity for businesses. Under Chrétien, Canada appeared to take the notion of commercial diplomacy seriously, with the government playing an active part in seeking and facilitating business opportunities. Clarke (1998, p. 26) explained:

> TCTM are among the biggest shows the Canadian business and government communities can mount. These treks to distant lands are meant to impress, to put Canada's name on the map in far-off markets by placing our corporate and government heavyweights on display. And box office has been boffo.

For the government officers working behind the scenes, much background work is involved. This may mean continual expansion of trade databases of eligible companies, sending out thousands of invitations with telephone follow-ups, and consultations with key stakeholders both within Canada and abroad to produce publications such as the World Information Network for Exporters (WINS), which lists over 30,000 Canadian exporters and businesses and makes this available to foreign importers (Longenecker 2009). Also, with the array of information available, DFAIT can get TCTM participants to 'join networks in China or Taiwan by introducing them to new customers, distributors or agents' (Groen, Cook, & Van der Sijde, 2015, p. 44). Further, as Boyer (2003) explains, the Department of Foreign Affairs and International Trade (DFAIT) organised meetings for would-be Team Canada trade mission participants in order to provide them with the political and economic overviews of target countries as well as put them into contact with foreign business representatives, ambassadors, and trade specialists. In fact, 'special attention is given to culture and language training, which will provide a background for subsequent meetings and social events abroad' (Boyer 2003, p. 144).

The seriousness with which Canada approached the TCTM demonstrated that Team Canada was more than just a matter of trade missions. Prior to Chrétien embarking on his fourth major trade mission in 1997 with nine premiers and about four hundred businesspeople, McCarthy (1997, p. A2) noted that, 'the Team Canada mission is a chance to highlight its effort to expand exports as a key job creation tactic.' Eight years later, Wadhva and Woo (2005, p. 14) affirmed that the trade missions were a 'unique partnership in Canada's international business development efforts to increase trade and create jobs and growth in Canada.'

Ruel et al. (2013) considered commercial diplomacy to be increasingly important because it typically involves the gathering of information, lobbying and advocacy work and the representation of a country's commercial interests by businesses and government representatives. In the case of Canada, commercial diplomacy included the foreign ministry's support of TCTM and the enlistment of embassy staff and commercial attachés to facilitate meetings and accommodate the needs of business participants. According to Ruel et al. (2013, p. 15) this kind of government intervention on behalf of businesses can facilitate trade and contribute to the growth of investments.

In fact, while export promotion often gets attention as a key element of commercial diplomacy, the term encompasses 'investment support, promoting the country's brand, country image building and facilitation in trade disputes' (Naray & Bezençon 2017, p. 334). The Canadian government played a part in all the four areas mentioned above. For example, in terms of investment support, one of the companies that is the pride of Canada and has continually received government investments and subsidies for expansion and export is Bombardier, a company that started out manufacturing snowmobiles but now has become well known for its 'railcars and jets' (Mackinnon & Marotte 2001). In 2001, the Chrétien government provided a $2 billion loan to 'help Bombardier compete for a contract' (Mackinnon & Marotte 2001). Also, the Export Development Corporation of Canada is a Canadian government entity that is charged specifically with providing 'credit insurance, financing, bonding services, and foreign investment insurance to Canadian companies. Under the Export Development Act, the Government of Canada is authorised in prescribed circumstances to undertake certain activities, of a financial nature, directly to facilitate and develop export trade' (Ariff 1998, p. 36).

One area in which the Canadian government has been at pains to try to change the image of Canada is in the high-technology sector. Canada is a nation that manufactures airplanes, contributes to medical innovations, and has played a part in some of the greatest engineering marvels, including the development of the Canadarm that is part of the International Space Station. And, yet, the perception persists that Canada is a snow-laden prairie wasteland. As James K. Bartleman, who worked closely with Prime Minister Jean Chrétien, explained, the image of Canada continued to be that of a raw materials supplier 'even though manufactured goods had long dominated Canadian export sales. This 'branding' problem made it that much harder for Canadian exporters of high technology products to penetrate the European market and discouraged European investment in our hi-tech sector' (Bartleman 2011, p. 79). Thus, the government felt a responsibility to build the image of the country and to let it be known around the world that Canada was so much more than the old perceptions. Finally, when it came to trade disputes, Canada was one of the architects of the development of the World Trade Organisation, a dispute settlement organisation. But more than that, since the Canadian government perceives successful export of Canadian products as being a plus, it does a great deal to support such companies when they run afoul of other countries' laws. One of the more prominent examples is the longstanding Canadian softwood lumber dispute with the United States. The Canadian government has intervened in many ways to seek a solution that would ensure the viability of the softwood lumber industry in Canada (Duckenfield 2017).

Some TCTM participants were cultural emissaries in the sense that the products they promoted abroad were of a cultural nature, associated with the arts, film, or education. While proponents of cultural diplomacy might not tout the direct economic benefits of such efforts, the interchange of ideas, sharing of information, art and other elements of culture that might foster cultural understanding is not trivial. Only when nations enjoy peaceful relations and mutual respect can they build upon this foundation to extract the benefits that might accrue from trading relations. While cultural diplomacy might be characterised as 'soft power,' it:

> Can also have a harder edge in that it can actively leverage and positively energise diplomacy in such areas of concern as human rights, concern for the environment, disaster relief, overseas aid and development and the potential dangers of climate change for future generations. (Hurn 2016, p.80)

The matter of human rights was a frequent topic of discussion even while the Chrétien government barrelled forward in its export promotion activities. The softer image that Canada frequently projected in the world might have made it easier for the country to be accepted, opening up the way for the country to let others know the country's true capabilities.

The European Union has been very serious about the use of commercial diplomacy especially when it comes to the energy sector. It has done so by establishing the Common Commercial Policy (CCP), which allows member countries to speak with one voice. Stoddard (2017, p.5) highlights two kinds of commercial diplomacy, namely, one geared towards 'investment promotion' and another focused on 'investment protection' and points out that with regards to investment promotion, governments are not unwilling to pass on market intelligence to companies or match companies with the right overseas partners.

Separately, the Netherlands has been paying closer attention to the deployment of commercial diplomacy. For example, embassy staff or trade commissioners provide background assistance for trade mission participants. This falls under the aegis of commercial diplomacy, and may include intelligence, networking, or matching services. In studying Dutch officers filling roles in commercial diplomacy, Ruel (2012) suggests that both officers with an affinity for business and those with a more political bent can be useful in serving client firms, that is, as long as they see business promotion of companies from their country as their primary purpose (Ruel 2012). Also, in the case of Croatia, two key goals of the government's commercial diplomacy efforts have been to increase exports and attract foreign direct investments (Boromisa, Tisma & Raditya-

Lezaic 2012, p. 37). In these respects, the Canadian government under Chrétien was not a complete outlier for seeking to help domestic businesses make breakthroughs in the international arena.

Firm size

Katsikeas et al. (1997) attempted to make fine distinctions among exporters by noting that some companies only have experimental involvement, whereas others may have active involvement and still others, committed involvement. In the Katsikeas et al. (1997) study, this classification was used as a basis for gauging the degree of success of export-oriented companies. The authors argued, as did Ogunmokun and Ng (2004), that firm size plays a major role, not only in a company's inclination towards exporting, but also in its potential success. Katsikeas et al. (1997, p. 53) explained that larger organisations may have more resources that allow them to make more effort towards their export goals and to deal with the risks that attend such efforts.

TCTM made it a point to reach out to smaller firms because such firms might have been reluctant to go into foreign markets due to perceived risk factors and the possible lack of slack in their operations. For smaller companies, participation in trade missions could launch them into foreign markets within an environment of trust, which is provided through the support they receive from their government. For example, as part of their functions the TCTM organisers found potential matches for Canadian companies. For small firms, the fear of making major mistakes in that area is virtually eliminated, which facilitates their entry into international markets in a way that they might not have been able to do by themselves.

Katsikeas (1997) found that market accessibility appeared to be a major consideration for small firms in comparison with medium-sized ones. The relatively smaller resource base of these smaller companies meant their having to devote more resources to the task of accessing foreign markets. It appeared that the TCTM organisers took an inclusive approach by not limiting themselves to large firms. While some take it for granted that greater firm size provides a better foundation to venture abroad because of greater access to financial and human resources, others consider the potential to absorb risk as the advantage possessed by larger firms when it comes to internationalisation.

Calof (1993) considered whether there was a relationship between size and internationalisation and if size was a barrier to internationalisation. Despite the common perception that it is the larger firms that have a better chance of success in internationalisation, much of the growth in exports, in Canada has come from SMEs. Small companies often benefit from using a niche strategy and are vital to the country's economic prospects (Goldenberg, 1991). Research conducted by Statistics Canada near the beginning of the TCTM program suggested that small companies do better in local job creation than their larger counterparts. Small businesses comprise up to 98 per cent of businesses in Canada and are demonstrably important for net job creation, having been responsible for creating 77.7 per cent of private jobs between 2002 and 2012 (Key Small Business Statistics – 2013). While Industry Canada defines small businesses as being firms with fewer than 100 employees, statistics show that small businesses employed around five million people by 2011, which represented 48 per cent of the total labour force in the private sector (Key Small Business Statistics, July 2012).

The literature provides conflicting reports, with some indicating a relationship between size and export intensity (e.g., Czinkota & Johnston 1983). Others (e.g., Bonnacorsi 1992) find no discernible relationship between size and export orientation and suggest that small firms are not at a significant disadvantage in exporting. Conversely, Spence and Crick (2004) found that those with some experience in the export field benefited more from participation in a trade mission. Calof (1993) explained that part of the problem for this inconsistency may be the differences in methodology and how size is measured. While some researchers used the number of employees, others used the amount of sales. There has been little interest in focusing on the particular markets served, which may also account for some of the disparities in the results.

Calof (1993) used two archival sources: a database of 38 Ontario exporters that had sales between $10 million and $250 million, and a database known as Business Opportunity Sourcing System (BOSS), which was established by the Canadian government. The firms in the BOSS database were encouraged to update the information yearly. Calof (1993) argued that the sample size of 38 limited the generalisability of the results. In addition, it seems more likely that the firms that responded fit into the category of medium-sized rather than small or large. Further, only companies in Ontario were included, which raised the question of whether these companies could be taken to be representative of Canadian companies.

Calof (1993) found that even the smallest firms were able to successfully engage in international trade because more than half of those in the BOSS database had some form of international operation:

> Small firms had higher levels of export intensity than large firms. Forty-six percent of all small firms' observations were in the highest sales intensity class compared to 15 percent for large firms. (Calof 1993, p. 60)

However, larger firms served a greater number of markets compared to smaller firms. Calof (1993) concluded that large firms were better able to find and take advantage of international opportunities due to their greater resources. However, their export intensity was lower compared to smaller firms, which indicates that the latter often depended to a greater extent on foreign trade for their survival and profits. The implications are that managers ought not to view size as an insurmountable hurdle to internationalisation. Small firms may have fewer resources, but Calof (1993) asserted that this should not deter them from entering foreign markets. Resources are required for any successful internationalisation strategy, although the number of resources can be pegged to the scope of the strategy (Calof, 1993). It seems that the Team Canada strategy of including SMEs in its efforts was not misplaced and that these companies had an opportunity, through internationalisation, to help their companies grow and to potentially contribute to the country's balance of payments. The Canadian economy grew steadily in the 1990s at an average of 3.2 per cent each year from 1991 to 2001 and by 2002, exports represented 41.2 per cent of GDP, which indicates a strong orientation to exports (OECD 2004).

Product type

A further aspect considered by Katsikeas et al. (1997) was product type. While manufacturing firms seem to be a common target for research, an examination of the TCTM participants revealed that export success was not confined to those in the manufacturing sector. For example, educational firms were among the service firms that enjoyed success through the efforts of the trade missions.

A key to success was the establishment and development of a competitive distribution market overseas. In some countries, such as China and Japan, the distribution network seemed opaque to foreigners, success required bringing some knowledgeable insiders within the target market on board. Holley (1994, p. 1) explained:

> Japan's infamous multilayered system not only jacks up prices by 30% or more, due to profit taking at each level of the network, but it also ends up blocking foreign manufacturers from contact with their customer base.

Katsikeas et al. (1997) found that firms exporting industrial products had a tendency to use a more direct distribution approach due to concerns about meeting product quality and technical standards. Also important may be the need to guarantee a reliable product along with after-sales service support (Thorelli & Glowacka 1995). It is understandable why companies, worried about opacity in markets such as that of Japan, would seek assistance to establish themselves in those markets.

Market selection

Companies that want to export require a concrete strategy to identify relevant markets. Katsikeas et al. (1997) argued that making the right choice of markets has a bearing on whether a company attains success, which applies to all areas of exporting. There are many different markets with great differences in characteristics. While some companies have been able to assure the ubiquity of their products in major markets around the world, the issue of where to begin such an undertaking is one that appears to be daunting to companies that perceive themselves as lacking the necessary expertise to succeed.

Market selection is also a decision that should not be made on a whim. Quite often, the selection process for trade mission participants involves ascertaining a measure of correspondence between the applicants and the target market. Beyond this, if a company has developed an export plan, this would help define more clearly where it wants to direct its efforts. As Cavusgil (1993, p. 1) writes, 'To succeed in exporting, a company must identify attractive export markets and estimate the export potential for its products in them as accurately as possible.'

2.9 Trade Fairs

Trade fairs have been a popular way by which a company can showcase its products to a wider market. Each year, thousands of trade fairs are held around the world, often with specific product themes such as watches, jewellery, or medical equipment. Trade fairs provide a convenient means for manufacturers and distributors to expose their wares to their potential customers and may offer an opportunity to sell directly to potential customers. For example, in the field of luxury watches, trade fairs have always been a place to display new products and to make some sales, as noted in this report:

> Watches costing more than $100,000 were plentiful at the fairs and timepieces in excess of $1 million emerged as the new benchmark for the extraordinary, largely because of demand from Asia, Russia, the Middle East and the US. (Murphy 2007, p. 1)

Seringhaus and Rosson (2001) debunked the notion that trade fairs usually focus on domestic buying and selling and that the minimal buying and selling of foreign products does not require serious study. The recognition of the importance of trade fairs to businesses is evident from the sizeable marketing budget that many companies devote to these shows. In this respect, some areas of study that have engaged the attention of scholars include understanding what drives people to attend trade shows, the ways in which visitors interact with those exhibiting their wares, financial and other costs associated with attending the events, how much it might cost to participate and how governments use such events to promote their countries' exports (Seringhaus & Rosson 2001).

Companies that decide to participate in trade fairs often have to consider the type of products they wish to showcase and the geographical region in which the exhibition would take place. Concerning the vast array of trade fairs available, Seringhaus and Rosson (2001) suggested that only through research and analysis can a company make the right decision regarding where and in what trade fair to participate, often with the view to maintaining or boosting current business. Participation in a trade fair requires substantial planning, including booth design, display, production and pre-fair promotion. With regards to the potential benefits of participation in trade fairs, Seringhaus and Rosson (2001, p. 881) argued:

> The reality for most companies is that it is qualified leads that are generated at the fair, to be converted into sales through subsequent contact or sales calls. In some industry sectors, where the sales cycle is long, conversion will likely take months (or even years).

Important as trade fairs may be, they appear to be of greatest benefit to companies that have already made a name for themselves and are easily recognisable. A company without name recognition requires help of the kind that trade missions appear to offer.

B. Trade Missions
2.10 Trade Missions

Seringhaus (1989, p. 5), declared that 'research on trade missions is scarce. This is particularly interesting since trade missions are found in the export promotion programmes of many trade-oriented nations.' Reducing the risk of entry into a foreign market is one of the key issues of international trade and marketing. Commitment and a deep understanding of a new environment and culture are crucial. This 'usually means adapting the company's products, programmes and approaches to the special needs and circumstances of each new global market' (Kotler & Armstrong 1997, p. 527). There are benefits to participation in trade missions, with Hibbert (1995, p.141) suggesting that trade missions play a positive role by:

- facilitating market research
- allowing participants to collectively develop more effort to market investigation
- having greater promotional impact on market
- carrying a certain news value that serves trade publicity
- gaining access to high-level business and government officials
- providing wider and deeper contact coverage by raising general consciousness in the home country regarding foreign markets
- providing important educational experience in the home country for inexperienced exporters
- providing beneficial intra-group exchange and contacts for experienced exporters.

Seringhaus (1989) identified two main types of trade missions: incoming missions, in which potential buyers and importers visit exporters in the host country under the auspices of a government or private organisation, and exporters entering a foreign market selected by the organiser of the mission. Seringhaus (1989) argued that because a firm's initial move into a foreign market may be potentially risky, trade missions are likely to be of most benefit to firms just starting out in their exploration of foreign markets. This raises the question of why some companies, including those associated with TCTM, kept participating in trade missions long after they had passed the neophyte stage. This suggests the possibility that beyond the facilitation of personal visits and contacts, trade missions offer something more, which serves the needs of companies with some years of experience in international markets. Seringhaus' (1989) research took a different approach to that of Nummela et al. (2004), who had sought an association between global orientation and export performance. Seringhaus (1989) argued that planning orientation in a company's international marketing strategy was a key success factor, which suggests that companies in which global orientation might be lacking, but where planning and strategic marketing exist, can succeed in international markets. As such, the emphasis was not on past associations, travel or education, but focused on what managers were willing to do in the present and future to achieve their export goals. Oudalov (2013) emphasised that the needs of organisations might change depending on how far along they are situated on the export experience continuum. A beginning exporter might seek to reduce uncertainty, whereas a more experienced exporter may attempt to deepen or expand connections with trade counterparts abroad.

Seringhaus (1989) used a sample of 90 respondents, 59 per cent of whom were trade mission users and 41 per cent non-users. These SMEs were involved in manufacturing, including machinery making, metal fabrication and the electronics sector in Canada. Seringhaus (1989) found that trade mission users were more systematic and oriented to research and planning in their domestic and export-related activities. Having comprehensive information and contacts such as those offered by TCTM could be attractive to companies that had an interest in planning their entry into foreign markets regardless of whether their managers have a global orientation. Another element considered by Seringhaus (1989) was market entry, for which trade missions emerged as being important. The research indicated that without the assistance provided through trade missions, it would have been very difficult for some companies to make connections with potential business partners and to effectively evaluate the quality of opportunities or garner sales. For participants who are new to the host country, having organisers set up meetings with potential business partners and arrange meeting places helps to 'generate more leads and larger sales' (Spence 2003). Some non-users may already have regarded themselves as being quite successful and felt that there was no need to participate in trade missions. They might have believed that they had the knowledge or knew of other means besides trade missions to obtain the required information. Seringhaus (1989) found that while users expected specific export performance, non-users considered trade missions to simply be sources of information.

Firms that believed their lack of knowledge might hamper successful entry into foreign markets were more likely to take advantage of opportunities offered by trade missions. Seringhaus (1989, p. 5) argued that 'trade mission users experienced greater knowledge-related barriers (such as conducting market research and coping with foreign business practices) than non-users.' In terms of the market entry process, it emerged that non-users were slower to generate customers within the target market. With regard to market entry effectiveness and export market diversification, Seringhaus (1989) found that while non-users generally displayed more rapid expansion, they exited the market at a greater rate than users. Although non-users might enter foreign markets confidently at the beginning on the basis of their perceptions of what knowledge is adequate for success and might attempt to do so without the support of trade missions, they are likely to falter along the way. There is a compelling case for continual involvement in trade missions over several years until a solid basis for success has been established though Palangkaraya and Webster (2019, p. 1) report that after some time there may "diminishing returns for repeat participants.' Those participating in trade missions may have access to current knowledge and often the services of various government officials and consultants who can help them adapt to different scenarios, thus helping to increase their chances of success in a foreign market. However, non-users that lack any credible conduit to upgrade their knowledge may lose their enthusiasm and confidence as they come upon one roadblock or another.

Seringhaus (1989) and the few studies that have been undertaken on trade missions generally used quantitative measures and may have missed some elements that are not necessarily capturable as quantifiable data. For companies that have exhausted their possibilities for domestic expansion, they may need to look to international markets. It is evident from the literature that there are hidden dangers for unwary companies that venture abroad. Trade missions provide an opportunity for companies to establish contacts with other companies or individuals with the ultimate goal of making a profit. Success may come from achievements such as gaining market access, establishing a joint venture with a knowledgeable person or company or setting up a branch.

Figure 4. Trade Missions Concept Map: Tapping into International Markets

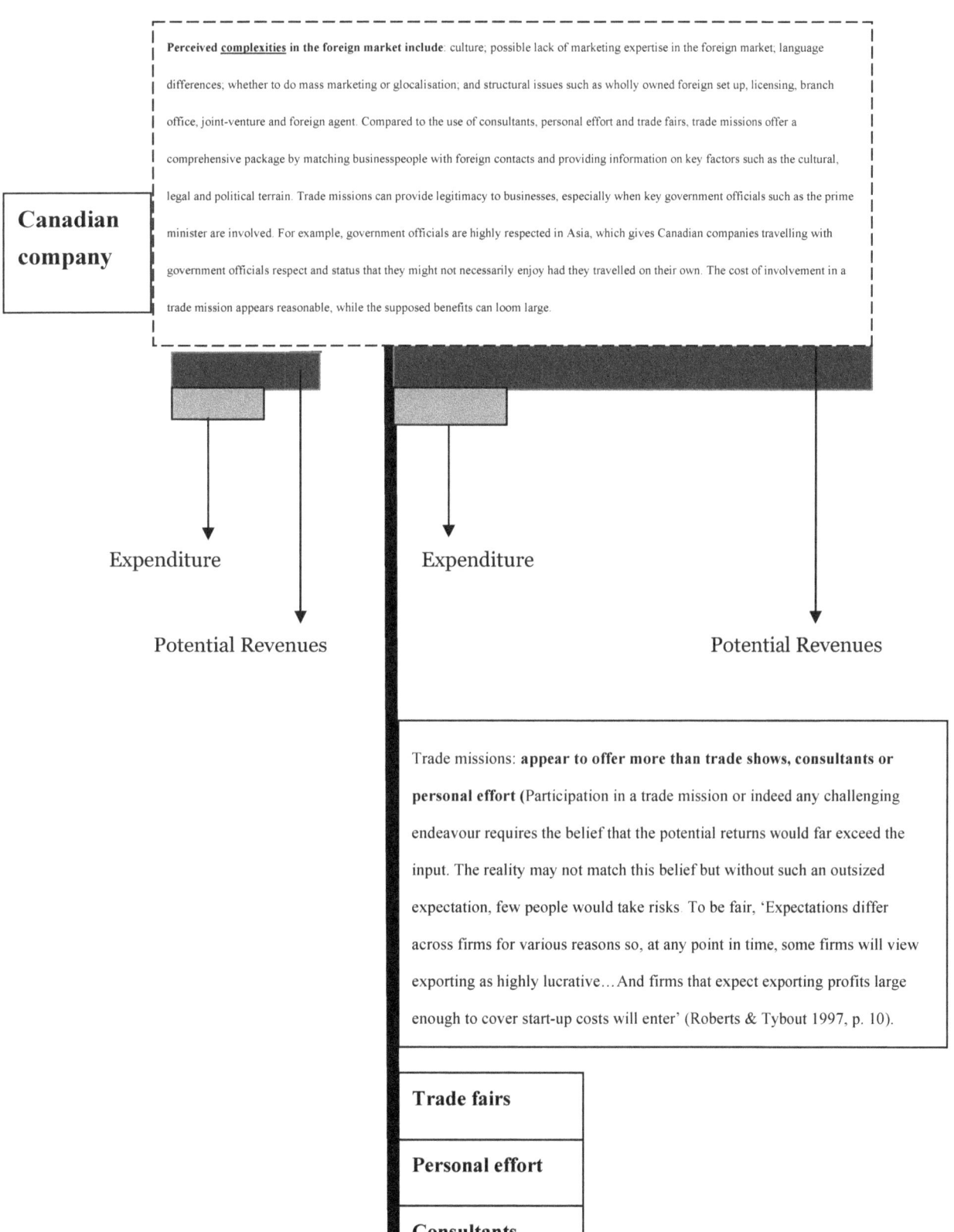

Figure 4 presents a concept map that was developed for this study, which details how trade missions might help increase profitability for companies that are limited in their possibilities for domestic expansion. Similar to trade shows, trade missions can facilitate the transition from an exclusive focus on the domestic market to extending into international markets. Trade missions and trade shows usually involve a host of organisers. As such, the individual or company is not left to negotiate the challenges and potential pitfalls in the international market alone. From trade show and trade mission organisers, business representatives going abroad may learn about customs and preferred business practices in different parts of the world. For potential participants, TCTM may have seemed like the best source for such information. Figure 4 demonstrates that a company might, because of the limits of the domestic market, spend more money on advertising, product quality or other elements of the business, without getting significantly more revenues commensurate with that investment. However, when this investment is made with the international market in mind, new market opportunities might open up and generate revenues that considerably exceed those earned in the domestic market. Trade missions are one means by which a company can enter the international market, using the expertise of government or trade association consultants and by leveraging the power of a respected group rather than taking a chance without sufficient knowledge or confidence. Because trade missions offer a range of services that encompass and surpass what consultants or personal effort might accomplish, they hold the possibility of yielding results that are worth the time, money and energy expended.

Apparent Success of Trade Missions

For the most part, businesses exist because they seek to make profit, which need not be measured only in terms of money. Many possible outcomes can count as success for a company: establishing contacts, acquiring distributors, setting up an overseas office or making a sale. Following some trade missions, organisers take the time to evaluate the extent to which the trade mission has been a success. For example, Oudalov (2013) asked trade mission participants to complete forms that had quantitative and qualitative assessments. Commercial diplomats in charge of the trade missions asserted that 'the most important criterion is whether the participants are satisfied with the values that this trade mission has brought to them' (Oudalov 2013, p. 43).

While some companies thinking of expanding abroad might be lured into going on a trade mission for the first time out of curiosity, it is unlikely that they would continue to do so unless there was a perception that the investment of time and money yielded benefits. No trade mission organiser guarantees that those participating will make sales or come back home with large orders. However, if participants benefit from widening their contacts and attracting new customers, it is within the bounds of reason for them to assume that such connections might translate into the kind of financial results that every business ultimately seeks.

The difficulty of measuring whether a trade mission has been successful notwithstanding, Ruel (2019) did not consider it realistic to look to trade missions to make a significant dent in a nation's balance of trade. Further, trade missions rarely lead directly to the signing of contracts, although contract-signing ceremonies are often made the highlight of some missions. In addition, as just one aspect of the internationalisation process, it is difficult to single out a trade mission as having been the deciding factor in any boost to exports:

> Trade missions should … not be considered in isolation; they are part of an internationalisation cycle …They are a perfect instrument for supporting firms and other organisations intending to internationalise their business and relationships. (Ruel 2019, p. 20)

While Head and Ries (2010) did not find that TCTM garnered significant positive returns to national export trends, there are several studies that presented a more nuanced picture of the success of trade missions. For example, Milic et al. (2017) found an increase in exports by as much as 172 per cent for Australian firms that participated in trade missions between 2010 and 2013. In addition, the probability that a participating company would become an exporter within 12 months of going on a trade mission increased by 26 per cent. While some studies indicated that trade missions were useful for businesses with little or no experience in the export sector, Milic et al. (2017) only studied companies with experience in exporting or those considered export ready, and were thus allowed to participate in the trade missions.

Conversely, Martincus and Carballo (2010) found that some Colombian companies needed to fill an information gap in order to achieve their export goals. Among the means used to assist export-oriented companies in Colombia were counselling, trade missions and trade fairs (Martincus & Carballo 2010). Using data from PROEXPORT, which assists an average of 2,500 companies per year, Martincus and Carballo (2017) compared how the different programs performed in comparison with one another. They found that bundled services combining counselling with trade missions and trade fairs in an integrated whole were more effective than the isolated use of trade missions or trade fairs.

Conversely, Martincus and Carballo (2010) found that some Colombian companies needed to fill an information gap in order to achieve their export goals. Among the means used to assist export-oriented companies in Colombia were counselling, trade missions and trade fairs (Martincus & Carballo 2010). Using data from PROEXPORT, which assists an average of 2,500 companies per year, Martincus and Carballo (2017) compared how the different programs performed in comparison with one another. They found that bundled services combining counselling with trade missions and trade fairs in an integrated whole were more effective than the isolated use of trade missions or trade fairs.

2.11 Trade Mission History in Canada Prior to Team Canada Trade Missions CTM operated under the ambit of the Criteria for TCTM

Canada, both the Federal government and organisations within the nation, throughout the country's history, have had a steady participation in trade missions. Before World War II, a number of Canadian business executives went on a trade mission to the United Kingdom with the purpose of securing contracts for 'the weapons it needed in the war looming with Germany' (Cuthbertson, 2012, p. 1). In 1957, a Canadian trade mission that visited the United Kingdom did so, not for the purpose of boosting Canadian exports but for boosting sales of British goods to Canada, leading to an increase in the share of Canadian imports from the U.K. to increase from 8.5% in 1956 to 10.7% in 1960 (Buckner, 2004, p. 121). In May 1961, in order to acquire knowledge of the potential uses of rapeseed, the Prairie Regional Laboratory and Industry, sent a delegation to Europe comprising not only grain handling companies but also research scientists and 'trade officials of the federal government' (Kramer 2002, p. 78). As reported in the Canadian newspaper, Medicine Hat News of Friday, March 12, 1976, similar trade missions were sent to Singapore, the Philippines, and Japan under the federal Department of Industry, trade and commerce in 1976 to explore the prospects for selling rapeseed in the aforementioned countries. In 1961, on the same issue of rapeseed, a rapeseed delegation visited Japan, 'Canada's largest customer for rapeseed' (Kramer 2002, p. 78) and various other countries. That the interest in trade missions remained steady throughout Canadian history is revealed in a government initiative reported in 1970, in which the Senate foreign affairs committee was advised to send 'a stream of trade missions to China, Japan, Australia and South-East Asia to hunt and bag select contracts' (Mika, 1970, p. 35). In the 1970s, in search of economic resources, Canada embarked on a number of trade missions to the Arab world. In this regard, 'Between 1970 and 1980, trade between Canada and the Arab world increased twentyfold and was predicted to double again by 1985' (Ismael, 1985, p. 15). Non-government organisations have also consistently organised their own trade missions throughout Canadian history. The Drumheller Mail of Alberta reports in its February 17, 1982 issue, the goal of the Alberta Canola Growers' Association to dispatch 'two producers as members of an Alberta trade mission leaving this month for Japan. It is hoped that as a result of the mission, additional canola planting will be encouraged in western Canada.' It is apparent from the foregoing that trade missions have almost always been a part of the story of Canada's relationship with the outside world. What Prime Minister Chrétien did was to take what had been a mundane, often boring and neglected part of Canadian business and to elevate it to front-page status and, with that, the heightened attention of both supporters and detractors.

2.12 Criteria for TCTM

TCTM operated under the ambit of the prime minister, who participated in almost all of the trips. Provincial premiers and senior government officials were often part of the delegations. This meant that the program had a higher profile than other regionally or locally sponsored trade missions. The delegation that accompanied the prime minister was usually larger than those that went on other trade missions from Canada, such as the 1996 Ontario trade mission to Texas and California (Young 1996) or the industry specific Team Textile Canada trade mission to South America (Leclerc 2006). Usually, the duration of TCTM trips were longer than other trade missions.

2.13 Selection Paradigm

TCTM were open to the Canadian business community and companies that had an interest in internationalisation and demonstrated potential to add to the national economy. There was a screening process to ensure that the needs of the applying business matched the expectations associated with a particular trade mission (About Canada Trade Missions). Part of the preparation for the trips included participants being afforded the opportunity to attend business briefings, market and sector discussions and presentations, networking events, business-to-business meetings, site visits and 'face-time with the minister or senior government officials' (About Canada Trade Missions). For the companies that signed on to the TCTM, there was a desire to get their services and products widely known overseas. However, the government wanted to upgrade the nation's image, knowing that 'there is evidence that familiarity with and attitude towards the country impacts on how consumers evaluate products and brands from that particular country' (Caemmerer 2009, p. 524).

2.14 Before a Trade Mission Takes Place

Before a trade mission, there are usually mission organisers who take responsibility for the logistics, travel arrangements and meetings (Aarts 2011). In one case of a trade mission organised by the Canadian-based Manitoba Trade and

Investment Corporation to Russia, one of the participants, Wade Barnes, 'had no idea then that the trip's structured meetings, networking opportunities and site visits would lead Farmers Edge Precision Consulting Inc., his agricultural-mapping firm, to its next growth market' (Aarts 2011, p. 75). Aarts (2011) describes trade missions as a fast-track to exporting and suggests that the 'biggest benefit of participating in a trade mission is strength in numbers. A group of Canadians tends to get far more attention at a foreign trade show or convention than an individual firm could garner alone. Plus, many participants find immense value in the networking they do with each other, particularly between mission veterans and newbies' (Aarts 2011, p. 75). Though any businessperson would be happy to make sales on his or her first business trip, the reality is that it is the first step in cultivating relationships that could potentially become lucrative in the future. In the case of Wade Barnes, 'The mission to Russia allowed Barnes to see farms in action and talk face to face with potential buyers about their needs – prospecting that's difficult to do remotely. (Conversely, the mission experience can also demonstrate that a target market is not a good fit.)' (Aarts 2011, p.75).

As with Canada, in the United States, there are hundreds of local and state-run trade missions to foreign countries. One such is the Washington-state based Spokane Regional International Trade Alliance (SRITA), which has co-sponsored trade missions with the Spokane Area Chamber of Commerce. In one such week-long trade mission to the Kansai region of Japan in 1997, prior to the trip, the twenty-two businesses and government representatives that were participating were told not to expect quick results because of the 'heavy emphasis Japanese place on establishing personal relationships before making business transactions' (Crompton 1997, p. A1). Despite such warnings, Buckeye Beans & Herbs Incorporated of Spokane 'sold two cargo containers of pasta, gathered information on the growing Japanese consumer movement toward organic certified products, and took some initial steps to expand its distribution network' (Crompton 1997, p. A1). We learn from this that nothing beats personal experience. SRITA is one of those organisations that undertakes follow-ups with trade mission participants to help them turn leads into actual sales. The United States government, which runs specialised trade missions for various industry groups, has a number of guidelines for participants, such as the need to keep all appointments, the importance of being both patient and courteous, and being generous enough to refer other American companies if one's company' products are not what the prospective customer wants. One has to remember that the tables could be turned, in which case one could be the beneficiary of another participant's recommendation. Participants are also warned not to be 'fooled by a foreign competitor posing as a prospective customer. Such firms sometimes seek appointments with U.S. trade mission members merely to scout their prices, terms or technology' (United States Bureau of International Commerce 1974, p. 13).

2.15 The Canadian Government's Marketing Communications Efforts

In promoting the TCTM program, the Canadian government attempted to achieve national rebranding through public diplomacy and the marketing of its capabilities to the business community. Reports highlighting the success of the trade missions communicated subtly and overtly the power of the government to make a difference in the business fortunes of export-oriented companies.

2.16 Government Targets for Marketing Communications

Integrated Marketing Communications has been defined as the integration of advertising and public relations with direct marketing and sales promotion into a comprehensive plan (Caywood 1997). Kotler and Keller (2012, p. 27) argued that 'marketing is about identifying and meeting human and social needs' and 'meeting needs profitably' (Kotler & Keller 2012, p. 5). The American Marketing Association defined marketing as 'the activity, set of institutions and processes of creating, communicating, delivering and exchanging offerings that have value for customers, clients, partners and society at large' (Kotler & Keller 2012, p. 27). Success at marketing means ensuring that one's stakeholders, which comprise a wide range of people or groups connected directly or indirectly to an organisation, are satisfied. In terms of promoting the TCTM program, the Canadian government needed to communicate with its major stakeholders, including:

(1) Potential participants of the program—these are the companies and individuals that would join the prime minister and other government delegates on the trade missions.

(2) The Canadian public—who needed to be assured that government spending and involvement in the program was a benefit for the whole country.

(3) The targeted countries—where Canada wanted to rebrand itself as a nation worthy of being taken seriously as a business partner.

By promoting Canadian companies abroad, the government aimed to provide some benefits to Canadian society through the expectation of increased prosperity. Initiating and organising the TCTM involved communicating with the business community, from which TCTM participants were drawn. The TCTM website provided regular updates of events surrounding the trade missions. It was a one-stop site where prospective participants could obtain links to other related services and resources.

However, the public constituted another group to which the Canadian government had a responsibility to communicate its policies and intentions. It was claimed that the government wasted 'taxpayers' money' (Ruel 2019, p. 18) on ineffective trade missions and merely provided what amounted to corporate welfare. A counter-narrative on the importance of having the Canadian government work hand-in-hand with the business community in light of the highly competitive nature of business today was provided by the US ambassador to Canada during the Chrétien era (Cellucci 2005).

Marketing communications from the Canadian government were multi-pronged, involving the use of websites, speeches, press releases, testimonials and newspaper articles from reporters embedded within TCTM. The government wanted Canada to be known around the world for something other than the traditional images for which it had become recognised. Saner (2001, p. 650) argued that the government's role includes 'reinforcing the underlying determinants of national advantage.' Over the years, Canada had developed itself beyond the primary resources it has been known for. However, the images of a snowbound country, full of loggers and Mounties (Brown

2005) has persisted, which prompted Heinbecker (2011, p. 228) to call for a Canadian public diplomacy that would seek to convey 'an image of Canada as a culturally sophisticated, economically successful and technologically savvy' nation. In this same vein, Potter (2011, p. 291) highlights an attempt by Daryl Copeland, a DFAIT official during the Chrétien era, who advocated a new message—'Canada. Cool. Connected'—as a way to counter the 'outdated foreign images of Canada.' The government wanted to convey that Canada was a country with substantial expertise, which it was willing to share with the world. This is in line with research that found that countries or territories that lacked branding have a difficult time trying to attract political and economic attention (Van Ham 2001).

At this point, the question arises as to what is meant by nation branding. Szondi (2005, p, 285), described it as 'the strategic self-presentation of a country with the aim of creating reputational capital through economic, political and social interest promotion at home and abroad.' This effort then has the potential to 'change the behaviour, attitudes, identity or image of a nation in a positive way' (Gudjonsson 2005, p. 285). That the TCTM was an effort in this direction is supported by the comments of Potter (2004, p. 57):

> These high-visibility missions, with the Canadian prime minister leading a Canadian delegation consisting of his minister for international trade, provincial premiers and territorial government leaders and hundreds of Canadian business people to different priority markets, had evolved into a key component of Canada's international business development efforts.

Marketing communications involved providing assurances to potential participants that the government had the necessary expertise and resources to provide opportunities for them abroad. Canadian businesses that responded eagerly to participate ran the gamut from those focusing on goods, services and events, others that focused on experiences, people and places, to companies specialising in properties, organisations or information and ideas (Kotler & Keller 2012).

It seems that the Canadian government understood what marketing stalwart, Philip Kotler, had called attention to as far back as 1994: 'Now more than ever, places must think, plan, and act on their futures, lest they be left in the new era of place wars' (Kotler, 1994, p. 15). Individual companies competing in a global arena can only speak for themselves, and the lone voice of a company, especially one that has not yet garnered widespread recognition or fame, is likely to be drowned out. In contrast, the unity that comes with corralling several companies together and going on a trade mission has the potential to turn ripples of interest into a wave that would redound to the benefit of the country, now and into the future.

Porter (1990), in considering the matter of competitive advantage, sees a role for governments, albeit a limited one. Rather than giving direct government assistance, the government can 'create an environment in which companies can gain competitive advantage rather than those that involve government directly in the process' (Potter 1990, p. 87). While there are many forms in which such government assistance can take, 'The ideal is to deploy the nation's limited pool of human and other resources into the most productive uses' (Porter 1990, p. 77). To this end, one of the key emphases of the Team Canada trade missions was to 'tell the world that Canadians can provide state-of-the-art equipment and technology and not just metals, logs and other unrefined resources' (Sato 1999, p. C6).

2.17 Message Strategy

Finding the right themes and appeals was a key challenge. The image of Canada as a nation poised for business with the rest of the world was a fundamental one. To create a successful message strategy, the themes and appeals needed to delineate areas of difference and areas of parity so that what was being marketed could stand out clearly, including the quality or profitability of products and services or extrinsic considerations such as whether the brand was popular, contemporary or traditional (Kotler & Keller 2012). It appeared that the government was eager to let the world know that the country was versatile, innovative and highly advanced. These and other elements, including the emphasis on teamwork among Canadians, were meant to send a bold message to the rest of the world that Canadians valued interaction with others. In any case, the Chrétien government appeared to be aware of the importance of the reputation of the country, seeing it as equivalent to a brand image for a product or company (Anholt 2007). This was also underscored by Chrétien's participation in most of the TCTMs.

2.18 Hierarchy of Effects

Marketing communication encompasses the use of a large number of tools, including 'advertising, publicity, public relations, reseller support—merchandising, sampling and packaging changes' (Ray 1973). The notion of hierarchy of effects has gone through several iterations and essentially seeks to address marketing and advertising effectiveness and the process from a potential client's unawareness through to the point of purchase. In its recent incarnation, the hierarchy of effects is perceived as a six- or seven-step feature, from unawareness of a product or idea, through awareness, knowledge of what the product has to offer, the development of a favourable attitude towards the target product, a favourable attitude that chooses a particular product over others, a desire to purchase and then the actual purchase (Barry 2012). In another incarnation, the hierarchy of effects appears as the acronym AIDA—attention, interest, desire and action (Wijaya 2011).

2.19 Evaluation of Integrated Marketing Communications

Integrated Marketing Communication includes the use of data to assess the extent to which a message directed to a target group might be getting through. Quantitative and qualitative measures can be used to analyse data to ascertain how best to proceed towards the goal of satisfying the future needs of the target group or helping the communicator to achieve a particular goal. However, this is not always easy. Kitchen et al. (2004b) argued that a key problem centres on the question of how the effects of an integrated marketing campaign might be measured. Kotler and Lee (2007, p. 265) declared that 'measuring marketing performance is one of the most complex, even frustrating, of all marketing tasks. It is often expected and then questioned; it can be applauded and then forgotten.' The traditional approach for many communicators has been to market and to wait and see if there is a response or an increase in response compared to previous efforts.

In much simpler times, it was an easy matter to gauge whether marketing communications were successful, such as having a circus visit a town or holding a parade and advertising the program. Later, the organisation would count 'the number of paying patrons that attended the event. A direct correlation between expenditures and returns' (Schultz & Block 2003, p. 51). However, the landscape of business has become more complex, with competitors and customers, different channels of distribution to monitor and an increased time lag between marketing communications and results, which has made measurement more challenging. In other cases, outside organisations have been engaged to collect data for companies and provide analyses and measurements of success (Schultz & Block 2003). The measurements have usually involved the development of messages and incentives, the purchase of media time or space to get messages to target audiences and the measurement of their impact through media delivery or psychological methodologies (Schultz & Block 2003). Taking an interest in the issue of measurement is also a matter of concern for governments, which face constant pressure to become more effective even when resources are low. Riege and Lindsay (2006) found that governments are increasingly being held to account and expected to be transparent in their dealings. Monitoring a project can be useful for making changes mid-course (Kotler & Lee 2007). However, a full evaluation involves measurements that seek to answer the outcomes at the end of the program. The kinds of questions to be answered by comprehensive evaluation include:

- Did you reach your goals?
- Can you link outcomes with program elements?
- Were you on time and on budget?
- How do costs stack up against benefits?
  Were there unintended consequences that will need to be considered going forward—maybe even handled now?
- Which program elements worked well to support goals

(Kotler & Lee 2007, p. 266)

For governments that have not calculated the results from their marketing efforts, it might seem like a daunting task. A UK government publication stated that 'while some difficulties exist, activities upon which no financial value can be placed are rare' (Government Communication Network 2011, p. 4). The same publication suggested that the time to consider measurement is not at the end of a marketing communication campaign, but from the beginning. Having clear, realistic and measurable objectives is a first step and should consider:

> Outputs (such as the percentage of target audience reached); outtakes (such as awareness of your activity and understanding of its messages); intermediate outcomes (responses such as signing up to a website or calling a helpline); and outcomes (such as changed behaviour or a change in a population statistic). (Government Communication Network 2011, p. 5)

Other metrics that can be measured include payback, net payback, return on marketing investment and cost per result.

2.20 Canada: A Nation's Image

During Chrétien's leadership, Canada attempted to shape its image in the eyes of the world and to build upon the generally favourable view of the country held by people. Canada adopted a public diplomacy approach, which involved 'effort by the government of one nation to influence the public or elite opinion of another nation for the purpose of turning the policy of the target nation to advantage' (Potter 2002/2003, p. 46).

In achieving this end, Canada appeared to successfully employ the internet, membership in major international organisations and trade missions. By working together, the three levels of government were able to leverage Canadian diplomatic assets for the benefit of image and trade. Potter (2002/2003, p. 60) considered the TCTM to be an attempt to take advantage of the synergies of federal and provincial activities 'and to promote a single unified image of Canada. By all accounts, such an approach is working.'

The Canadian government realised that the era of globalisation was one in which individuals and governments needed to be highly aware and nimble to survive, to not allow the global economy to 'roll over cultural diversity, fragile social and political systems and state sovereignty itself' (Potter 2002/2003, p. 43). The Canadian government saw the potential threat from globalisation to businesses and the country if it did not go on the offensive and make Canada a potent force in international business rather than a marginal player. Globalisation had already begun to make various population groups around the world more assertive regarding their identity. The Canadian government recognised the importance of making use of varied means of discourse to capture hearts and minds internationally, which was an effect that could translate into security and better trade relations. Potter (2002/2003, p. 51) argued that public diplomacy was seen as a 'third pillar' of Canadian policy, besides the emphasis on economic growth and that of international peace and security.

Part of the reason for Canada's push towards the use of media and avenues such as trade missions to influence other countries included the recognition that with round-the-clock media, it was more important than ever to be the shaper of your message lest someone else shapes it for you. Citizens were able to easily access information and contribute to the dissemination of information through their websites, blogs and newsletters, which made the context of image-making much more complex, because the nation was not the sole conveyer of information and does not have a monopoly on truth.

DFAIT made extensive use of culture to burnish the national image. This department was able to select Canadian cultural artefacts that helped project Canada's image abroad, which was a form of communication and discourse. Scholarship programs to foreign students were also used to improve Canada's image abroad. Despite these efforts, Canada's efforts were rather on the cheap compared to cultural promotion efforts by countries such as the UK, France and Japan, with the latter two each spending more than a billion dollars (Potter 2002/2003).

Canadians like to think of the nation as being a high-technology enclave, whereas perceptions from outside the country do not necessarily concur. Despite Canada's success in influencing global organisations such as the UN, Potter (2002/2003) argued that the perception of Canada remained as a resource economy, rather than a dynamic, innovative, competitive and technologically advanced country. In 1997, an international survey conducted by the Angus Reid research organisation found that more than 50 per cent of Germans and Japanese associated Canada with lumber, pulp and paper and food, but fewer than 1 per cent associated Canada with telecommunications or other technology-based products (Potter 2002/2003). Valls (2010, p. 57), reporting on the brand image of Canada a few years back, maintained that:

> Canada was not among the countries drawing most international attraction still a few years ago. Moreover, traditional postcards represented it as a land of snow, Mounties and huts (together with old-fashioned folklore). It was a still undiscovered tourist country and most economic transactions were done with its big neighbour to the south, the US.

The persistence of this quaint image of Canada long after the country believed it had attained scientific and technological maturity points to the government's concerted effort to play a part in changing Canada's trade image. Team Canada Inc. spearheaded annual reviews of all Team Canada activities, which encompassed more than the trade missions. Head and Ries (2010) concluded that the trade missions did not provide tangible monetary benefits to Canada. However, following the May 2003 trade mission to Bulgaria and December 2003 trade mission to Chile, this report was issued:

> An evaluation of the TCTM program was undertaken with key stakeholders, including provincial officials, SME's, big business, cultural and educational institutions. While some changes to the existing format have been suggested, most consulted felt the Team Canada concept is useful in promoting Canada in key international markets. (Team Canada Inc. – Annual Report 2004)

Since 'there is no consensus on what makes a trade mission successful' (Ruel 2019, p. 18), supporters of the TCTM program were apt to agree with the government's view, whereas detractors rejected the terms of evaluation as being flawed or biased.

2.21 Summary

This literature review has traced reasons why, in the face of globalisation challenges, some companies might not have felt that they could enter foreign markets by themselves. Real and perceived challenges were highlighted, along with key success factors and different modes of entry into foreign markets, which demonstrated the apparent attractiveness of trade missions over some of the other choices. In launching the TCTM program, the government needed to be aware of three main groups: the businesspeople and companies that could potentially participate in trade missions; the Canadian public, to whom the government owed a responsibility of transparency and the international market, specifically those countries that were a target of Canadian export designs.

The issue of the value of trade missions in Canada is a persistent one. If trade missions are successful for participating companies, federal and provincial governments can add to their revenues through those generated from exports. However, at the level of individual companies, the facts are far from well established. The question remains as to whether the benefits are real or whether some of the companies seek to bask in the reflected glory of government ministers only to come back and bemoan the time, energy and money spent on these trips. After all, there are problems and roadblocks faced by companies dealing with the export market. For SMEs, it is worthwhile to consider the opportunity costs of trying to build a business abroad compared with focusing on the domestic market. David Bond, senior consulting economist for Hong Kong Bank of Canada, warned:

> It isn't just that a small company finds it harder risking capital on business development. It's the time spent pursuing the opportunity. Time is one of the most important assets an entrepreneur has. Spending it going back and forth trying to establish relationships in a foreign environment can be disastrous for a small firm. (Clarke 1998, p. 30)

In some cultures, relationships and trust-building are critical to establishing a firm business foundation, which can be a lengthy process (Hakanen et al. 2016).

C. Conclusion
2.22 The Gap: Discourse Analysis and Thematic Analysis

Analyses of trade missions in Canada have followed two pathways: evaluations of the benefits of the trade missions based on a comparison between participants and non-participants (e.g., Seringhaus 1989); and analyses of possible increase in the volume of export trade over the course of the trade missions such as the TCTM program (e.g., Head & Ries 2010). However, these studies did not go behind the numbers to capture the perceptions of participants. Additionally, the studies did not focus on the different constituencies in society that might have questions about the opportunity cost of having government resources inordinately expended on one sector of the economy to the exclusion or detriment of others (Ayob & Freixanet 2014). It is this conflict in perceptions of the TCTM revealed through the discourse that this research sought to address. The power relations and discourses that surrounded the TCTM program are examined, the government and business participants' criteria for success of the program are explored and how other constituencies perceived the program and sought to make their voices heard as citizens of Canada are analysed. Further, the vast amount of discourse surrounding the TCTM program, including from newspapers, government bulletins, magazines, speeches and dedicated websites are thematically analysed.

Chapter 3: Methodology

3.1 Introduction

This chapter presents the data collection methods, outlines data analysis procedures, provides a justification for the paradigm and methodology and considers issues pertaining to rigour, quality and ethical considerations. It is conventional to apply a rational approach to examine government policies and practices. O'Connor and Netting (2011, p. 78) claimed that 'there is an assumption that a single "best" policy truth is within the universe and it is the task of the policy maker to figure out what that is.' The rational approach was used in research undertaken by Head and Ries (2010) regarding whether TCTM added value to the Canadian economy. However, Head and Ries's (2010) research reduced marketing communications, nation branding, public diplomacy and ancillary discourse surrounding the promotion of the TCTM to simple cause-and-effect or profit and loss. However, the approach used for this research assumes that there are multiple truths competing with one another and that based on the context, 'one truth might be pragmatically better than another for now, but maybe, not forever' (O'Connor & Netting 2011, p. 140).

The TCTM program was instituted by Chrétien to 'promote Canadian products and expertise abroad, in order to encourage job creation at home' (Iftody 1997, p. 5A), and to burnish the government's image as a dynamic regime with solutions to create jobs, reduce unemployment, and to improve the international image of Canada (Plamondon 2017). Over time, various interest groups, including labour, NGOs, think tanks, political opposition members, the academic community and the general public, began to question aspects of the trade missions, from their purported success to whether the government should be so heavily involved. The wildly differing perceptions from disparate camps—the government and business participants, and critics of the trade missions, and the clash that ensued led to the central question of the research: what power relations and discourses surrounded the TCTM?

This section provides the background to the methodology used to analyse relevant texts and justifies why discourse analysis and thematic analysis were used, along with email interviews with Canadian academics to add breadth and depth to the research (Denzin & Lincoln 2000, p. 2). To undertake an analysis of the discourse surrounding the trade missions, it was essential to go back prior to 1994 to capture the prevailing socioeconomic and political currents and sentiments. Scheurich (1997, p. 97) argued that 'the territory of policy archaeology, contrary to that of traditional and postpositivist approaches, begins prior to the emergence and social identification of a problem as a problem.' Discourse analysis—one of the primary modes of analysis in this research—suggests that discourse may have greater significance, because, although conventional qualitative analysis attempts to gain insights into social reality and to subject it to interpretation, discourse analysis considers discourse to be 'constitutive of the social world—not a route to it—and assumes that the world cannot be known separately from discourse' (Phillips & Hardy 2002, p. 6). Understanding social reality may translate into new policy directions. Foucault (1980, p. 131) posited that discourse or knowledge are inseparable from power and highlights the need to take seriously what governments say as well as what they do. In fact, communist and socialist governments take seriously the idea of discourse and ensure control of the organs of communication. And of course, capitalist and democratic governments also have their means of influencing public discourse. In a society such as Canada, citizens often consider it their obligation to lend their voices to the public discourse as a way to help advance society.

Foucault used discourse in reference to 'text and the analysis of text' (Jansen 2008, p. 109), which are disseminated, shared, stored, and reproduced in a society, and carry the potential to affect future social reality. Studying texts can yield clues to how problems become visible and how a variety of solutions are weighed, allowing for the 'study of the social construction of a social problem' (O'Connor & Netting 2011, p. 153). From the range of words and meanings expressed in debates, dialogue and disagreement, there is the hope that enough good sense and understanding can be extracted to forge a meaningful path forward. Discourse analysis, in other words, provides a means to highlight difference and shows a means of according respect to other beliefs, interrogating one's own beliefs, synthesizing different strands of knowledge and opening a dialogue 'on different beliefs and opinions' (Jansen 2008, p.

108). Using this approach, which centres upon 'unequal power relations' (Jansen 2008, p. 108), it is possible to untangle conflicting statements and criticisms of TCTM by framing questions in terms of power relations expressed in the prevailing discourse.

3.2 Justification for the Paradigm and Methodologies

Differing notions surrounding the concept of knowledge inform research design, including ontology, epistemology, axiology, rhetoric and methodology. Researchers bring certain assumptions about ontology (what constitutes reality) and epistemology (theory of knowledge) to their research. Of the four main paradigms competing in the world of ideas—positivism, postpositivism, critical theory and constructivism—the last was selected as being appropriate for this research for reasons that are explained below. Positivist epistemology is based on an objectivist stance. Methodologies associated with this worldview include the use of experimentation, manipulation and verification of hypothesis (Guba & Lincoln 1994). While postpositivism regards reality as being apprehensible in an imperfect sense, it focuses on an external reality. For this reason, positivism and postpositivism were deemed to be unsuitable paradigms for this research, which sought to untangle discourses represented through documents and communications. Critical theory holds that society is shaped largely by socio-political forces, culture, class and gender, and that values permeate society over time. Its epistemology is transactional or subjective and research may be based on dialogic or dialectical approaches. This approach was not inappropriate for this study, as it has a critical element. However, the constructivist paradigm aligned with the thinking of Foucault and had a better fit to the data selected for analysis and the research questions that were developed. Moreover, constructivism does not make claims of a universal truth, but allows for the possibility of 'multiple perspectives and the researcher's role in constructing interpretations' (Lauckner et al. 2012, p. 6).

Indeed, quantitative analyses have contributed a great deal to the world of knowledge, although there are cases when they have fallen short in revealing the totality of 'truth' surrounding an issue under investigation (Teddlie & Tashakkori 2009). Without discounting the incredible value that quantitative analysis has contributed to human understanding, qualitative analysis usually allows for the voices of subjects to be heard, thus lending greater understanding to a phenomenon (Creswell & Plano-Clark 2007). For a study that gave primacy to voice, text or discourse, relying solely on quantitative measures could not do justice to the research. Qualitative methodology may be used for the benefit it affords in understanding complexity, and its findings, sometimes presented in narrative form, can be accessible to a wide range of audiences. In the end, qualitative research may be conducted because 'quantitative measures and the statistical analyses simply do not fit the problem' (Creswell & Plano-Clark 2007, p. 40). Nevertheless, as emphasised by Creswell and Plano-Clark (2007), rigorous data collection methods must be followed, in which the research design is clearly identified and defined.

In considering the role of discourse in the promotion of TCTM and the power of the interplay of supportive and opposing messages in the marketplace of ideas, the presentation of numbers was insufficient. It was necessary to allow the data—messages trapped in marketing communications, bulletins, newspapers, or speeches by the prime minister and cabinet ministers and policy papers—to yield their knowledge towards a greater understanding of TCTM. It was also important to consider the context within which the TCTMs emerged and the role that they were supposed to play in a world that was undergoing rapid change. It is important for Canadians and their government to understand how the clash of discourses shaped society's views of trade missions in general and the TCTM program, in particular. The perception of whether the program was a success did not occur in a vacuum. The perceptions of the public came from what they heard, read and were exposed to. In the absence of multiple, rigorous and impartial studies to assert whether the trade missions were a success, the public's perception would be influenced by two factors: the extent to which the government successfully communicated its message and the extent to which detractors had done the same. Research that seeks to examine the discourse of the two opposing camps from a 'neutral' position has the potential to yield insights that can benefit both parties and Canada as a nation.

3.3 Discourse Analysis: Reaching Back to Foucault

According to Foucault (1972), discourses are made up of bodies of statements that are regulated and systematically organised. To come to a proper understanding of the production process, it is important to 'identify the discursive mechanisms (e.g., research evidence, statistics, media influences and so on) involved' (Stevenson & Cutcliffe 2006, p. 716). Through discourse—the web of statements and techniques emanating from certain quarters in society—problems become visible. Through persistent dissemination of discourse, people may come to imbibe that worldview over time, which becomes entrenched as a matter of course and accepted as though it were natural. Foucault's (1972) policy archaeology looks past the façade to unearth the conditions, elements of discourse and competing forces within a period that may have given birth to a new notion or norm. Prior to presenting the examination of Canadian policy documents to consider how Canada projected itself to the world, it is useful to consider recent historical documents and to examine what policymakers have said about the nation, along with the practices that accompanied the rhetoric. Fairclough (2003, p. 46) explained that both Foucauldian and critical discourse-based research 'draw upon historical and other sources to make connections between the texts or utterances and wider social practices.'

According to Foucault, traditional history focuses too much on linear representation (see Figure 5). Traditional history attempts to make cause-and-effect linkages and to smooth out discrepancies and differences, including the exploration of connections between disparate events or seeking causal connections (Foucault 1972, p. 4).

Figure 5. Traditional View of History

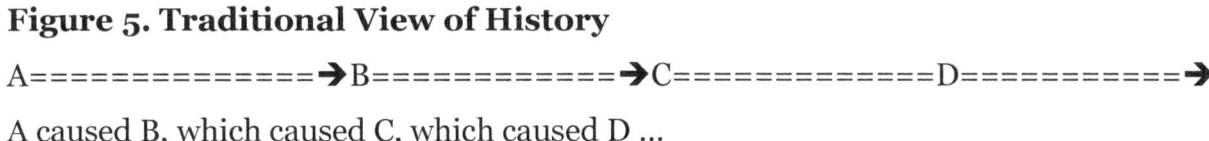

A caused B, which caused C, which caused D …

Foucault (1972) argued that this way of looking at history is fundamentally wrong and an oversimplification. In effect, Foucault (1972) challenged scholars to ponder matters differently and to consider 'how certain systems of thought and practices come to be conceived in a particular way, highlighting paradoxes [and] difficulties' (Motion & Leitch 2007, p. 264).

Research that seeks a direct financial outcome from the promotion of TCTM may derive from the traditional view of history that attempts to make cause-and-effect connections. However, Foucault suggested that instead of thinking of history in terms of a straight line, with one thing causing another, it is more useful to consider the history of a period as a field of events and that these events or discourses include all kinds of utterances such as rumours, statistics, newspaper articles, magazine pieces, news conferences, speeches, lectures, or professional articles. Examples can be observed in the ways in which rumours can affect movement on the stock market (e.g., Schmidt 2018) and how statements by the US Federal Reserve Bank can affect the stock market (e.g., Osterland 2019). However, Foucault looks more to the accumulation of discourse over time rather than focusing on a specific moment. The effects of discourse are powerful and run through all areas of life.

At the base of Foucault's archaeological terminology is the term 'statement', which is not used in its regular grammatical attribution, but rather as a unit of discourse—a distinctive idea that stands on its own as a meaning unit and is part of 'a series or a whole and always plays a role among other statements' (Bourke & Lidstone 2015, p. 835). These statements are not inert but have real-world effects. The government, with its mandate from the populace to govern, makes pronouncements that are imbued with a sense of authority in policy statements, prime minister's speeches, ministers' press releases and ministry bulletins, which become part of the networks and fields of use, with some discourse eventually disappearing, with others being replaced, and still others enduring over time (Bourke & Lidstone 2015, p. 835). Beyond statements as basic units of discourse, Foucault also described discourse as individual groups of statements (Foucault 1972, p. 80) and how 'human beings are made subjects' (Foucault 1982a, p. 208). The different modes by which human beings are made into subjects may at times be presented as being in the interest of the subjects themselves, when specific institutions or the government may be the true beneficiary.

While suggestive discourse can have a major impact, this was not considered in this research because indirect speech—namely, 'the phenomenon in which a speaker says something he doesn't literally mean' (Pinker 2007, p. 437)—cannot properly be judged because one cannot get into the mind of the speaker. Therefore, all discourse considered for analysis in this research was assumed to have been meant to be taken seriously.

According to Foucault (1972), discourse may be linked to the production of knowledge in the form of the plethora of books, authoritative documents and reports that are produced by people in authority (see Figure 6).

Figure 6. History as a Field of Multiple Discourses

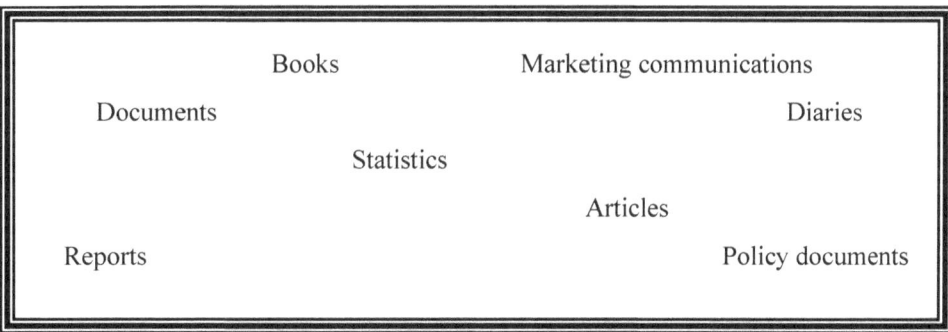

Over time, these may become accepted as normal, although new forms of discourse may also arise in time to permeate the consciousness of society. However, it is not the aim of archaeological analysis to examine the discontinuities with the view to solving or overcoming problems (Foucault 1972, p. 152). Budd (2006, p. 65) declared that the goal of archaeological discourse analysis is less concerned with what should be or the search for a solution to a puzzle but rather focuses on discourse practices at a particular period in time that have also been influenced by events, practices, or discourses from the past.

Marketing communications disseminated by the Canadian government, including policy documents that set out the government's intentions, advertisements, speeches by government officials on regarding the TCTM program, media reports, commentaries by think tanks and inputs by social activists, each contributed to a pool of discourse with the potential to influence the thinking of society. The multiplicity of documents, statements and speeches were not benign pronouncements. Rather, they aimed to carve out a place as the truth (Bourke & Lidstone 2015, p. 836). The ideas of decision makers were apparent in the vast majority of documents reviewed for this research, including newspaper articles (see Appendix 1) and TCTM promotional materials.[8] The researcher sought to have an unbiased approach by relying mostly on the existing public record and searching as widely as possible through the public record, such as newspaper archives covering the whole range of perspectives across Canada. It was not considered necessary to interview staff associated with organising the trade missions because there was extensive information issued by the Team Canada organisers as a matter of public record, which served as a proxy for the perceptions they sought to engender at the time. However, in a democracy, competing voices are important and can present messages that disrupt, differ or detract from those of the government. In Foucault's words (1972, p. 182), 'The analysis of archaeological breaks sets out…to describe the dispersion of the discontinuities themselves.'

At its heart, Foucault's methodology forces researchers to look at 'differences and changes in relation to a problem' (Kendall & Wickham 1999, p. 42); it focuses on statements and visibilities and avoids psychological explanations. In focusing on the power of the Canadian government and the voices of critics in this research, it is worth noting what Stevenson and Cutcliffe (2006, p. 715) said regarding Foucault's idea of genealogy, that, 'Foucault was concerned with the enactment of power. So, genealogy is a means (a methodological device) to explore how a practice was brought into being or developed.' Similarly, Perkins (2008, p. 7) claimed that 'by showing how past discursive formations have changed, altered, been transformed, Foucault's genealogies assert the potentiality for social change and reformed power relations.' The government of Canada is perceived to have power, although its legitimacy comes from the people. The government may enact its power through legislation and continually use the power of discourse to cement its authority. However, 'there are always contradictory discourses

---

[8] https://works.bepress.com/everettofori/58/

about what is right and what is normal, and these circulate and compete with each other at different points in time' (Bourke & Lidstone 2015, p. 835). Foucault (1972) argued that discourse emerging from entities other than the government had its own sense of power.

3.3.1 Power/Knowledge

Foucault (1980, p. 131) contended that language plays an important part in establishing 'regimes of truth'. It is through these regimes of truth that social problems are formulated and addressed. Based on Foucault's (1972) writings, discourse analysts have come to understand that power is not a matter of individual agency, but is embedded in a network of relationships, which Jacobs (2006, p. 41) expressed as 'the recursive relationship between language and power rather than…language as simply a reflection of power relations.' Whereas it is commonly believed that some institutions possess power, this was not how Foucault understood power. For Foucault (1982a), the effects of power on others was not through a direct and immediate enactment. Power makes the production of knowledge possible, which is used to select and deploy techniques of power. Power is productive and provides the link between what can be said and what can be seen—the sayable and the visible. Discourse invariably serves someone's needs and the question must be asked as to who benefits from it.

3.3.2 Governmentality

Another way of considering the issue of productivity is to understand the government's desire to subject its citizens to the will of the state. According to Foucault, governmentality may be considered to be a 'subtle comprehensive management of life drawing from a top-down exercise of power over conduct … with a subjectivity constituted in a sense of personal responsibility, rights, freedoms and dependencies' (Fox 1993, p. 32). Further, power is practiced as a set of actions exerted upon other actions (Stevenson & Cutcliffe 2006, p. 710). For example, in an organisational setting, managers usually set forth various protocols to which workers are expected to adhere. Foucault challenged the traditional notions of power (Wandell 2001, p. 368) and posed the question of how we can be sure about things around us that seem self-evident and natural. If it is only the government's voice that we trust, we are apt to believe whatever the government tells us is true. Fortunately, in democratic societies such as Canada, there are other voices that command attention and respect, which can either bolster the government's case or undermine it.

3.4 Policy Archaeology: From Foucault to Scheurich–O'Connor

In compiling the textual archive for this research, two policy documents—*Canada in the World: Government Statement* (1995)[9] and *A Dialogue on Foreign Policy: Report to Canadians* (2003)[10] — along with other forms of marketing communications discourse from the TCTM archive, including newspapers, bulletins and news releases, were analysed in terms of regularities, motifs, repetitions and discontinuities. Fairclough and Wodak (1997, p. 19) explained the interpretive, descriptive and explanatory nature of discourse analysis and how those who make use of its approaches attempt to make prominent the crucial role that language plays when it comes to issues in the political field or the urban governance arena. The two policy documents chosen for analysis were released between 1994 and 2005 and can be regarded as reflective of the thinking of the government of Canada as it sought to energise the economy and to seek a place of national recognition and prominence in a rapidly changing world. While the documents covered broad policy terrain, they yielded rich information regarding the direction in which the government sought to take the country. The attitude of the government towards other countries in the North and the South can also be discerned in these documents. This mode of analysis can provide insight into the relations of power that other non-governmental entities and individuals possess, vis-à-vis the government and how each seeks to reify its position through discourse and other media.

Discontinuity is an important feature of historical investigation as are systems of dispersion, which may underlie the reality of discursive statements (Foucault 1972, p.

---

[9] *Canada in the World* 1995, Ministry of Foreign Affairs, Ottawa, Ontario, viewed 1 December 2006, http://gac.canadiana.ca/view/ooe.b2644952E/1?r=0&s=3

[10] *A dialogue on foreign policy: Report to Canadians 2003,* Minister of Foreign Affairs, Ottawa, Ontario.

4). As such, this investigation included the search for disunity of objects, forms, or concepts and an exploration of the perceived powers behind them, while ensuring that the key research question centred on the power dynamics between the government and its critics on TCTM.

Scheurich (1997) developed a framework that captured the essence of the grid of social regularities hinted at by Foucault. According to Graham (2005), Foucault's purpose for writing was to provoke, to disrupt equilibrium, and certainty. Concerning the framework that Scheurich has developed out of Foucault's work, Lincoln (2001, p. 694) argued that 'Foucauldian genealogical analyses are not well laid out as a method, with the best and most accessible proposal having been made by Scheurich (1994; 1997)'. O'Connor (2005) further applied Foucault's method of analysis. Therefore, bringing Scheurich (1997) and O'Connor (2005) together (Scheurich–O'Connor) provided an effective template for understanding the range of discourses before and during the period of the TCTM. Additionally, while discourse analysis is largely based on the examination of texts, it does not divorce itself from consideration of social practices but seeks to find connections between what is avowed and what is practiced, in order to determine the 'relationship of language to other social processes and of how language works within power relations' (Graham 2005, p. 4). This juxtaposition of text and practice finds ample resonance in the government's policy documents (text) and social and business engagements (practices) such as TCTM, including trips and signing ceremonies.

With Foucault's ideas and methodology as a backdrop, it is possible to provide a historical critique that helps illuminate the nature of the relationship between knowledge and power. One key element in Foucault's (1972) policy archaeology is the question of the existence of a social problem or issue and how it comes to occupy a place of importance in society (Scheurich 1994, p. 6). Policy archaeology examines 'the grid of conditions, assumptions, forces, which make the emergence of a social problem possible' (Mawhinney 1995, p. 7). Jacobs' (2006, p. 44) understood discourse to be a complex set of ideas and values competing with one another in our daily lives and claimed that the 'key task for researchers is to identify how discourses exemplify conflicts over meaning that are linked to power.' Sharp and Richardson (2001, p. 196) claimed that discourses arise from power conflicts, with each group trying to make its agenda supersede those of others. Foucauldian-inspired scholarship has the potential to present a discourse regime that veers from well-accepted modes of research. Jacobs (2006) contended that for Foucault's methodology to be properly applied, researchers must explore power relations, provide sufficient political and social context, as well as sufficient description and explanation of texts.

Public policies, which are government pronouncements invested with ideology, may be interpreted with consideration for the role and function of the modern state. A capitalist state recognises the centrality of capital accumulation on the part of the government to meet social needs and to keep the engine of capitalism running (Stevenson 2001). The use of the two policies that fell within the period under consideration, provided a basis for understanding the thrust of the government's policies, while the broader literature of the era, including newspaper accounts, offered insights into the reversals, discontinuities, specificities, ambiguities and support attending the government's TCTM efforts.

Policy archaeology aims to expose 'in a systematic way, multiple ways a text can be interpreted' (Martin 1990, p. 340), which reveals various ideological assumptions that are 'particularly sensitive to the suppressed interests of members of disempowered marginalised groups' (Martin 1990, p. 340). It is not uncommon for texts to suppress societal conflicts by glossing over or denying issues of disruption among the various centres of power in order to present and promote a view of society that is at once united and harmonious. Martin (1990) explained that deconstruction removes the layers of ideological obscuration to reveal the conflict that has been made invisible. Deconstruction displays the 'power operating in structures of thinking and behaviour that previously seemed devoid of power relations' (White 1986, p. 421). Deconstruction exposes silences in texts and lays bare the gaps and absences within an ideology. The researcher must bring alive these dead silences, in effect, 'reveal its gaps and silences, what it is unable to articulate' (Eagleton 1976, pp. 34–35)

The starting point for deconstruction is an intense focus on conflicts that have been suppressed, along with multiple interpretations of a text, to expose weaknesses in any claims to truth and objectivity. While positivism espouses detachment and the search for an objective truth, 'deconstruction requires subjectivity and reflexivity' (Martin 1990, p. 341). Although historical documents are used, the goal was not simply to make a historical analysis, but to examine the 'grid of conditions, assumptions, forces, which make the emergence of a social problem possible' (Scheurich 1997, p. 7). In Scheurich's reformulation of Foucault's ideas, social problems are not accepted *a priori*. Rather, the emergence of the problem is sought and the issue of why it is seen to be a problem is investigated. O'Connor (2005, p. 8) argued that the archaeological approach requires an understanding of how problems become socially visible.' Foucault argued that power is revealed through a variety of force relations that exist in the sphere in which they operate and constitute their own organisation. Continual struggle and confrontation may end up in transformation because, while some notions become reinforced and strengthened, others wither through isolation, neglect, disjunctions and contradictions.

3.5 Thematic Analysis

Thematic analysis can be used for the identification, analysis and interpretation of meaning and themes found in qualitative expressions or data (Clarke & Braun 2017), which allows for compacting an extensive array of raw data into some semblance of structure (Nowell et al. 2017). It is useful as much for a small dataset as for large ones and with 'virtually any data type' (Clarke & Braun 2017, p. 298). The hundreds of pages of marketing communications data and dozens of newspaper articles covering the TCTM covered the entire period of the program and represented the gamut of Canadian media, from national newspapers and magazines such as the *National Post*, the *Globe and Mail* and *Maclean's* to those of local or regional importance, such as the *Toronto Star*, the *Winnipeg Free Press* and *CanWest* (see Appendix 1).

Thematic analysis is a tool that can be used across a wide range of theoretical frameworks, which means that it is not confined by paradigmatic strictures (Clarke & Braun 2017). This approach makes it possible to generate codes as the first step (Clarke & Braun 2017) in identifying key themes and comparing and contrasting them. Close reading of the information can enable the researcher to offer an interpretation that the raw unanalysed data might not readily yield. For example, it has been determined by Clarke and Braun (2017, p. 298) that 'what distinguishes thematic analysis from most other qualitative analytic approaches is its flexibility, leading to a wide range of applications' in qualitative research. When it comes to thematic analysis, rather than the criteria of validity and reliability, which are often sought in quantitative research, elements such as 'credibility, transferability, dependability and confirmability' (Nowell et al. 2017, p. 3) are more important.

3.6 Research Procedures

The Scheurich–O'Connor framework was first applied to the analysis of two key documents issued by the Canadian government during the TCTM period. These documents and other discourses within that period helped to establish some of the motivations for the government's active involvement in partnering with business to promote Canadian products and the nation's image. Second, thematic analysis was conducted using the marketing communications data[11] released by DFAIT, which included trade mission itineraries, success stories, information about participating premiers and organisations, drafts of the prime minister's speeches, activities engaged in during the trade missions and foreign counterparts met. This was supplemented by more than 160 newspaper articles from across Canada, which actively reported on the trade missions while they were in progress, including editorials, letters to the editor, comments by trade experts and think tanks and responses by the government and ministers on the utility of the trade missions (see Appendix 1). Third, an email panel interview was conducted. Because of the length of time that had elapsed between the trade missions and this study, few respondents were able to respond with useful

---

[11] https://works.bepress.com/everettofori/58/

information; this has been included, not because of their validity, but because they lend an interesting perspective to the rest of the research (see Appendices 3 and 4).

In my initial research efforts, I contacted some officials at the Department of Foreign Affairs and Trade office in Ottawa, Canada, for possible interviews. They declined. My request to interview trade commissioners at the Canadian embassy in Tokyo, Japan, where I reside, was also rejected. The choice to include the email interviews was not to make it the primary mode of enquiry. Rather, it was to complement the two other methods of discourse analysis and thematic analysis centred on analysing thousands of pages of material relevant to the Team Canada trade missions. Table 2 presents the sources of texts that were used as the basis for the analysis (A and B). An email survey of Canadian academics is also considered (C).

Table 3. Data Sources

DATA

- A. 1. *Canada in the World: Government Statement* (1995)[12]

    2. *A Dialogue on Foreign Policy: Report to Canadians* (2003)[13]

- B. 1. TCTM (testimonials and marketing communications; TCTM Archives)[14]

    2. Other discourse surrounding the TCTM (e.g., newspaper articles and public pronouncements; see Appendix 1)

- C. Email survey of Canadian academics on their insights into the TCTM debate/used after the analysis of the two was done (see Appendix 3)

---

[12] *Canada in the World* 1995, Ministry of Foreign Affairs, Ottawa, Ontario, viewed 1 December 2006, http://gac.canadiana.ca/view/ooe.b2644952E/1?r=0&s=3

[13] *A dialogue on foreign policy: Report to Canadians 2003,* Minister of Foreign Affairs, Ottawa, Ontario.

[14] Team Canada Trade Missions – Database: https://works.bepress.com/everettofori/58/

There were two key domains of analysis:

Part I: Broad context using Scheurich–O'Connor framework, which used data mainly from (A).

Part II: Thematic analysis with a focus on differences, discontinuities, similarities, rupture (Foucault 1972), using mainly data from (B).

3.7 Method I: Setting the Context—Using Scheurich–O'Connor Framework

Discourse refers to text, speech, or actions on a particular subject related to human experience in which power is deployed 'in the form of productive knowledge in the social world' (Powers 2013, p. 6). Foucault demonstrated how the production of discourse in various domains served to elevate one strand of ideas while suppressing or ignoring others. Power does not emanate from one unchanging location or only 'engendered from the top downwards' (Motion 2005, p. 505), but is a set of relations, which is also why resistance can emerge from known or unexpected quarters (Motion & Leitch 2007) to challenge the dominant discourse. Policy archaeology excavates these power relationships to understand how power plays out. Foucauldian analysis focuses on a review of the history of the targeted discourse, considers how the discourse functions in a chosen period and explores the 'effects of the discourse on power relations' (Powers 2013, p. 7). The Scheurich–O'Connor approach used in this study focused on applying the four phases of the Scheurich–O'Connor framework to the two policy documents and to other texts and data that reflected discourse before and during the TCTM.

In policy archaeology, dimension one assumes that problems in the social sphere are socially constructed (O'Connor 2005, p. 9). Social construction is understood to entail the naming and defining of a problem and the rendering of certain other problems as being invisible. A historical lens is used to critically investigate the process of construction and this investigation should begin before 'the emergence of the problem as a problem, but this is not just historical recounting of events' (O'Connor 2005, p. 9). The analysis went farther back than 1994 to trace the genealogy of globalisation and to capture the moment when it came to be characterised as a possible problem within the Canadian political and social spheres. The importance of going farther back was affirmed by Scheurich (1997, p. 97), who argued that when it comes policy archaeology, it is important to begin 'prior to the emergence of social identification of a 'problem' as a 'problem' (though there must be a social identification of the problem before its antecedents may be studied).'

Scheurich (1997) briefly demonstrated how the four arenas and the concerns raised within each might be applied to a topic of interest to a researcher. The focus of Scheurich's (1997, p. 107) application was the poverty of lower-class children in the American school system. O'Connor's (2005, pp. 13–14) application was on Megan's Law, which mandated that violent social offenders register with the authorities in their local area every 90 days for 10 years.

Table 4. Four Dimensions of Policy Archaeology

ARENA I: Social Problem/Social Construction	ARENA II: Social Regularities/ Identification of Network of Problems
- Identification of the problem - Process by which the problem emerged - How the problem was privileged over other problems - How the problem gained the attention of the state	- Objects/concepts behind establishment of trade mission - Social regularities: competing social agents/ideologies - Role of dominant social agents - Emerging power blocs in shifting social landscape
ARENA III: Policy Solutions	**ARENA IV: Policy Studies**
- Range of possible/impossible solutions - How such choices were 'shaped by the grid of social regularities' (Scheurich 1997, p. 101) - Language used to constitute the problem - Meaning to all stakeholders of implementation	- Consideration of 'conventional and postpositivist policy studies' (Scheurich 1997, p. 102) immanent in the broader social order - Why the social problem has not been examined by conventional and postpositivist policy studies - How policy archaeology differs from other approaches

Source: Adapted from Scheurich (1997) and O'Connor (2005)

Considering that the Scheurich–O'Connor framework is not as well-known as some other more established theories, the different dimensions of the framework are explained below, with subsequent application presented in Chapter 4.

Arena I

While focusing on documents, including those that may have been ignored in the past, Arena I, begins with a consideration of the grid of conditions, as well as assumptions and forces that contributed to the naming of the problem in question. The aim here is to determine the set of regularities and history that allowed the problem to emerge. According to Scheurich (1997), one must consider why a particular group or issue rather than another might become visible as being a problem. This is rooted in the perspective of policy archaeology, for which Scheurich (1997, p. 107) claimed that, 'the grid of social regularities produce or construct this problem population.' Every dynamic society is confronted with a vast array of issues, some of which bubble to the surface, whereas others remain below public consciousness. Who 'speaks' of the issue and persists in holding it up to public gaze, often has an impact on how significant the society comes to hold that issue. Powers (2013, p. 9) argued that genealogy delves into the social conditions of the discourse, including the original power relations and how they are expressed in application to 'some realm of human experience.' Likewise, O'Connor (2005) considered interrogating why one issue might have become privileged over another. Some questions that arise: 'How did it become noticed? How was it moved from invisibility to visibility? What was its naming process? What were the existing conditions?' (O'Connor 2005, p. 14).

Arena II

It is assumed that social problems are not recognised by sheer accident but that there are elements in society that contribute to the production or generation of the kinds of ideas relating to the emergent issue in question. Social regularities are those elements that are considered to be visible and credible. One may conceive of a grid of problems and issues, some of which stand out for recognition. Rather than being static, the grid of social regularities is dynamic, and the relative influences of different elements shift over time. By identifying what the social regularities are and noting the shifts that occur, it is possible to identify the emergence of problems. According to Scheurich (1997, p. 107):

> Social regularities 'arrange' the 'seeing' of this target group, the seeing of it as a problem group. This targeting, naming, labelling is the reproductive work of the grid of regularities; the grid attunes its listeners to hear (see) a particular frequency (the problem group) and constitutes the frequency (the problem group) itself.

In this vein, O'Connor (2005) considered what the subordinate and dominant values of the period might have been and what objects, ideas and concepts contributed to the enactment of Megan's Law. In Arena II, the role of social agents and shifts in power and influence are also considered.

Arena III

There is an assumption that certain policy choices exist under the influence of social regularities. There is also an assumption that some of the choices at this point have privilege over others (O'Connor 2005, p. 12). This raises the question: which are the foundational categories, and which are the circumstantial ones in a grid that might include race, family values, gender, class, or professionalisation? A close examination of texts and stakeholders, along with current definitions can be useful in this arena. Questions highlighted by O'Connor (2005, p. 15) included what the range of possible and impossible solutions might be, along with what consequences might be considered to be acceptable. In following through with the application of policy archaeology to the issue of impoverished children, Scheurich (1997, p. 109) argued that the problem is constituted by social regularities through several avenues, including public performances 'both popular and academic.' How the problem is portrayed 'also constrains the choice of policy "solutions" or treatments' (Scheurich 1997, p. 109). In this connection, the power relations among the major players might be considered for the potential to either extend the status quo or for one player to dominate. Attention ought to be paid to dominant discourses and alternative discourses that undermine or resist them (Powers 2013, p. 11).

Arena IV

The policy analysis process is also subject to interrogation, including seeking answers to such questions as how the analysis undertaken fits with the social order. O'Connor (2005, p. 16) highlighted issues relating to preferred social order and how policy archaeology might be implicated, and raised the question: what, if, anything different in understanding of policy intent, implementation, or experience is provided by policy archaeology? Additionally, Arena IV focuses on the social functions of policy studies because, as with other functions that are visible in a society, policy studies and policy solutions are 'constituted by the grid of social regularities. Policy studies is but one governmental apparatus that produces grid-congruent problems, problem groups and policy solutions' (Scheurich 1997, p. 110). The identification of the problem and the emergent solution have roots in the prevalent discourse of an era.

Policy analysts often achieve their aims by valorising certain ideas while devaluing others. In distinguishing between postpositivist analysts and conventional analysts, Scheurich (1997, p. 111) maintained that both 'make the problem and the problem group visible through sanctioned performances and they both discuss only those policy solutions which sanction that order.' In his conclusion, Scheurich (1997, p. 114), admitted that 'policy archaeology and its attendant assumptions are complex and sometimes ambiguous.' While policy archaeology does not claim to deliver a solution, it provides a wider canvas upon which to seek understanding of the issues surrounding problems. The 'problem' in this case, unlike that identified by O'Connor (2005), did not centre on a population group but an idea or force—globalisation.

3.8 Method II: Thematic Analysis
3.8.1 Data Collection

In the early days of the TCTM, the researcher was a self-employed small business owner who took an interest in the trade missions because of the heavy publicity that attended each trip. This interest has been sustained for more than 20 years, during which time a great deal of material on the trade missions was collected, read, reviewed and analysed for this study. The sources used for the analysis were documented, with much of the data available either through the Canadian government archives or through commercially accessible Canadian newspaper archives (e.g., www.newspaperarchive.com) and scholarly databases such as EBSCOHost and ProQuest (see Appendix 1).

3.8.2 Thematic Analysis: Process

Much of the marketing communications were read in real time by the researcher while the TCTM were active. In later years, this researcher reread the materials and reflected upon them. The marketing communications data from the program were collected and saved and the newspaper articles were printed out and bound into two saddle-stitched booklets. Using a green felt pen, each page was numbered. This system allowed codes to be traced back to their sources if required. Initial coding was undertaken through highlighting and underlining of phrases that captured key ideas associated with the trade missions, particularly those related to criteria for success. Because context was important, codes were allowed to retain their complete meanings so as not to provide distortions (see Appendix 2). Phrases were written in a notebook to isolate and categorise them.

In the first complete review and coding of data, the focus remained on two broad categories: criteria for success established by the government, participants and critics. In subsequent close reading and reflection on the data, it began to emerge that the voices of the critics were not monolithic and that the sources of those critiques varied widely. Some critics could not see any scenario in which the government should have any involvement in trade missions. For such critics, criteria for success meant nothing. The next phase involved painstakingly identifying different voices and to do so with attention to the context and the speaker. For example, some of the criticism came from the media through editorials or journalists, while in some cases the source of the critic was a professor or opposition leader who was quoted in the article. Taking stock of these differences was important to obtain a better understanding of the range of voices that contributed to the discourse. Beyond identifying the proponents and resistant voices, it was important to highlight the key themes that were the outcome of the coding, analysis and reflection. The use of thematic analysis was undertaken in the spirit of Bazeley's (2013, p. 191) assertion that effective thematic analysis requires the use of data to 'build a comprehensive, contextualised and integrated understanding or theoretical model of what has been found, with an argument drawn from across the data that establishes the conclusions drawn.'

3.9 Method III: Email Survey of Expert Panel

To lend a different perspective to the research, an email survey was conducted, which drew upon the experiences of Canadian academics from business and government-related fields such as management, international business, international marketing, economics and international marketing to elicit information regarding how they viewed the trade missions. There were 11 respondents, whose insights added to an understanding of the debate concerning power relations and whether the TCTM program was worth pursuing. As many as 315 academics were contacted but, because of the length of time that had passed between the Team Canada trade missions and the research, very few respondents (eleven) were able to provide useful information. This information has been included, not because of their validity, but because they lend an interesting perspective to the rest of the research, in effect, providing an open-ended way to check perceptions. Even though the number of respondents was small, that by itself, does not negate the value of the comment shared by respondents. Unlike a quantitative survey that requires a large number of respondents, a qualitative survey, can, for pragmatic reasons, such as money or time, be limited to a small sample size (Jansen 2010). The small sample garnered for this research is in accord with the definition of purposive sampling offered by Padgett (2008) as 'a deliberate process of selecting respondents based on their ability to provide the needed information…[it] is done for conceptual and theoretical reasons, not to represent a larger universe' (p. 53). Even where data saturation is used as a criterion for determining sample size, Guest et al. (2006) found that 12 interviews sufficed (Guest, Bunce, & Johnson 2006), and that 'the basic elements for themes were already present at six interviews' (Hennink 2017, p. 3). The results of this survey similarly exhibit hints of such saturation (see Appendices 3 & 4).

3.10 Ethical Considerations

The marketing communications put forth by the government in its aim to attract participants to the program, focused on presenting a positive story about TCTM. Although some of the testimonials included information that appeared to balance the overly positive tone, it is undeniable that it was the government's stance that TCTM was hugely successful. To capture other critical voices, a wide net was cast to consider what newspapers, magazines and books had written about the trade missions between 1994 and 2005. Although it was unlikely that participants with serious negative opinions about the trade missions might have found ready reception at the government's promotional websites, there was nothing to prevent anyone from publishing grievances or deficiencies about the program in other media outlets. An active search was launched to find such information and there were some strong examples of criticism of TCTM uncovered. Marketing communications are often skewed and puffed. Communications relating to trade missions, as with many other promotions, may have been presented in ways that were meant to affect the emotions and to attract the attention of potential participants. Seringhaus (1985) and Head and Ries (2010) have undertaken quantitative studies on trade missions in Canada. This researcher did not seek to replicate those results but sought to broaden the field of enquiry to encompass qualitative factors and to unearth theoretical and practical insights that might enable further understanding of trade missions in general and TCTM in particular.

An application to undertake this research was sent to the Human Research Ethics Committee of Southern Cross University. The approval number issued by this committee for the conduct of the research was ECN-09-010. The research was conducted in accordance with the Australian National Statement on Ethical Conduct in Human Research, which included the provision of a detailed statement on the kind of research that was to be conducted. Because the human aspect of this research involved having participants answer a four-question survey and did not involve the participation of vulnerable groups, it was considered to be of low or negligible risk for harm to participants.

3.11 Conclusion

This chapter focused on clarifying the texts and discourse that were subjected to analysis and additional data collection and analyses methods. For this study, documents, newspaper articles, editorials, journal pieces and other sources of information with supportive or critical insights were examined because these discourses reflected the ideas that were current at the time of the missions. It was important to keep in mind relevant research questions for this research and to not lose sight of the interplay of power through discourse and a search for greater understanding of the differences in perception, differences in definition and differences in the assignment of criteria for success of TCTM. Additionally, Foucault's research focused on periods spanning decades or even centuries, whereas this study was confined to a period of 11 years. Events and discourses from several years prior to the beginning of the program were considered in order to understand what might have led up to the government's decision to use trade missions to boost exports. Discussion of the years beforehand also helped to explain the range of precursors that led to globalisation becoming a major consideration or 'problem' for the Canadian government.

Chapter 4: Data Analysis

4.1 Introduction

Chapter 3 made the case for using discourse analysis to examine the emergence of government-supported trade missions in Canada. Policy documents issued within the period 1994–2005 provided some clues to the dominant discourses emanating from the government and other official sources and demonstrated how TCTM fit into the government's overall national and international agendas. This chapter presents results of data analysis. Section 4.2 provides an analysis of discourse in two policy documents—*Canada in the World: Government Statement* (1995) and *A Dialogue on Foreign Policy: Report to Canadians* (2003)—using the Scheurich–O'Connor framework (see Chapter 3). Section 4.3 focuses on a thematic analysis of the Canadian government's marketing communications and discourses in ancillary documents such as newspaper articles. Sections 4.4–4.6 present extensions of the thematic analysis. Section 4.7 examines the email survey of 11 Canadian academics regarding their views on TCTM and trade missions in general.

4.2 Part I: Analysis of Policy Documents using Scheurich-O'Connor Framework

Foucault's formulation of discourse has been elucidated by Scheurich (1997) and O'Connor (2005) through a four-part framework. Using this four-part framework, this section analyses two policy documents: Canada in the World (1995) and A Dialogue on Foreign Policy: Report to Canadians (2003). Because of the need for intertextuality, these two policy documents are not exclusively used.

4.2.1 Arena I: Problematising Globalisation

The emergence of globalisation as a problem

When Levitt (1983) first coined the term 'globalisation', he did not present it as a problem. Rather, he saw the potential problem surrounding globalisation as one of myopia on the part of companies that failed to grasp the idea that a new commercial reality and marketplace had emerged. This new reality was described by Kennedy (1989,

p. 92) as 'global markets for standardised consumer products on a previously unimagined scale of magnitude.' Some of the earliest hints of problems associated with globalisation came, not from the view of globalisation as being an obstacle to progress for advanced countries, but as being detrimental to the progress of developing countries. It was the view of the detractors of globalisation that advanced Western nations would automatically win and that the ones that needed protection were developing countries. Hints that businesses in Canada had reason to fear were echoed in the following comment: 'Structural changes in the world economy—globalisation—means that we have to learn a different bag of tricks' (Kennedy 1989, p. 86). Further, Stollery (1989, p. 56) argued that we were living in an era of discontinuity and that there was 'no question that people are finding it difficult to adapt to change and they are resisting it because they feel convulsed, somewhat disconnected by the rapid pace of technological advancement.'

Globalisation refers to the garnering of efficiency that comes with free trade around the world. Over time, it includes aspects of life that are social, political and cultural (Ghosh 2004). Whether complaints were accurate that globalisation was neo-colonisation of developing countries by their more advanced peers or a disguised effort to spread American culture, it was a view that merited close examination. Ghosh (2004, p. 89) argued that the combination of fast technological change, allied with globalisation and instant communication and information mobility posed a great challenge and that the 'issues are not merely the technological preparation for global competition and an information-based economy, as living and working in an increasingly interdependent world requires international knowledge and intercultural communication skills and also has moral and ethical dimensions.'

Although there are major differences in cultural outlook, globalisation has made once-impervious seeming cultures highly susceptible to influences from abroad. Ghosh (2004, p. 93) claimed that it was a constant source of worry for Canadian leaders that a high volume of US ideas, images and values transmitted through the media permeated Canadian society. There has always been an underlying fear in Canada that national values and culture, in the form of literature and visual arts, would be eclipsed by the torrent of materials from the US. Although it offered potential benefits, globalisation presented a grave threat to the identity of nations. What kind of response would Canada make in the face of such a threat? *A Dialogue on Foreign Policy* (2003) used terms such as 'diverse population,' 'microcosm,' 'the world's people,' and 'global interests' to paint an image of a Canada that appealed to Canadians and the rest of the world. A policy document is not only for the present, but also, a 'document for future use' (Foucault 1977, p. 191). As such, the document does not merely present wishes, but eventually the document becomes a historical record that shapes perceptions, including how the government is viewed. More than that, the contents of the document can also help to shape how other countries view Canada and how Canadians look at themselves as a nation.

According to *A Dialogue on Foreign Policy Report* (2003), Canada sought to align itself more closely with the rest of the world. The document asserted that Canadian society mirrored the population of the world in its diversity. Since diversity has become a desirable concept, at least in North America, Canada could indirectly burnish its image as a caring, fair and inclusive nation. The policy document claimed that Canada was keenly interested in the world beyond its own borders. The idea of becoming engaged in shaping the future was a strong undercurrent in this document. It was geared towards dispelling the notion that Canada was a weak nation that engaged the rest of the world out of fear. The attempt was made to create the impression that Canada's engagement was based on the courage to do what may be difficult for other countries. While *Dialogue on Foreign Policy Report* (2003, p. 4) did not explicitly label globalisation as a problem, it recognised the importance of sharing the benefits of globalisation 'more widely within and between countries to fulfil the promises of market economies, democracy and free trade that have so reshaped the global order in recent decades.'

In this policy narrative, Canada was cast as a responsible nation, one that recognised that globalisation had perils and prospects and that the positive elements ought to be more widely shared. This document also established a firm view that Canada had a distinctive presence in the world and that other countries may not be as considerate, caring or as concerned as Canada. Voices of Canadians that advocated for a more equitable form of wealth and resource distribution were featured. In making this appeal, citizens acknowledged and legitimated the power that the government had to give direct support and create and facilitate opportunities for growth through the nation's foreign aid programs.

Privileging of the problem of globalisation over other concerns

Although problems such as First Nations Land Rights, racism and homelessness were part of the everyday consciousness of Canadians, these problems seem to have been pushed to the margins of government concern during Chrétien's leadership of the ruling Liberal Party. The need for greater competitiveness in the face of global competition and the effort to eliminate deficits (Gordon & Mintz 1998) became an impetus for the government of the day to reduce social spending and to decentralise and contract out public services to the private sector. For example, there was increased attention to privatisation in the healthcare system (Willson & Howard 2000, p. iii), which women's groups feared would have an adverse effect on women working as healthcare workers. Examples of privatisation included the termination of government-sponsored school-based dental programmes, the privatisation of catering and cleaning services in hospitals, 'the use of private, for-profit medical laboratories, the expansion of private personal care homes … and the expansion of private health clinics' (Willson & Howard 2000, p. iii).

While attempts to reduce state expenditure fell heavily on social programs because of the perception that these contributed to expanding the national debt, the reasons for the rise in public debt stemmed from 'the combination of high interest rates, lower employment rates and economic growth rates' (Jiwani 2000, p. 35). The increasing recognition that globalisation was a challenge appeared to go hand-in-hand with the government's withdrawal from the third sector, the network of private and public institutions, which helped to foster a sense of wellbeing across the nation. Some scholars have argued that globalisation and the neoliberal ideology have 'worked to magnify the pre-existing cleavages' (Jiwani 2000, p. 31) in Canada. *A Dialogue on Foreign Policy* (2003) highlighted views from a cross-section of the Canadian public, with some stressing the notion of security, while others considered the significance of human rights and democratic freedoms as being of paramount importance. Still others believed that addressing socioeconomic, cultural and environmental problems should be part of the government's efforts.

It seems that the rise of globalisation and the rapid acceleration in social and technological change around the world appeared to have forced a reappraisal of the government's approach, changing what had been a profound concern for the weak in society to one in which the first priority for the government became economic survival and prosperity. The policy paper *Canada in the World* (1995, p. ii) stated that 'influence depends increasingly on the strength of economic relations.' Unsurprisingly, in listing the three key policy objectives, it appeared that pre-eminence was given to economic success:

- The promotion of prosperity and employment.
- The protection of our security, within a stable global framework.
- The projection of Canadian values and culture (*Canada in the World* 1995, p. ii).

The extent to which the quest for economic success lay at the core of the Chrétien government's agenda can be surmised from the following comment: 'The promotion of prosperity and employment is at the heart of the Government's agenda. International markets present tremendous opportunities for Canadians' (*Canada in the World* 1995, p. ii). Building a prosperous Canada was seen as the linchpin to developing global clout.

Jiwani (2000) claimed that the Canadian government likely decided to reduce its spending on social services because globalisation presented the government with the perfect excuse to do so. Jiwani (2000) argued that at the beginning of the Liberal Party's tenure, the leadership was adamant that public programs were out of control and that something needed to be done to curtail them. Additionally, some respondents to the government's policy document felt that Canada should pursue additional trade and investment opportunities in 'important emerging countries of the developing world (with China, India, Brazil and Mexico among those most frequently mentioned)' (*A Dialogue on Foreign Policy* 2003, p. 14). While many developing nations traditionally found themselves in a position of needing aid, there were some such as China and Brazil, who had been able to place themselves in favourable economic and trade positions. These countries, which continually increased their GDP, became important markets for countries such as Canada, which had a relatively small domestic market.

Factors that made the emergence of the problem possible

In an address at the Kruger College Leadership Forum, Canadian Maureen O'Neil, Director of the International Development Research Centre, answering the question of whether Canada was ready for globalisation, said that Canada was not ready and needed to better understand 'our place in the world. My definition of 'ready' is that Canada be prepared to lead in the search for greater equity, at home and internationally' (O'Neil 2001).

O'Neil argued that globalisation was nothing new if viewed in terms of the flow of money and goods. However, it had moved on in fits and starts, with many gains interspersed with setbacks and efforts at protectionism (O'Neill 2001). Levitt (1983) had made it clear that those who clung to the old ways would be in trouble. Globalisation emerged as something more than trade among nations, the kind of interdependence that meant that both the good and the bad could happen on a global scale whether it was war or a climate catastrophe '—all could affect the lives of Canadians in potentially ruinous ways'(O'Neil 2001).

Between 1978 and 1988, there was annual growth in Canadian exports to China of about 18 per cent (Holden 2008) and by 1987, the figure had grown substantially to a little over $2 billion, and then, 'one year later, it had increased to $3.6 billion. By 1988, China was Canada's sixth largest trading partner worldwide' (Holden 2008, p. 6). The 1994 TCTM, in the choice of China as the first destination, appears to have been part of the government's stance that Canada was ready to engage the world to demonstrate its influence and economic clout. Evidence that the Chrétien government was aware of the need to be engaged in the wider world and to pay attention to globalisation and its potential impact emerged from a speech he gave in New York in 1998. The prime minister said that his government had restored foreign aid cuts that had been made in more challenging times, but that, he believed that Canada was going to do more 'because we believe that wealthy countries as they get their books in order—have a responsibility beyond their own borders' (Chrétien 1998, p. 12). While urging maintenance of the economic links with the US, there was also a sense that Canada should not allow the relationship to limit taking actions in its own interest. In line with Canadian values, there were calls for fair trade so that Canada would not be counted among the countries that exploited others, but to be seen as one that cared about its citizens and those of other countries. Part of the effort to address this huge disparity between the developed world and the developing world involved opening up Canadian markets to less-developed countries.

Problem moved from invisibility to visibility

Globalisation and the inescapable rise of new players on the global scene made it easier for Canada to look beyond the US for new business relationships. Chrétien claimed that business and friendship with the US should not be confused (Dingwall 1994). The perceived lack of respect by the US also played a part in driving a willing Canada into the arms of foreign players. Dingwall (1994, p. 46) explained that despite incredible Canadian successes in areas such as sports and literature, the perception that Americans held of Canadians remained dim, a fact that became clear during the 'Larry King Live' NAFTA debate, when United States Vice-President Al Gore, did not seem to know the name of the new Canadian prime minister. While the US was likely to continue to be Canada's leading trade partner into the foreseeable future, the government under Chrétien decided to make the Asia–Pacific region the new focus of its trade promotion efforts. Regarding the need to engage new players on the world scene beside the US, Dingwall (1994, p. 46) maintained that a few decades ago it would have been difficult to predict the enormous changes in industrialisation that occurred in Asia with countries such as Malaysia, Singapore, Thailand and mainland China replicating the Japanese model of economic success. In the past, these nations had been seen by Canadian industries as possible competitors in the manufacturing sector, whereas their successes had turned them into a market (Dingwall 1994). Such a realisation may have sown the seeds for the government to seek solutions that would move Canada from the fear of globalisation to one of potential benefit.

Socio-political context prior to the emergence of the problem

Before the emergence of globalisation as a potential threat, the world was largely viewed through the prism of North and South, with the more advanced countries of the North controlling most of the major decisions related to trade. For example, many advanced countries used their technological expertise and capital as leverage to obtain access to mineral resources or markets. The result was that Western governments and companies and their local contacts became rich, while the vast majority of people continued to live in poverty. The Asian Tigers and others proved that through education and hard work it was possible to be as successful as their more advanced counterparts (Morris 1996). Such success sent a message that other countries, whether in Africa or Latin America, could also find a way to achieve a sense of parity with advanced countries. In 1994, when several Canadian provinces seemed on the brink of bankruptcy, 'financial markets responded with hostility to the Liberals' business as usual budget; interest rates rose; fear gripped senior mandarins that foreigners might dump Canadian dollars' (Richards 2004, p. 6). The government needed to send a strong signal to the business community that it was on their side. Chrétien's election victory was based on promises to boost the domestic economy, expand the number of jobs and draw the country together (Dingwall 1994). The government needed to show by deed that it was in favour of business.

The naming process

Although Levitt (1983, p. 100) is credited with coining the term 'globalisation', he admitted that others, such as the Japanese had been taking advantage of the world as a single market for a long time. Although the meanings associated with globalisation have come to be highly contested, the greater intensity of interrelationships among the peoples of the world are considered a key factor (O'Rourke 2001). While the initial conception of globalisation used by Levitt (1983) focused on aspects of technological change and markets, the term has come to be understood as being full of contradictions and ambiguities (Kellner 2002). Whereas some see globalisation as the culmination of the success of the world capitalist economic system, which strengthens the hand of multinationals while weakening nation-states, others see a postmodern break in history with the past or as a network society, which is based on a foundation of technology and the global Internet. Further, there are those who stress increased fragmentation in society. According to Kellner (2002, p. 286), for some individuals, globalisation is seen as providing not only economic opportunities but also democratisation and cultural diversity, but then, critics viewed 'globalisation as harmful, bringing about increased domination and control by the wealthier overdeveloped nations over the poor underdeveloped countries, thus increasing the hegemony of the 'haves' over the 'have-nots'.'

Canadian leaders were willing to generate a response that would ensure that the potential downside of this phenomenon was adequately dealt with. Maureen O'Neil (2001, p. 1), explained that globalisation was paradoxical, being at once a force for integration and a force for fragmentation. Further, O'Neil (2001, p. 1) observed that globalisation had the potential to enrich and impoverish and that it could empower as well as disable:

> So doing, it generates vast and turbulent inequalities. To give you just one statistic. The average GNP per person in the richest 25 countries is down to about $25,000 (US). That is, 58 times the average GNP per person in the poorest 50 countries. These disparities between rich and poor are growing worse in many countries and between countries.

Finally, globalisation being understood as a problem in Canada was expressed by Pearlstein (2000, p. 1) who feared that Canada was falling too strongly under the sway of the United States both from an economic and cultural perspective. These comments reflect ideas that were becoming more widespread within Canadian society and raised concerns among Canadians about their place within such a rapidly interconnecting world.

Existing conditions at the time

For years, it appeared that there was some kind of barrier, psychological or otherwise, between the developed world and the developing one. Through communications such as the internet and increasingly linked financial systems, there were indications that globalisation might be the solution to some of the economic woes that had afflicted those in developing countries. There was also a sense that the old paradigm, in which the rich North crafted contracts in their favour and exploited the developing world, might meet with some resistance. Such challenges came increasingly from young people in developed nations such as Canada, who stood up for the just treatment of people globally who had been unfairly treated by more advanced countries (Gopal 2001).

Societal assumptions at the time

It may seem as though any potential problems associated with globalisation ought to have concerned only the developing countries that had traditionally operated without much power in the world trade system. That the Canadian government regarded globalisation to be a force to reckon with can be observed in the following statement:

> All societies are having to respond to the pressure of economic globalisation; the increasing capacity of industries to distribute production, the power of financial markets to influence the value of currencies without regard to political geography and the enormous volume of investment capital which flows daily across borders at the push of a button. International capital markets have the strength to affect the independent capacity of governments to guide economies. Globalisation means that economies respond less to political control than before. Societies look to their governments to foster economies that succeed in the global system but produce benefits locally. (*Canada in the World* 1995, p. 3)

The last sentence provides a sense of the justification the Canadian government may have put forth for establishing the TCTM. In a turbulent world, the government realised the ease with which it could have become sidelined, as the forces of the market became increasingly more powerful. Therefore, helping to shore up small Canadian businesses was a way of legitimising itself while ostensibly enriching the country.

As recounted by a newly-elected Member of Parliament, Fen Hampson, who was summoned to meet the newly-elected Prime Minister in 1993 to discuss the new government's focus on the Asia Pacific region, 'The Prime Minister was determined to fulfill Liberal campaign commitments to increase exports and get more of Canada's small- and medium-sized enterprises (SMEs) trading, particularly in the rapidly expanding markets of the Asia Pacific' (p. 105). This vision seems to have materialised as the government had envisioned, because in a few years, Gordon Duncan, owner of Total North Communications, which installed, designed, and repaired phones, participated in a 1997 trade mission to Asia, and got into active discussions for a partnership with a South Korean company. As Seguin (1997, B7) reports, 'Mr. Duncan's personal experience is but one of a dozen examples of how small and medium-sized Canadian businesses are benefiting from the high-profile Team Canada mission.' Also, in a January 1988 trade mission that Jean Chrétien led to Latin America, 'The business delegation was composed of representatives from every region of Canada and included women and young entrepreneurs. Nearly three-quarters of the companies were small and medium-sized enterprises' (Courchene, Savoie & Schwanen 2008, p. 473).

Societal forces involved

In addition to the forces of the marketplace, the Canadian government was aware that 'culture now has assumed a global character' (*Canada in the World* 1995, p. 3) and that it was possible for Canada to influence and be influenced by others. Canada, which struggled for years under the shadow of the US, had to contend with potentially more powerful forces from elsewhere. *Canada in the World* (1995, p. 4) declared that globalisation 'has given greater scope for vibrant cultures to flourish across borders; it has raised, however, concerns about global homogeneity stifling local expression and identity'. For Canada, seeking a balance between protecting the nation's culture while being open to others was a challenge. Globalisation allowed for the greater flow of ideas, and technological innovations opened new ways by which people could connect, and for trade relations to evolve.

4.2.2 Arena II: Network of Social Regularities

The Canadian government attempted to act from a position of knowledge. Rather than allow itself to be overwhelmed, it appeared that the government sought to confront or neutralise the potentially devastating effects of globalisation by positioning Canada as a strong player in the emerging new order. Two elements seem to have shaped Canada's decision to include trade missions as a countermeasure to this world of uncertainty. *Canada in the World* (1995, p. 2) suggested that the downfall of the former Soviet Union was not just a matter of its inability to match Western military might but that it had a flawed economic system that did not 'generate an acceptable standard of living for its people. The new powers among developing countries are generally those whose influence derives from striking economic success.' With this continual emphasis on economic success, trade missions seemed a perfect fit because they opened up the opportunity for the government to engage businesses while showcasing Canada's main points of attraction to the world.

Objects and concepts that went into the establishment of the trade missions

It was the contention of Chrétien that a focus on trade would provide Canada with greater clout in the world. This included an intense focus on China (Cao & Paltiel 2015). However, the target was much broader. The government was determined to cut down Canada's debt and eventually spend on social and economic needs (Liberal Party of Canada 1993). There was a sense that Canada needed to spread its wings beyond its traditional dependence on the US. A focus on trade, under these circumstances, seemed reasonable. The framework for organising and implementing the trade missions came from the Ministry of Foreign Affairs and International Trade, which created a special office in the trade section to handle organisation and coordination. Although the trade missions were not established on a parliamentary bill or order in council, the program appeared to have had the broad support of the government. At the time, Chrétien was strong in his defence of trade missions and participated several times in travels to other countries along with other government ministers and provincial premiers (Price 2007).

Prevailing modes of thinking at the time

Canada recognised that it could not remain aloof from the world and that this increased need for international communication and trade offered two sides: one of threat to prosperity for those who failed to plan and one of possible profit for those who had a plan for survival and prosperity. However, there were other interrelated issues. Concerning the prospects for trade, one policy document reiterated that the government would seek to strengthen global prosperity because when 'when other parts of the world prosper, we benefit in many ways. Prosperity helps to anchor international stability and enables progress towards sustainable development' (*Canada in the World* 1995, p. ii). There was an increasing awareness that Canada could spread its values abroad and bring other nations into the country's sphere of influence. *Canada in the World* (1995, p. ii) contended that the promotion of Canadian values such as appreciation for human rights, respect for democracy, 'the rule of law and the environment - will make an important contribution to international security in the face of new threats to stability. Acceptance of such values abroad will help safeguard the quality of life at home: Canada is not an island able to resist a world that devalued beliefs central to our identity.'

Human rights were part of the government's language, although it was one of the areas that came under challenge when the government did not respond forcefully enough to countries such as China, which were seen by critics of the TCTM as not having a sterling human rights record. Although not a new term, critics tried to reintroduce the government to the concept, a move that Motion (2005, p. 509) highlighted as 'a crucial part of discourse transformation; changing the way that people speak about things aims to change attitudes and knowledge.'

The dominant and subordinate values prevailing at the time

From the government's point of view, the Canadian people needed to be partners in shaping the policies of the state and to have a hand in how Canada engaged with the rest of the world. It was important to the government that the policy document *Canada in the World* (1995) come from wide-ranging consultations with ordinary Canadians and experts alike:

> Canadians volunteered ideas and proposals on foreign policy throughout 1994, many making outstanding contributions to the review process. The government has also met and continues, to meet, with Canadians of all backgrounds and from all regions to seek their views on specific questions—on aid, trade, human rights, the international environmental agenda and nuclear non-proliferation. The Ministers of Foreign Affairs and International Trade have each met with groups of Canadians for these purposes. (*Canada in the World* 1995, p. iv)

The inclusion of Canadians and other groups, including experts, to chart the nation's foreign policy course was not an accident. It was rooted in the government's realisation that to remain relevant in a global environment of dispersing authority, it would need to engage the populace as much as possible. In effect, the government could regain some of its waning influence by relating to its citizens as partners. However, the government's engagement with citizens was not across the board because poverty groups continued to chide the government for sidelining the poor (Krauss 2002).

The second policy document, *A Dialogue on Foreign Policy* (2003), did not simply detail what the Canadian government desired to do. It also emerged out of consultations with Canadians across the country, which was a signal that the government respected the voices of the people. From a Foucauldian point of view, this effort may be understood as an attempt on the part of the government to draw closer to the people in a moment of great uncertainty and to exercise control over them. The government attempted to join hands with the people, who were reminded of their diverse origins and how this invested meaning into what being Canadian represented. Through its diverse policy statements, throne speeches and other forms of communication, the government contributed to helping Canadians construct a very specific image of themselves. One of the key points to emerge in this document was that the diversity of the Canadian population made the country 'a microcosm of the world's people; our geography and population give us broad global interests ... we have a unique basis for asserting a distinctive presence in the world' (*A Dialogue on Foreign Policy* 2003, p. 3)

Through repeated assertions of what Canada was and aspired to be, sets of statements (discourse) were made that sought to manifest Canada's new dream self-image. This need for repetition stemmed from the reality that there were numerous other interests, data, communications and news bulletins, which were published daily from a multiplicity of sources, and that might inadvertently drown the government's message. An entity that did not release its own statements amid the jumble of texts and discourse could be inadvertently shaped or 'misshaped' by the discourse of others. The government sought, through myriad ways and increasingly the internet, to shape Canadians' view of themselves and how the world should see Canada.

Possible factors influencing the emergence of the 'problem' of globalisation and policy solutions

The problems raised by globalisation were of such a nature that Canadians could not deal with them by further withdrawing into themselves. It was imperative for Canada to be a part of the international trade regimes because these had implications on the domestic scene. Another response was the need for states to cooperate with one another. Foucault (1982b) declared that power does not reside in one place, person or country, but is a system of relations. This recognition on the part of the Canadian government, may have partly fuelled the country's efforts to engage the rest of the world. China, which had been considered economically underdeveloped by many in the West for years, was becoming a force to reckon with.

For several years, the idea of globalisation as a 'problem' continued to permeate Canadian national consciousness. On the surface, it was difficult for democratically minded people who valued openness in their society to criticise the notion of greater cooperation and openness around the world. However, others observed that expanding markets, as well as communications advances and the development of more open societies could bring tremendous benefits to millions and increasing global interconnections would spread knowledge 'and facilitate transnational networking of many kinds, including media and civil-society activism' (*A Dialogue on Foreign Policy* 2003, p. 7)

Moreover, Canadians had to be aware that social tensions could arise from the increasingly open approach to borders and that 'global openness and interconnections also enable the spread of new forms of terrorism, criminal activity, infectious diseases and economic instability' (*A Dialogue on Foreign Policy* 2003, p. 7). In a world of diminishing US influence, as Asian countries anchored by Japan and China continued to rise, it was necessary for Canada to make new alliances, to keep connections with old friends, but to recognise that, in this new reality, 'partners will choose each other to attain specific objectives or to reflect diversity in pursuing new long-term prospects. Variable alliances will increasingly become a pattern in international relations (*Canada in the World* 1995, p. 6). The regionalism emerging in response to the challenges of globalisation possessed unique challenges and opportunities. Although Canada had long been closely allied with the US, it sought to practice multilateralism, and use its image as a haven of multiculturalism to engage other countries 'prudently and effectively as the regional systems themselves evolve' (*Canada in the World* 1995, p. 7).

Other social regularities not seen in this solution

Over the years, Canada has sought to fill the gaps in its low-growth population by accepting immigrants from around the world (Webb & Wood 2009). In the past, Canada's immigration policy was tinged with racism (Price 2007), although the country has moved toward the notion of equality for all and the desire to attract highly educated immigrants without regard to their national or racial origin (Webb & Wood 2009). This open-door policy to the world also helped to shape Canada's image in the world as a welcoming haven for people who might have felt politically, socially or economically repressed.

In addition to the attraction of immigration, Canada took significant steps towards repairing some of the distrust between the government and the country's First Nations people. In fact, 'Aboriginal spending was maintained and even increased slightly at a time when the Chrétien government was reducing almost all other line items in the federal budget' (Flanagan 2000, p. 102). These internal issues helped to support the image of Canada as a fair, peace-loving country, which was an image that supported the nation's ambitions to become a bigger player on the world stage.

Canada sought to capitalise on its connections with other influential players on the world stage and to use its geographic location to its advantage, to harness the dual benefits of its Anglophone and Francophone communities 'as well as to the homelands of Canadians drawn from every part of the globe who make up its multicultural personality' (*Canada in the World* 1995, p. i). The government saw a chance to capitalise on and highlight the presence of immigrants who were part of a trade mission to the immigrants' home countries. *A Dialogue on Foreign Policy* (2003, p. 5) sought to push Canada to step forward in the world and to assert itself and to 'clearly articulate Canadian values and interests.'

Canada could not relax and simply hope that the world would understand its pacifism, benevolence and myriad acts of charity towards the rest of the world. These values had to be shared and actively promoted. Even as Canadians asserted the need to make their values widely known, they expressed fear of seeming to impose these values on others. This self-questioning and reflection demonstrated a mature view on the part of Canadians seeking to use globalisation as an opportunity to put national ideas into the international marketplace. Soliciting comments from Canadians also demonstrated how considerate the government was, serving to shore up Canada's image as an enlightened nation and to highlight how different the country was from others. By continuing to talk about globalisation and to weigh Canada's place among the family of nations, the problematic nature of globalisation continued to take centre stage, even as Canada strove to define or redefine its own identity vis-à-vis the US and the rest of the world.

How emergent answers have deepened understanding of the problem

When the Liberal government came to power in 1993, they had a good idea of where Canada stood as far as economic strength was concerned (Chrétien 1998). The government saw an opportunity to achieve several goals at once—focus on the needs of business as a way to generate more revenue, improve the image of Canada abroad through Team Canada activities and use Canada's image and economic might as an opportunity to influence other countries. While the government's discourse on the success of TCTM appeared to satisfy some Canadians, others were unsure. Some of the latter wondered if the program was worth all the attention and money the government was putting into it (Head & Ries 2010). There were many criticisms of the trade missions even though Chrétien never wavered in his support for the project.

The last TCTM under Chrétien occurred in 2003. His immediate successor, Paul Martin, who ended up as a short-term placeholder until federal elections were held, participated indirectly in a trade mission in 2005. Martin may have felt the need to continue to strengthen the relationship that Canada had forged under the former prime minister with countries such as China. However, he also slightly distanced himself from the trade missions by not travelling on the same plane with the businesspeople, which his predecessor had often done. According to Poy and Cao (2009, pp. 63–64), in 2005, Liberal Prime Minister Paul Martin visited China and oversaw the handling of 80 trade and bilateral deals, and thus laid 'the groundwork for both sides to discuss an approved destination status agreement in relation to Chinese tourists visiting Canada.' Prime Minister Martin had an opportunity to clarify his continuing interest in countries such as China, when he was interviewed by the Harvard International Review (Canada leads … 2006, p. 67) and was asked about his having proclaimed a strategic partnership with China in September 2005. Martin responded that Canada was indeed ready to do business not only with China but also India. The interest was not in only one direction because 'several dozen Chinese delegations visited Canada soon after Paul Martin's trip to China in January 2005' (Evans 2005, p. 163). This visit to China, which had become even more successful since the 1994 visit, could be read as a signal in terms of Canada's growing clout and the understanding that there were mutual benefits.

4.2.3 Arena III: Assumptions—Range of Policy Solutions
Range of possible and impossible solutions

Canada could have become protectionist by restricting businesses from other countries from taking advantage of its domestic market. Canada's population is about 37 million people and a protectionist stance would not have been a good move because other countries with larger markets could have retaliated by shutting off those markets to Canada. Whether in terms of the promotion of prosperity, the protection of national security or the projection of Canadian values, the government of Canada, it appears, saw no value in closing its doors. Rather, the government believed that Canada was sufficiently strong to 'compete with the best in the world' (*Canada in the World* 1995, p. ii). The government realised that Canada required a policy framework at home to support economic development, access to markets abroad, 'fair and predictable set of rules governing trade and investment; and means to ensure that Canadian firms are able to take advantage of promising foreign market opportunities' (*Canada in the World* 1995, p. 10).

Another consideration involved how Canada could express its values around the world and share its culture with others. Some saw Canada's model of plurality as a possible solution for the problems plaguing other countries and regions. For others, charity had to begin at home and the country's influence abroad would garner greater credibility if the government paid attention to 'enhancing the place of women, visible minorities, disabled persons, First Nations peoples and immigrant communities in Canadian society' (A *Dialogue on Foreign Policy* 2003, p. 20).

While policymakers were touting the need to share Canadian values with the rest of the world, there were problems related to the treatment of First Nations people, women and the visible minorities in Canada, such as Indians, Pakistanis and Blacks. Kufeldt et al. (2011, p. 410) argued that although Canada was consistently ranked by the UN as one of the best countries in which to live, First Nations people residing in reserves were very low on the human development index. Cultural diplomacy was also considered to be a good approach to developing positive international relations, which included greater promotion of Canadian artists abroad. Another suggestion was the promotion of people-to-people exchanges. While Canadians wanted to contribute to the education of developing countries, they expressed concern about contributing to the brain drain of those societies. Further, Canadians expressed sensitivity about the stereotypes that persisted about their country and wondered whether the time was right to promote a new image of the country. *A Dialogue on Foreign Policy* (2003, p. 21) stated:

> There are calls for targeting educational and promotional campaigns in key markets and for creativity in presenting our values and culture. The point is also underlined by provincial government contributions encouraging the 'branding' of Canada as a location for economic partners, visitors, students and skilled immigrants. Among other suggestions is a proposal to improve international knowledge of Canada by reaching out to the more than 7000 Canadian scholars around the world who influence large numbers of students, foreign media and publics.

The document also suggested that there ought to be an expansion of internships, partnerships, exchanges and other outreach programs working in collaboration with government, parliamentarians and private sector associations and NGOs. However, Canada's interests were not to be given short shrift. Increased trade was the key.

Grid of social regularities that allowed this particular response

The Liberal government that ushered in the TCTM program had won an election in 1993 with a large majority. The policies of the previous Conservative government, which had included the establishment of free trade with the US (Gaston & Trefler 1997), had worried some groups that Canada was going to be subservient to the US. In this context, the new government sought to demonstrate its independence by reaching out to potential business partners besides the US.

Although Canada can be counted among the major capitalist countries in the world, the welfare state, which had provided free healthcare, low-cost mortgages, pensions and welfare money, was accepted as part of the government's benevolent attitude (Guest 1980). Before it became clear that the government's focus on business also meant less attention to other issues, it would have been difficult to find anyone who seriously challenged the idea that a country's exports deserved attention.

Throughout Canadian history, trade missions were a fact of business and government life, but they were not the high-profile affairs that they became under Prime Minister Jean Chrétien. Indeed, in a total free market, there would not have been any need for government to be actively involved in business. But the Canadian government has, for many decades, sought to influence business both through regulations and support to various business sectors. The government's involvement in business has not been without critics. For example, the Canadian Taxpayers Federation has called the Team Canada trade missions 'junkets' (The Canadian Taxpayers Federation 1997, 4A). Also, as one critic, Michael To, president of the Federation for a Democratic China, put it, 'The last Team Canada trade mission to China in 1994 achieved little on the trade front and even less on the human rights front...I think the result was questionable economically, and at the same time we seem to be very ineffective in terms of our human rights agenda' (Scoffield 2000). These criticisms, however, have done nothing to dampen the interest of the government in continuing to offer its support to the business community where export promotion is concerned.

The early 1990s were also a time when Canada could bask in the confidence of being the best country in the world according to the UN, and to use that reputation to improve its international economic standing and image. This was expressed in *Canada in the World* (1995, p. 12):

> The UN Human Development Index has rated Canada as among those countries with the best quality of life in the world. The protection and enhancement of that standard is a key goal of Canadian foreign policy. the Special Joint Committee pointed out, Canada's prosperity depends on more than sound domestic economic policies, although they are essential. It depends as well on one side global prosperity and on our ability to take full advantage of the opportunities this presents.

The Liberal government, via *Canada in the World* (1995), emphasised that domestic initiatives were necessary to get the nation's house in order. Although this point was not made directly in connection with trade missions, there was a sense in which it was clear that the government found need to be creative in setting up initiatives that would ensure Canada a place of advantage in the emerging global order.

Possible acceptable or unacceptable consequences

The discourse surrounding globalisation during the early 1990s was one of great uncertainty. The government of Canada appeared to realise that the new regime was one that would make winners and losers of nations and individuals. It seemed that Canada—a country that the UN had repeatedly proclaimed as being first among equals—could not end up a loser. Since the government could not trust the private sector to succeed on its own, the government prepared itself, keenly aware of the goodwill that Canada enjoys around the world, to help Canadian industries fight in the global market to win. Canada had an image of itself that the nation needed to maintain. *Canada in the World* (1995, p. 13), emphasised that Canada was a major world trading power and that acting in concert with other members of the G7 and the Quadrilateral Group, it has been able to remain at the centre of the world economy, and so, Canada needed to 'continue to participate in the world economy today. We must continue to ensure that these relations are managed with care.' The policy document also acknowledged emerging challengers in global trade, including Korea, Taiwan, China, Mexico and Brazil, expressed in *Canada in the World* (1995, p. 13):

> These new players compete with Canada for market share and quality investments, while providing increasingly attractive markets for the export of Canadian goods and services. Using all available foreign policy instruments in a coordinated way, we must build relationships with them and with other dynamic developing economies to reflect their current and growing economic importance to us.

If the government had remained unconcerned and unwilling to do anything in the face of the globalisation juggernaut, it might have seemed like capitulation in the face of impending danger.

Whose needs were ignored?

In the new push for business success, the biggest losers were the poor and those who fell outside the world of business in the sense of being unemployed or unemployable. In the years before Chrétien's Liberal Party took office, Canadians who could not obtain employment were able to get welfare assistance. In the neoliberal era of the 1990s, the qualification for obtaining welfare was made tighter. Not surprisingly, the number of homeless people began to multiply on Canadian streets. The Liberal government did not make budget provision for 'social housing, although homelessness has emerged as a primary concern in Toronto and Canada's other major urban centres' (Jones 2000, p. 1).

One of the frequent critics of the Chrétien regime, the Canadian Centre for Policy Alternatives, pointed out that, 'The Liberal government balanced the books in the late 1990s thanks to swift and savage cuts to social programs. Program cuts allowed the government to balance its books, but also left a trail of growing poverty, widening income disparities, and deteriorating public services' (Campbell 2003). Also, Josephine Grey, executive director of Low-Income Families Working Together, 'said the federal government failed to adopt any program in recognition of the International Year for the Eradication of Poverty or provide any funds to promote its recognition in Canada' (Grange 1996, A10).

For a document that purported to have had considerable input from Canadians, the 1995 policy document appeared to be skewed towards business and lacking in concern for the poor and disenfranchised. The policy document also revealed that the government's consultations with the business community were extensive and that out of these consultations had emerged a policy for how Canadians should conduct international business. The government acknowledged that it could not do everything that demanded attention and that it would have to be selective (*Canada in the World* 1995, pp. 19–20), and concentrate the nation's resources abroad while scaling back some domestic operations. In that same document, the federal government declared its intention to work with provincial and municipal authorities as well as the private sector.

Kinds of language used to establish what constitutes the problem

The policy document attempted to not be alarmist but to point out that the environment then differed from the Cold War regime. In light of the expected peace dividend[15] in the post-Cold War era, the Canadian government's policy document appeared to highlight issues of Canadian interconnectivity with the world, which presented two interlocking possibilities: involvement and potential prosperity in the globalising new order. In *Canada in the World* (1995), it was suggested that prosperity could offer a pathway to influence and power in a way that the military could not. This meant that the way forward for Canada was clear: determine ways of profiting from the global uncertainties and use the government's accumulated goodwill, image, capital and connections so that Canadian export-oriented companies could get a jumpstart in their quests for economic success. The following are some significant areas of emphasis:

1. *Increasing the participation of Canadian businesses in the international economy*

With the nation's increasing stature in the world, the Canadian government realised it could use its influence 'to open doors to foreign governments and to key economic agents' (*Canada in the World* 1995, p. 21). Image building was seen as carrying the kind of capital or currency that could translate into business opportunities for Canadian companies. Trade missions could be a vehicle for achieving this goal.

---

[15]The peace dividend is a concept used to describe the economic benefits accruing from not having to waste money on military matters because of peaceful relations among former adversaries.

2. *Diversifying international business markets*

As important as the US has been for Canada as a market, the government seemed determined to expand beyond this single market to ensure that Canadian businesses could profit from opportunities elsewhere and that Canada would 'rely more on locally-engaged staff in the US and Western Europe and redeploy Canadian personnel resources to Asia–Pacific and Latin America' (*Canada in the World* 1995, pp. 21–22).

With a network of trade representations around the world, the Canadian government had access to an incredible amount of knowledge. The government also saw an opportunity in this wide-open global climate to promote Canadian culture and educational opportunities in Canada abroad 'as a way of creating an identifiable image for Canada and its goods and services' (*Canada in the World* 1995, p. 22).

3. *Attracting international investment and assisting science and technology*

In addition to supporting the export of Canadian products, the government saw the need to make a case for potential investors to choose Canada. Although attention centred on local businesses attempting to sell their wares abroad, the Chrétien government was also interested in foreign direct investment into Canada. For example, Toyota expanded its plant in Cambridge, Ontario. Holroyd and Coates (1996, p. 3) reported that 'the massive investment, totalling $600 million was hailed by Canadian politicians as evidence of the country's continued attractiveness and of the long-term benefits attached to the free trade deal.' The trade mission to China was not just a matter of Canadians selling their products abroad but an attempt to court Chinese investors.

4. *Building partnerships and a 'Team Canada' approach*

The 'Team Canada' metaphor was explained as a federal government partnership for international business, which was precipitated on three fronts: the federal government, the provinces and the private sector. It was the goal of the federal government to collaborate with the provinces to help companies that wanted to export their products, and for this, 'We have initiated discussion on a strategy that defines roles and responsibilities and seeks to eliminate overlap and duplication and instill one-stop shopping for export related intelligence and services' (*Canada in the World* 1995, p. 23).

The TCTM concept was one component of a much larger strategy of ensuring that the Canadian government leveraged its power and influence on behalf of Canadian companies to succeed in the shifting and uncertain new world of globalisation. The trade missions often included provincial premiers who came along with businesspeople from their province. For example, in 2001, New Brunswick Premier, Bernard Lord, led a provincial group of seven New Brunswick companies and schools on a trade mission to China that lasted from February 9th to 18th. As reported, 'The New Brunswick delegation is part of a larger Team Canada mission which includes Prime Minister Jean Chrétien and provincial premiers'... (Communications New Brunswick www.gnb.ca)

4.2.4 Arena IV: The Social Functions of Policy Studies
Function of conventional and interpretive policy regarding government involvement in supporting businesses

The traditional view of policy analysis held that with a range of subject backgrounds such as law, economics, organisational analysis and budgeting (Howlett & Lindquist 2004), those in positions of responsibility for policy could craft policies to fit perceived problems. However, real-world policymaking does not necessarily come in such a linear package. Before winning the election that brought them to power, the Liberal government of Chrétien outlined their policy positions, many of which appeared to be in line with the social responsibility that previous governments had taken in Canada, such as ensuring protections for healthcare, unemployment and women's empowerment. The promise of fiscal responsibility was also considered by many to be a positive aspect of their platform. However, upon taking office, the overriding ethos that seemed to drive the Chrétien government was the quest to cut the deficit at all costs. The policy moves that the government made appeared to be in line with neoliberal tenets that had begun to take root in many Western democracies a decade or so earlier.

A sampling of the broad goals of neoliberalism included internationalisation, privatisation, removal of restrictions on foreign investment and deregulation of capital and currency markets (Albo 2002). Within a few years, the Chrétien government succeeded in whittling down the deficit and accumulating a surplus. On the surface, this could be marked as a singular act of success. However, a deeper interrogation of this success reveals that it came at the expense of social benefits that many Canadians had come to take for granted. The federal government's drastic reductions in transfer payments to the provinces, which also cut back on their transfer payments to municipalities, exposed the middle class and those at the lower rungs of society to harsh realities that they had not been confronted with before. Dobrowolsky (2004, p. 175) explained that 'in his first budget (1994), Paul Martin declared that unemployment insurance would be slashed by $5.5 billion in 1994–1995 and 1996–1997.'

Women were hit hard when funding to women's organisations came under the chopping block. The large-scale reduction in the ranks of federal workers through an offloading of their work to the private sector raised the ire of feminist academics and activists, who highlighted the disproportionate impact of these austerity measures on women. Some 'federal departments saw reductions in spending of more than one-third over a three-year period' (Veldhuis & Clemens 2016, p. 1). With the appearance of increasing trade and the symbolism of the prime minister travelling from country to country fronting for the business community, all appeared to be well, although not every group in society would have attested to the incontrovertible success of the Chrétien government.

Preferred social response regarding the provision of government assistance to businesses

The government of Canada has traditionally given the impression that it cares about the people and will do whatever it takes to ensure a fair, equitable society. The government has also traditionally recognised the important role played by business through its contribution to the tax base for the successful implementation of social programs. However, there were legitimate questions regarding whether the government's contributions to the TCTM program were appropriate. Following a steady stream of criticism, the government's discourse began to lose some of its power to win popular support. TCTM were temporarily curtailed when a new government took power in 2006. Despite the highly publicised cases of success by the companies involved in the program, some individuals and organisations remained sceptical and thought that the program was a waste of money (Schiller 2008).

A Dialogue on Foreign Policy (2003) sought to question whether the earlier emphasis on security, prosperity and values presented in *Canada in the World* (1995), remained relevant in a world shaken by new events. There was a wide divergence of ideas and opinions regarding whether Canada should follow the US. For example, there was strong consensus that Canada should chart its own course, such as on the Kyoto Accords, rather than blindly following the US.

In answering the question of how Canada could use its geographical position for further economic advancement and to 'make the benefits of globalisation more widely shared' (*A Dialogue on Foreign Policy* 2003, p. 15), there was a key concern: not allowing economic considerations to dominate foreign policy. Canadians could not be true to the values they espoused if they allowed the quest for economic prosperity to dictate the nation's reaction and response to events around the world. Canadians wanted principle to override capital considerations, which reinforces the notion that Canada aspired to a higher purpose, striving to hold on to the values that made the nation a respected voice around the world.

4.2.5 Concluding Remarks

The Canadian government under Chrétien saw the need to enhance Canada's role in the world. While Canada had always sought to promote strong international organisations as a means to remain engaged in the world, there was the added reality that with its relatively small size, Canada was overshadowed by the US and needed to explore relationships with countries much farther afield.

To this end, Canada's embrace of the wider world beyond the US made sense to Canadians, who had steadily embraced the principle of multiculturalism and considered diversity to be a strength. It was also undeniable that economic might was a worthwhile goal, although some segments of society might not have envisioned having to be sacrificed in the process of pursuing greater fiscal responsibility.

The TCTM program was one strand of the government's effort to raise Canada's profile in the world. The involvement of the prime minister and other government ministers ensured that these events received substantial coverage. The TCTM also opened up the opportunity for Canadian leaders to meet their counterparts abroad while potentially contributing to the export volume of trade for Canada.

If the government's voice on TCTM had been the only one, its message, undiluted and focused, could have made a strong impression. The government, with its vast array of experts, could speak with the voice of authority and have its views permeate the consciousness of the people. Government actions, including relations with other countries, support of developing countries and trade missions, were supposed to support this collective viewpoint.

Part I set out the context, environment and regularities within which the TCTM and ancillary policies were enacted. Part II focused on specific extracts that pertain to the research questions, including the criteria by which the government and the business community, as well as other entities in society such as the media, academia and NGOs, judged the government's involvement in the TCTM program.

4.3 Part II: Thematic Analysis
4.3.1 Part IIa: Analysis of the Canadian Government's Marketing Communications and Other Prevailing Discourses Surrounding the TCTMs

From the perspective of the government and business community, the TCTM was an unqualified success. In addition to the volume of trade, contracts signed, memoranda of understandings agreed upon, friendships forged, and contacts initiated, there was little doubt that the trade missions were a success.

As powerful as the government's message might have been, Foucault explained that the notion of power as residing only in certain entities is incorrect. Power is a matter of relations and the voices of a few critics, who knew how to exercise their agency, could create a new understanding of the value of the TCTM program over time.

To promote TCTM to local businesses, thousands of pages of marketing communications were produced by the Canadian Ministry of Trade and Foreign International Affairs, which was responsible for administering the program. Since the curtailment of the program, these communications, including bulletins, testimonials from former participants, news releases, interviews with government officials and newspaper reports of the missions were archived at the National Library of Canada's TCTM Archive but seems now to be defunct. This researcher, however, managed to preserve most of the materials, which are now housed at a Team Canada Trade Mission website dedicated to the marketing communications produced by DFAIT. A sampling of these materials is accessible online.[16]

Canada successfully marketing its high-technology savvy abroad

An image of Canada as a land of vast prairies and beautiful natural scenery is held by many people around the world. Such an image, which does not make room for Canada's manufacturing technology development over the years, has remained irksome for Canadian businesspeople and the government. The TCTM program, through the publicity accorded these events and the marketing communications put forth by the Ministry of Foreign Affairs and International Trade, functioned in part to offset this viewpoint.

There were two broad areas in which Canada's technological savvy was highlighted. One was the superior technical expertise of Canadian companies, which placed them in high demand by other advanced countries such as Germany, the US and the Netherlands. For example, the Eco-Nova Group in Halifax, Nova Scotia, developed partnerships with countries such as Germany, Finland and the US:

---
[16]https://works.bepress.com/everettofori/58/

> The reputation of our high-quality underwater images means that when maritime museums around the world require video surveys of new wreck sites, we are the ones that receive the call. (TCTM Archive 2006)

This marketing discourse highlighted the unique expertise of this Canadian company and how it could benefit other countries such as the US, Germany and the Netherlands. This was a message in which Canadians could take pride, but was also one that had the practical purpose of making Canada's expertise better known around the world.

Demand exists for Canadian expertise in advanced countries

Considering that the US has many high-technology companies, it seemed impressive for a Canadian company to be chosen by an American entity. For example, it was reported that Trojan Technologies obtained a $15 million contract in May 2001 for the treatment of municipal wastewater and sewer overflows in Jefferson County, Alabama. That contract turned out to be the largest in the company's history, extending over two decades of operations and 'the largest ultraviolet (UV) disinfection treatment contract ever awarded in the UV disinfection industry' (TCTM Archive 2001).

Another company that was a world leader in technology was Proto Manufacturing Limited of OldCastle, Ontario, which developed expertise in residual stress and applied stress analysis systems. When the best of the best was needed to assist in technical work in the aftermath of the collapse of the World Trade Center, Proto Manufacturing Limited was called upon:

> Proto's Systems—currently the smallest and fastest of their kind are in demand around the world in various applications, mostly by major aircraft and engine manufacturers ... 'We have received letters of commendation from both the US Navy and Airforce,' says Michael Brass, company president, 'and we are known as the best in the world.' (TCTM Archive 2002)

As more people around the world came to know about Canada's high-technology industries, there was a chance that the image of a mere frozen land, farmland or prairie, would be dispelled.

Demand existed for Canadian expertise in developing countries

It was important to Canada and the Liberal government of Chrétien for the country to be seen as taking an interest in the needs of developing countries, which matched the government's goal of rebranding Canada in the eyes of the world. Using the BOOT formula (i.e., build, own, operate and transfer), Dessaus-Sojun Inc. of Laval, Quebec, was involved in constructing a 230-kilometre highway between Kingston and Montego Bay, Jamaica. It was anticipated that when completed, 'it will help boost the living standards of people in depressed rural areas by improving access to local and international markets' (TCTM Archive 2003). Another Canadian company, Summit Seeds, Oxford Station, Ontario, was involved in marketing hybrid seeds developed in Canada by Agriculture Environmental Renewal Canada Inc. of Ottawa, Ontario, which could improve foraging activity and boost milk productivity. The company's hybrid seeds, specially designed with cold climate in mind:

> Will extend the growing season to January. They may also allow year-round production in North and Northwestern parts of the country where the temperature can fall to 10 degrees Celsius. (TCTM Archive 2002)

Such opportunities gave the impression that Canada was not just interested in making money but was genuinely contributing to the wellbeing of other countries, which was an image that helped to boost the nation's standing among developing countries.

Canada presents a united front abroad: Federal government, provincial premiers and business community

The involvement of the prime minister was the first signal to businesspeople and government officials in other countries that Team Canada delegations merited attention. Dorothy Grant, a First Nations designer who participated in the 1999 TCTM to Japan wrote in her testimonial that the trade missions carried 'the prestige that attracts valuable contacts and serious enquiries because of the endorsement of all three levels of government' (TCTM Archive 1999). A travel group that included premiers, businesspeople, other government officials and the prime minister, held an image of a united front and gave the impression that there were smooth working relationships among Canadians and that they were people who could be trusted to work smoothly with others.

Another participant, Dr Henri Paupach, president of UltraDoc, who participated in the 2002 trip to Russia and Germany, claimed that 'the invitation from the Canadian government carries a lot of weight with these individuals' (TCTM Archive 1999), referring to foreign businesspeople and potential business partners. In that same 2002 trade mission, Harry Prout of Permaquik wrote in a testimonial, 'from Permaquik's point of view, the trade mission was a great success … Our distributors were particularly impressed by the functions organised by the Canadian government' (TCTM Archive 2002). Further, according to Herman Victorov, president and CEO of Technophar, 'the missions presented us with excellent opportunities and enabled us to sign lucrative contracts with China and Vietnam in the presence of the Prime Minister' (TCTM Archive 1999). The leadership and involvement of the Canadian government carried clout in the eyes of many people around the world.

Canada as a gateway for cultural products such as film

Behind the scenes, Canadian companies were heavily involved in supporting creative productions in the film and video game industries. Frantic Films, which employed 65 people in 2002 when the company participated in the TCTM, served 'a growing roster of clients that include Warner Bros, Paramount Pictures, 20th Century Fox, ABC Tel, History Tel and Life Network' (TCTM Archive 2002). Rhombus, which was founded in 1979 at York University's film department, worked in concert with 'internationally renowned cellist Yo-Yo Ma and other artists … and garnered several trophies in Brazil, Italy and France as well as two prime-time Emmys and the prestigious Rose D'Or' (TCTM Archive 2002). Those not familiar with Canada's clout in the film industry learned:

> The Toronto film market, the second most important in the world after Cannes, is the preferred gateway for foreign film and television professionals entering the North American market. Distribution agreements for Canadian and foreign films worth millions of dollars are concluded each year. (TCTM Archive 2002)

This information helped to remind readers that Hollywood movies were not the only products of worth in the movie business and that opportunities in television and cable existed, which provided a platform for Canadians to share their expertise with clients around the world.

Canada as a cooperative nation

The TCTM marketing communications made frequent references to cooperation between Canada and Canadian companies with other nations and their institutions and companies. This reinforced the discourse of Canada as being a peace-loving, caring and concerned global player. For example, Alternative Fuel Systems Inc. of Calgary, Alberta:

> Customised its proprietary Sparrow System to enable a well-known diesel engine to operate on natural gas, in collaboration with a Dallas-based company that intends to market the engine to beverage delivery and school bus fleets in Texas. (TCTM Archive 2002)

Additionally, Entrust Technologies, Ottawa, gained a reputation for successfully working with government agencies around the globe to improve internet security. Relationships between Canadian companies and other well-known global companies such as that between Fincentric Corporation of Richmond, which developed state of the art multicurrency and multilanguage platforms for such companies as Microsoft, Compaq and Japan's Nomura Research Institute, helped to position Canadian companies as among the very best (TCTM Archive 2002).

TCTM participants garner financial success

While not all companies were willing to share financial information, many were, which formed one of the key marketing tools for TCTM:

> Years after the Team Canada 1998 trade mission and the signature of a $200,000 contract in Mexico—a deal that has generated revenues in excess of $1 million—Massload Technologies is forging ahead in that region of the world. (TCTM Archive 2002)

Regarding Cubex Ltd., of Winnipeg, Manitoba, 'A $1.2 million contract for the sale of drilling equipment to Norilsk Mine, resulting from the TCTM to Russia this February, is just the latest example' (TCTM Archive 2002). Various Canadian newspapers also reported on the value of deals, often accompanied by pictures of beaming businesspeople and government officials. When rumours began that Paul Martin, who was slated to succeed Chrétien, might cancel the TCTM because of open discord between the two politicians, a spokesperson for Martin provided the assurance that Mr Martin would continue to promote Canadian trade around the world, either through the TCTM program or some other creative way (Dunfield 2003). The anxiety about whether the trade missions would continue or not reflected the continual divide between those who passionately believed the program was of benefit to Canada and those who considered it to be nothing more than a way for Chrétien to give the impression that he was doing something worthwhile.

TCTM repeat participants a clear sign of success

It was unlikely that a participant in a trade mission who obtained no benefit would return for future missions. Therefore, it is unsurprising that repeat participants' stories were given pride of place in the TCTM marketing communications. For example, in the 2002 trade mission, Dr Gabriel Pulido-Cejudo, CEO of Ottawa, Ontario-based Canbreal Therodiagnostics International Inc., sought to develop business connections in Africa. According to him, the most challenging aspect was persuading government leaders in the public health sector. Over two years, he participated in four TCTM and revealed that during one mission:

> Canbreal signed a memorandum of understanding with the *Institut du Cancer de Dakar* (Dakar Cancer Institute) to develop a national and international breast cancer early detection programme. The agreement is valued at

$10 million over five years, $7.5 million of which is Canadian content. (TCTM Archive 2002)

Ecolo Odor Control Systems Worldwide of Toronto, Ontario, under the leadership of Ian Howard, Vice-President, participated in several trade missions and saw firsthand how the insights gained into international markets provided 'an excellent climate in which to reach agreements in Latin America and in South-East Asia' (TCTM Archive 2002). Mitchell Brownstein, of Brownstein, Brownstein Associates, which specialised in immigration and international business law, shared the following:

> We've been on every TCTM since they first began … The advantages for participants are tremendous. For example, we often have the opportunity to meet in one room—representatives of all of a country's major law firms. On our own it would take us at least a month to establish the contacts we make in only three or four days per city with Team Canada. (TCTM Archive 1999)

TCTM allows companies to establish a presence in foreign markets

For companies that did not see much room for expansion within Canada, the opportunity to establish a presence in new markets abroad was an important draw for participating in the trade missions. For example, Marshall Macklin Monaghan Ltd of Toronto, Ontario, with experience in 40 countries and involvement in projects ranging from transportation to environmental engineering and water resource management and geomatics, saw an opportunity to expand into Turkey. The company had done its groundwork before the opportunity came and as a result, in 2002, Marshall Macklin Monaghan worked together with Turkish Consulting Company to finish:

> A project involving the preparation of a master plan for the expansion and improvement of 26 airports across Turkey. The $2 million contract was awarded to the company by the Turkish government against stiff competition from US and European firms. (TCTM Archive 2000)

For global integrated payment systems company, Paradata Systems Inc. (Whistler, BC), the 2001 trade mission offered an opportunity to establish global alliances that would 'allow us to build our export capabilities to enter large markets in the US, Europe and Asia' (TCTM Archive 2001). It was the drive for new markets that similarly encouraged Gary Pollack of ICEBERG Vodka to participate in the 2002 trade mission. Pollack signed a letter of intent with a Russian company to promote ICEBERG Vodka in Russia. Later, Pollack secured successful deals in Germany while travelling under the TCTM auspices. Pollack, a repeat participant in the trade missions has had doors open 'to negotiations in Mainland China' (TCTM Archive 2002).

TCTM raises the profile of participating companies

For some companies, the impetus for participating in the trade mission was to raise the profile within the industry or to make themselves better known around the world. This meant that even small companies could present themselves on the world stage with greater confidence. For example, Grand Derangement of Moncton, New Brunswick, a group of Acadian musicians, sought to break into the European market by working closely with a Parisian publicity firm. Although the company had only nine employees in 2002, they sought to present a more robust profile.

A web-based business run by Karen Hollet, operating from Yellowknife, North-West Territories, sought to improve its profile around the world. The company had 65 per cent of its sales from the US, although they wanted to expand their market further to increase the number of orders they received from Asia, Europe and countries such as 'Australia, New Zealand ... and even Algeria' (TCTM Archive 2002). Another small company with an expanding global profile was Asham Curling Supplies Ltd., of Winnipeg, Manitoba, which:

> Has grown from a one-man, home-based business to a factory employing 12 people in Winnipeg, manufacturing and distributing curling shoes and accessories to the US, Europe and Japan. Over the past five years, the company's sales have risen dramatically, due in part to its international activities. (TCTM Archive 2002)

Likewise, ASL Environmental Sciences Inc., a consulting firm in the field of oceanography and instrumentation, which specialises in frozen parts of the world, said that its reputation:

> Has led to sales of sea-ice related products and services in other parts of Russia, most notably in the Pechora Sea, as well as in northern Japan and Kazakhstan. Since 1996, this business has significantly increased ASL's revenue—as well as its staff, which has almost doubled to more than 25 people. (TCTM Archive 2002)

Jean-Guy Paquet, President of the National Optics Institute (INO), Sainte-Foy, Quebec, credited TCTM with raising the company's profile and with helping him and others 'get noticed' (TCTM Archive 1998). While participating in the 1995 trade mission to Japan, INO entered into a $1 million partnership agreement, with Moritex of Tokyo for the development of new optical telecommunications devices. 'We had been negotiating for months,' said Dr Paquet:

> When we received the invitation for the trade mission, the very day our Japan partner was visiting with us. The fact that we planned to participate really sped up the deal, which was actually finalised only days before the signing ceremony. (TCTM Archive 1995)

The National Optics Institute also participated in the 1998 trade mission. According to Dr Paquet, 'besides gleaning valuable information about the Latin American market—which we found to be not advanced enough for our technology—we established some important Canadian partnerships.' (TCTM Archive 1998)

Advice available for the TCTM participants from trade commissioners

The Canadian government maintained a staff of about 500 business professionals in more than 140 cities around the world. *Welcome to Canada: We Take Care of Business* (2011) stated:

At work in 150 cities around the world, Canada's investment and trade professionals can provide: Strategic market intelligence on your specific sector; Pathfinding for key government contacts engaged in supporting investment in Canada, in its provinces and territories; Referrals to investment support professionals.

These professionals provided market intelligence and advice to Canadians that sought to conduct business around the world. Being part of TCTM was not a requirement to avail oneself of the services of these professionals. However, when one travelled to another country on a trade mission and met face-to-face with professionals equipped with local knowledge and an understanding of the needs of Canadian companies, this was bound to provide encouragement that one would not struggle alone in achieving one's exporting goals. Canadian businesspeople could count on these professionals to support them even after the mission ended.

Participants in the trade missions quickly learned that beyond the potential benefits of the trip, they could have an ally in the form of the Trade Commission service in their target country that could continue to support their goals. Med-Eng Systems Inc., of Ottawa, Ontario, which participated in the 2002 trade mission to Mexico, obtained the attention of public and private sector partners in their intended market. According to Richard L'Abbe, President of Med-Eng Systems, the trade mission allowed his company to introduce their engineering expertise 'to several high-profile customers. It also served as a catalyst in advancing our current negotiations with the Mexican government' (TCTM Archive 2002). In addition, he added that 'embassy staff have provided us with local market intelligence and identified potential distribution partners. The quality of their services gives Canadian companies a real advantage over foreign competitors' (TCTM Archive 2002).

MassLoad Technologies, which specialises in the manufacturing of truck scales, wireless weighing, bulk weighers and load cells:

> Received support from the Trade section of the Canadian embassy in Mexico. This included giving pointers on how to approach the different business communities; providing contact information; helping with legal matters; and arranging meetings with the right people from the start. (TCTM Archive 2002)

It is not improbable to consider that for people not participating in the trade missions, the availability of such resources might not have come to their attention.

Awards to the TCTM participants signalled success

The highlighting of awards received by trade mission participants served the function of demonstrating that these companies were quality oriented, which signalled to potential participants that they would be in good company with the high-quality businesses attracted by the program. Among the awards linked with participating companies were the Canada Export Award, World Bank Award, Nova Scotia Export Achievement and BC Export Award (TCTM Archive 2003).

Participation in the TCTM provided companies with the chance to work with governments abroad

Governments are usually the entities of choice to deal with regarding infrastructure and other similar high-cost projects. For such opportunities, foreign governments are apt to have more confidence in dealing with a company that is recognised by the government of its home country. In this regard, participants in TCTM program leveraged their connections with the Canadian government to attract the attention of governments abroad to gain access to major infrastructure and other capital-intensive projects.

TCTM gave access to foreign government leaders

Government officials usually handled projects that involved major capital investments. It was imperative for Canadian companies with relevant experience to participate in major infrastructure projects or other government-supported projects to seek influence in those quarters. Buying a ticket and making an appointment with a foreign official did not provide the level of credibility to be taken seriously. However, through a program such as the TCTM, foreign officials would assume that the participants had been vetted and that the representations that they made were credible because they had their own government's backing. For example, Dessaport International of Halifax, Nova Scotia, was interested in handling projects in Eastern Europe and was slated to begin a terminal construction project in 2002 with a domestic partner when the company decided to participate in the 2001 trade mission. Donald Leblanc, CEO, said that he had joined the trade mission 'to meet with government officials and businesspeople in the agricultural sector' (TCTM Archive 2002).

Blair Nutting of Nascor Inc, Calgary, Alberta, which produces wood frames for housing in Russia using the company's advanced building technology, signed a US $1.6 million deal with a local home-building company called Sostnefteresus. This deal 'was reached after the company participated in a trade mission to Russia in 2000 led by Minister Pettigrew ... Nutting credits various federal government initiatives for helping secure the Russian contract' (TCTM Archive 2003). Participating in the 2000 trade mission to Russia increased the company's exposure and boosted its credibility. He added that 'partnerships between the public and the private sector are especially important in Russia, where government is significantly involved in business' (TCTM Archive 2003).

Participation in the TCTM gave companies a chance to expand their network

Participants in a trade mission have, as one of their primary goals, the chance to secure deals and to find international partners with whom they can have mutually beneficial relationships. However, forging relationships with fellow Canadians emerged as an important outcome for some participants in the trade missions. Hemat M. Shah of Cubex Limited, Winnipeg, Manitoba, stated:

> I'm there to support my colleagues from across Canada. If I hear of a lead in another sector, I can pass it on; and I can give moral support to new members because of my previous mission experience. It's important to be part of the team. The whole motive is to promote trade with Canada. (TCTM Archive 2001)

Ruel (2019, p. 19), who led the creation of a successful three-stage trade mission from the Netherlands to Turkey, learned that:

> It is not only contact with firms in the target country that participants in trade missions consider to be a positive aspect. They find interaction with other companies on the trade mission very important as well.

This view is supported by Dmitri Rojojanski of West Group Resources, Toronto, Ontario, which has gas-related construction experience in the former Soviet Union, North America and the Middle East:

> We've been working successfully in the region for more than 10 years … The Team Canada 2002 trade mission, our first, was an excellent opportunity to build on that success by meeting new business leaders and networking at a very senior level with other Canadian entrepreneurs. It also showed our Russian counterparts that we're part of a well-established community and enabled us to provide them with further opportunities by introducing them to other Canadian businesspeople. In the end, everybody wins. While on the 2002 mission, West Group signed three deals, one of which was a $4 million deal to implement software solutions for Tyumen Oil Co (TNK) of Moscow. (TCTM Archive 2002)

Another participant, Dr Harinder P.S. Ahumela, president of Info-Electronics Systems, joined the 2002 trade mission to make contacts:

> We held talks with personnel from the Indian Space Research Organisation, the Department of Science and Technology and several universities and institutes such as the Disaster Management Institute of India. (TCTM Archive 2002)

The trip was an excellent opportunity to network with other Canadian companies and government representatives. While acknowledging that he could meet other company representatives in Canada, he nonetheless explained that 'the friendships which develop from being together for a week in a foreign country are quite strong, from a business perspective' (TCTM Archive 2002).

TCTM helped companies to project credibility

For a company that was not well known, seeking opportunities abroad could seem daunting and any help to make the process less arduous might be welcome. The TCTM appeared to boost perceptions of greater credibility for the participating entities. That is what Sport Seats International of Calgary, Alberta, whose product, a walking stick that can be turned into a seat, achieved from participating in the program. During the 1998 trade mission to Chile, the company sold more than $50,000 for its Sport Seat and signed an exclusive distributor agreement. For Don McGillivray, president of Sport Seats, participation in the TCTM 'gave us momentum, credibility and access to organisations that we would otherwise not have had' (TCTM Archive 1999). Donald Berggren, General Manager at Sport Seats, who participated in the 1998 trade mission, expresses a similar sentiment:

> When you're part of a high-profile Canadian trade mission, potential customers look at you as a big player. And if you're seen as a big player, then you are one. (TCTM Archive 1999)

Participation in the TCTM accelerated deals

Several participants credited the presence of government officials and the limited time of the trade mission to the consummation of the deals in which they were involved. Ron Yuen, who participated in the 1996 trade mission as part of Kryton International Inc. of Vancouver, BC, commented:

> Team Canada not only encouraged our potential partners to move faster, it also ensured a timetable for signing, as everyone wanted to close the deal with their leaders present. (TCTM Archive 1997)

Further, Yuen claimed that 'meeting the political and private sector elite in other countries is not only important for export success—it is essential ... Team Canada is the best way to get the job done' (TCTM Archive 1997). Forensic Technology, WAI Inc.,

Montreal, Quebec, which helps law enforcement agencies around the world, participated in the 2002 trade mission to India. Mohammed Naeem, FT's International Sales Manager commented that 'our potential client was very interested in our products and our participation in the trade mission helped speed up negotiations' (TCTM Archive 2002).

Participation in the TCTM provided publicity/exposure/visibility

For each year that the TCTM operated, there was no shortage of businesses willing to participate. The trade missions received substantial publicity. It helped that there were embedded correspondents, which allowed them to report on their firsthand experiences, including the number of trade deals done on the missions and interactions with foreign leaders that became instrumental in opening doors to trade mission participants. The government used the full array of media, including the internet, books, press releases and television broadcasts.

Juice Zone Inc. of Mississauga, Ontario, which participated in the 2002 trade mission, did so partly 'to capitalise on the publicity associated with the signing ceremony which included International Trade Minister Pettigrew and Indian officials at the highest levels' (TCTM Archive 2002). It was the Indian customer, Cogent Group, that suggested that Juice Zone participate in the mission, with the rationale that, 'signing the contract in that venue would create wide-ranging exposure for our franchise in their country and new contacts in the region' (TCTM Archive 2002). On that same trip, Summit Seeds sought to capitalise on the local publicity because it could help the companies 'market our product' (TCTM Archive 2002).

TCTM was a gateway to a wide range of resources

Although many reasons were given for participating in a trade mission, another element of the discourse was the vast resources available to businesses in the form of databases, trade leads and letters of credit facilities, all of which were accessible on the TCTM websites.

4.3.2 Part IIb: Analysis of Critical Discourses Against the TCTM

The previous section highlighted a wide range of benefits that the TCTM marketing communications materials claimed to have arisen from participation in the program. These, along with the information from the two policy documents, suggest that the Canadian government had succeeded in expanding opportunities for local businesses while promoting and improving the image of Canada internationally. This section focuses on the critical discourses that emanated to challenge the one-sided view propagated by the government and the section of the business community that partook in the trade missions.

Between 1994 and 2003, the Canadian Ministry of Foreign Affairs and International Trade published more than 1500 pages of materials that promoted the TCTM program and highlighted the successes of the missions, including details on deals, letters of memorandum, statements of intent, testimonials and agreements made between Canadian companies and their foreign counterparts. These were accompanied by images in newspapers of Canadian businesspeople and politicians meeting their foreign counterparts. Headlines indicated that millions of dollars in deals were being struck. If this had been the only discourse, over time such positive news would have dominated the consciousness of Canadian society, garnering widespread support for the program. However, critiques from detractors began to cast doubt on the assertions of the government. As more criticism emerged, the government's message, powerful though it might have seemed in the absence of major critiques, began to seem dubious. Below are some of the critical discourses that were pitted against the TCTM and the claims of the government.

No cost–benefit analyses done on the TCTM

Even though the trade missions were accompanied by publicity pieces that highlighted the huge amounts of money in deals made by participating companies, critics maintained that this was not enough to determine that the government's investments and the efforts involved in organising the events were worth it. Opposition member, Morrison Lee, asked in Parliament:

> I would like to comment briefly on the puffery surrounding Team Canada's alleged success in snagging those ephemeral deals. The government needs to ask itself: What other factors play a role in determining our exporters' success? Really, if Team Canada's initiatives are all it takes to be successful abroad, then why would we not see our exports to China, Hong Kong, India, Pakistan, Chile, Argentina and Uruguay rising instead of falling after our big-ticket missions there?
>
> (Debates No. 147 1997)

Evidently, some expected the government to provide further concrete evidence that the money being spent on the TCTM program was not being wasted.

Team Canada deals were done in advance

Some critics pointed out that many deals were made before the trade missions occurred and that the deals had often been 'worked out and signed well in advance of the trade mission only to be signed again before the cameras' (Swimmer 1997, p. 120). This meant that there was really no value to the trade missions because those involved were capable of handling deals themselves. The logic was that if businesspeople could handle transactions on their own, what need was there for government personnel to be going on 'junkets' abroad? This had to be a waste of money. While acknowledging that improved networking might extend the number of deals signed during the missions, Head and Ries (2010, p. 755) argued that 'under the sceptical perspective, many of the announced deals do not actually come to fruition and most of the fulfilled agreements would have occurred anyway.'

Many deals promoted by the government were later cancelled

Some critics also contended that even though the amounts of money mentioned in press releases regarding deals sounded impressive, they did not accurately reflect the reality because deals arranged in the heat of the moment were sometimes overturned. These numbers were dismissed by critics as being of little empirical significance. Head and Ries (2010) used multilateral trade data and a gravity equation to assess the

Chrétien government's claim that the missions had led to billions of dollars in new business. Even though the objective of the TCTM was not to enhance bilateral trade, Head and Ries (2010, p. 772) declared that their research, 'does not support the use of missions as a vehicle for increasing bilateral transactions.' Thus, boosting Canadian exports through trade missions was not supported by the evidence (Head & Ries 2010).

Going abroad can be dangerous for Canadian businesses

There were concerns expressed that some markets posed a danger for Canadian businesses because of the potential for expropriation or fraud. In particular, Russia was identified as a major part of this concern from the head of Norex. Harper (2002) reported:

> One Canadian company, Norex, is said to have had a horrific experience in Russia leading its president to say of the 2002 Team Canada trip to Russia that the mission was like 'leading sheep to slaughter.'

Team Canada focuses on money and ignores human rights

The publicity often attending the trade missions, some of which focused on the dollar amounts of trade deals signed, appeared to be a sign of waywardness on the part of the Canadian government. Critics felt that the government was ultimately interested in money and not sufficiently concerned about pressuring countries, such as China, to accord human rights the importance it deserves. This was seen as a serious compromise of values that many Canadians held dear.

Over the years, Canada has built part of its identity on its support for human rights. Although Canada it has its own chequered past in the abuse and marginalisation of First Nations people, this has not stopped the state or various groups and individual Canadians from becoming champions of human rights at home and abroad. During the 1930s and 1940s, there were calls for the expansion of human rights among various 'ethnic, religious, libertarian and other organisations' (Tunnicliffe 2014, p. 808). The push for human rights and the recognition of civil liberties continued its onward march with fights for racial justice for Chinese, Japanese and Blacks becoming part of the historical record of rights expansion in Canada. However, the fight for human rights has not been confined to Canada. Strong proponents of human rights have often been quick to point out that Canada's efforts at fighting human rights abuses internationally falls short. The exasperation that concerned citizens felt at Canada's seeming impotence in the face of rights abuses around the world is captured by Wilson-Smith (1994, p. 20), who argued:

> The Liberals have made clear that their unbridled, unabashed enthusiasm for increased trade with China won't be tempered by concerns over human rights. The rationale is that, Canada, as a middle power of diminishing expectations, lacks the influence to bring about change. 'I am the Prime Minister of a country of 28 million people,' Chrétien told reporters last month. 'Am I supposed to tell the president of China what to do'?

Critics of Canada's increasing trade relations with China were not expecting trade to cease; they simply wanted their government to raise the question of human rights with countries that did not appear to respect such rights. The issue did not die with the departure of Chrétien from the leadership. Subsequent prime ministers have continued to make human rights an important part of the Canadian identity (Rochlin 2014). In summary, detractors of the TCTM raised the following points:

- The trade missions are a matter of hype/puffery (Debates—No. 147 1997).
- Unsubstantiated claims—no cost–benefit analysis done by the government (Head & Ries 2010).
- Polarisation within the TCTM team (Harper 2002).
- Trade missions are motivated by narrow self-interest (Rethinking Canada's International Priorities 2010).
- Leading sheep to slaughter (Harper 2012—Norex Petroleum/Archangel Diamond—Russia).
- Focus on money, not on human rights (Potter 2005, p. 58).
- Trade missions substituted for real planning (Janigan 2001, p. 30).

Table 5 juxtaposes contrasting discourses from government and pro-export business leaders versus critics.

Table 5. Contrasting Discourses: Government and Business v. Critics

Discourse of Government/Business	Discourse of critics of TCTM
Canada successfully marketing hi-tech savvy abroad (Gamble 1999; Crane 1996).	No cost-benefit analyses were done on TCTM; no follow-up studies (Head & Ries 2010; Aubry 2003, p. F1)
Canadian expertise valued in advanced countries (Chutter 1998; Sato 1999, p. C6).	Government ignores human rights (Scoffield 2000, p.B5).
Canadian expertise valued in developing countries (Talking trade and human rights in Asia 1996).	Unity among Canadians is just an image – not reality (Authier 1997, p. A3).
Canada presents a united front (Flaherty 1994, p. A3).	No real increase in exports from TCTMs (Jack 1999, p. A7; Team Canada trade missions of little value, says economist 1998, p. E11).
Canada a gateway for cultural products such as film (Government of Canada Launches Cultural Trade Program 2001, p. 3).	TCTMs are no substitute for real planning on the part of government and businesses (Do your homework 1998, p. S5).
Canada cooperative – partners with other nations (Cooper 2006, p. 53; Sheikh 2003, p. 10).	TCTM deals done in advance (Swimmer 1997, p. 120; Beauchesne 1998, p.1).
TCTM participants garner financial success (Pettigrew 2000).	Waste of government money (Gamble 1999, p. A8).
TCTM repeat participation is a clear sign of success (Team Canada Trade Missions – Database https://works.bepress.com/everettofori/58/).	Lack of consideration for human rights record of targeted countries (Defining Canada's role in the world 2004, p. H06).
TCTM – helps establish a presence in foreign markets (Das 1997, p. G4).	Just travel junkets for government officials (Inwood et al. 2011, p. 225).

TCTM raises the profile of participating companies (The Government of Canada Helps Farmers and Agri-Food Exporters Develop New Markets 2010).	Many deals promoted by TCTM were later cancelled (Cordon 2001, B05).
Advice available from trade commissioners (International trade 1999, p. 37)	Going abroad can be dangerous for Canadian companies, e.g. Russia
Awards to TCTM participants signals success (Team Canada Trade Missions – Database https://works.bepress.com/everettofori/58/).	TCTM focuses on money; ignores human rights, which is a value cherished by Canadians (Robertson 1996)
Gives access to foreign government leaders (Infrastructure program called major success: Chrétien taunts Manning 1996, p. B1).	
TCTM gives participants a chance to expand their network of both international and domestic contacts (Team Canada Trade Missions – Database https://works.bepress.com/everettofori/58).	
TCTM helps companies project credibility (Team Canada Trade Missions – Database https://works.bepress.com/everettofori/58; Marchi defends value of Team Canada 1998, n/a).	
TCTM provides publicity/exposure/visibility (Team Canada Trade Missions – Database https://works.bepress.com/everettofori/58).	
TCTM is a gateway to a wide range of resources (Team Canada Trade Missions – Database https://works.bepress.com/everettofori/58).	

Table 5 demonstrates that both sides were able to articulate reasons for why they believed in the position they took. Some of this rhetoric was emotionally charged, which probably did not encourage the two sides to look for an objective way to address what the opposing parties were saying.

4.4 Breakdown of Critical Voices

Table 6 displays the sources from which strong opposition arose towards the TCTM. Before focusing on the individual categories of opposition, a brief summary is presented regarding how the TCTM participants, government and the media were connected.

Table 6. Proponents versus Critics: A Closer Look

PROPONENTS OF TCTM →	TCTM PARTICIPANTS		GOVERNMENT	MEDIA	
FOR/AGAINST	BUSINESS GROUPS: Mixed responses to TCTM				
FOR/AGAINST	ACADEMICS: Mixed responses to TCTM				
CRITICS→	MEDIA	THINK TANKS	NPOs/ACTIVISTS	CITIZENS	POLITICAL OPPOSITION

4.5 PROPONENTS: TCTM Participants, Government, Media

The government and TCTM participants were wedded together. Both parties appeared to believe in the importance of the program. Although the successes were highlighted in the promotional materials, participants were advised to learn the importance of patience and to understand that it would take time to become established in another country (see Appendix 2.1). The number of contracts signed, and the number of sales were important, and these were usually announced in banner headlines by local and national newspapers and often through editorials that extolled the benefits of the trade missions. However, equally important was the opportunity for Canada to build a good reputation around the world and to demonstrate that Canadian companies could compete with the best. This was the case with one participant whose technology was so advanced that there was no competition for those products even in such a technologically advanced nation as Germany (see Appendix 2.1). Many participants went back repeatedly, which suggests that they got something of value from their involvement in the trade missions. Some of the media outlets, reporters and editorialists appeared to buy into the notion that the TCTM was successful and presented economic and other benefits to Canada.

Figure 7. Proponents

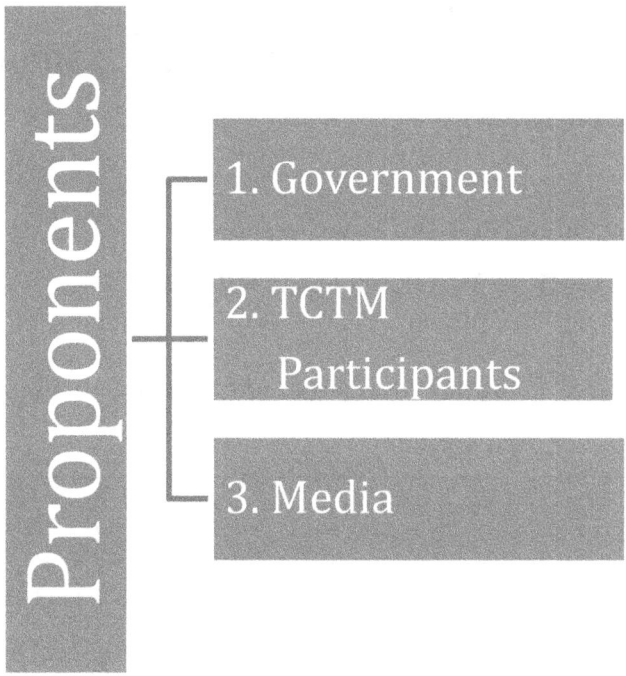

Note: The chart does not show the relative strengths of the proponents

4.6 CRITICS: Media, Think Tanks, NPOs/Activists, Citizens and Political Opposition
4.6.1 Media

While part of the media reflected the government's viewpoint in their reporting, another section struck a more sceptical tone. For this group, having so many government ministers go on a trip was a sign that they were incompetent. The trade missions were not under attack, merely the fact that so many ministers participated appeared to be the major bone of contention. It was also a point of marvel for some media critics that despite the effort to engage Asian countries and others outside North

America, Canadian trade with the US continued to grow, whereas there was no palpable increase or expansion in market share with the target countries. Charges that the trade missions were merely photo opportunities for ministers, or that the quaint images that countries such as Japan and China had of Canada continued, with the occasional use of a mocking tone included for good measure. The seemingly farcical nature of the TCTM program appeared to reach its apogee when it emerged that not only were special sponsorships of $50,000 being offered to select organisations, but that some of the recipients were government entities like Canada Post. For others, the problem with these sponsorships lay in their apparent lack of fairness for small companies that could not afford such a large amount (see Appendix 2.3).

Figure 8. Critics

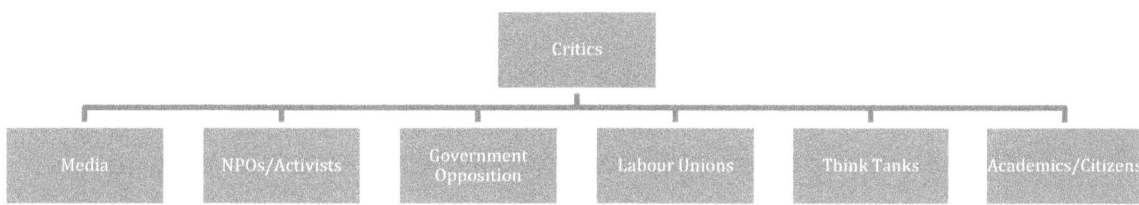

Note: The chart does not show the relative strengths of the proponents

4.6.2 Think Tanks

Much criticism came from think tanks, although they were not just blunt instruments of opposition. For example, the Asia–Pacific Foundation, while not claiming that the trade missions were bad, suggested they probably did not go far enough in helping Canada to wean itself off the US (see Appendix 2.6). For others, such as the Council of Canadians, international human rights and Canadian values were at the centre of their concerns. The exploitation of workers in the countries to which Canada went on trade missions and the maltreatment of indigenous people such as the Mayan Indians in Mexico were of concern. Likewise, the Council of Canadians shared its concerns about the Labour Union (see Appendix 2.5) that workers' conditions should be improved whether in South Korea, Bangladesh or China.

4.6.3 NPOs/Activists

For the East Timor Alert Network, the Canadian government could use some of its leverage over Indonesia to stop the abuses of power and the inhumane treatment of the Timorese activists in East Timor. The organisation deemed it unfair for Canada to continue to empower the Indonesian government while the abuse continued. Concerns regarding child labour frequently flared up, particularly when Free the Children, which was an organisation made up of children, sought to make their voices heard by having their 13-year-old leader, Craig Kielburger, meet with Chrétien, in an effort to persuade him to take the issue of child labour seriously (see Appendix 2.7).

4.6.4 Citizens

Through interviews, editorials and letters to the editor, ordinary citizens made their voices of opposition heard. For some, the involvement of Canadian government officials in the trade missions did not demonstrate good business sense. Additionally, the ease with which the Canadian government was willing to offer loans to foreign governments such as China or Romania was a concern. There was a fear that these countries might default in paying the loans. Many of these loans were tied in with the TCTM because government banks were sometimes involved in guaranteeing payment to the Canadian businesspeople while the payment from the foreign entity slowly made its way towards the Canadian bank. Another fear was that the main beneficiaries of the trade missions and the easy credit attached to it were big corporations, which took advantage of these facilities to expand abroad (see Appendix 2.10).

4.6.5 Political Opposition

As in most democracies, opposition parties were always on the lookout for the weak points of their counterparts. Opposition parties in Canada displayed scepticism towards the TCTM. The discovery that between 1993 and 1998, the prime minister's travel bill was in excess of $12 million became a point of derision that the government was wasting money in travel junkets with nothing to show for them (see Appendix 2.11).

4.6.6 Others: Business Groups/Academics/US Ambassador

One might have assumed that business groups would be unanimous in their support of Team Canada trade missions even if they were themselves not interested in participating in such missions. There was not unanimous support from business groups for the TCTM. For example, the Canadian Federation of Independent Business wondered why the premiers and the prime minister appeared to work so well while overseas and yet failed to deal with long-term intractable problems of protectionism and trade barriers among Canadian provinces. For the Canadian Federation of Independent Business, which stood with small businesses, the $50,000 sponsorship fee effectively shut out small businesses. By contrast, the Saskatchewan Trade and Export Partnership saw great value in the TCTM program for its potential to raise a company's profile. The US ambassador to Canada at the time suggested that the trade missions should consider the southern part of the US as a potential target. Although this was construed by some in the media that the ambassador thought that the trade missions were not achieving their aims outside the US, the ambassador clarified that he considered them a success and wanted some of that success in the country that he represented.

4.7 Email Survey of Expert Panel

An email interview was conducted with 11 academics in Canada. The responses were not meant to provide material from which to generalise any findings (see Appendix 3). Rather, they offered insights regarding the TCTM from what might be considered to be a neutral perspective. The responses were of historic importance in that these were the voices of unaffiliated individuals who observed the Canadian business and political scenes. While the number of respondents is too small to statistically assess, these voices are presented to lend perspective to the textual analysis. Responses to Question 1 were grouped and the same was done for Questions 2 to 4 for analysis. Key phrases were highlighted, and comparisons made. These were then examined in light of the findings from the discourse analysis, which focused on the differences in criteria between the government and trade mission participants and critics. Rather than considering this as a method for triangulating results from a discourse analysis, it might be better considered as a way to deepen insight into the issues surrounding the TCTM program within the broader policy goal of branding the nation. Although these responses fell under the purview of discourse, they were taken at face value and examined in light of the differences in perception they presented regarding trade missions in general and the TCTM in particular. The following questions were posed:

1) What do you think are/were the criteria for success of TCTM (1994–2005)?
2) Why do you think TCTM was curtailed in 2005?
3) In your view, of what value, if any, are trade missions?
4) In your view, should TCTM be reinstated?

The questions flowed from the central questions that underpinned the research, which focused on the dichotomy between the government and the business community and critics of the program. From the views of the expert panel, additional insight was gained into the divergent claims of the two opposing sides. The second question regarding the curtailment of the trade missions sought to crystallise the perceptions of this group regarding the impetus for ending the program and to determine to what extent it agreed or disagreed with insights that emerged from the research. The third and fourth questions also attempted to establish what the perceived value of trade missions were and to explore what governments ought to do in terms of continuing or terminating the trade missions.

Question 1: What do you think are/were the criteria for success of TCTM (1994–2005)?

Of the usable responses (n = 11) to this question, the dominant answer was 'number of contracts signed' (n = 5). Others mentioned 'building connections/networks with overseas businesses' (n = 2) and 'opens doors' (n = 1). It is possible that these responses came from the emphasis that the marketing communications efforts of the Canadian government had placed on the number of contracts and memorandums of understanding signed. This focus on the number of contracts signed may be taken as a proxy for success, which can be easily understood by the public. There was almost always an inclusion of dollar figures accompanying the reference to the number of contracts signed, which may have embedded a strong association in the minds of those familiar with the program's marketing communications. If the contracts signed were real and the dollar figures accurate, it might appear to be a legitimate way by which to judge the success of a trade mission.

Question 2: Why do you think TCTM was curtailed in 2005?

With regard to this question, 6 out of 11 respondents identified the change in government as the reason. However, 3 out of the 11 indicated that cost in time, effort and money, could not be properly justified. The program, which was strongly associated with Chrétien's Liberal Party, began its season of neglect in 2003 when the Liberal Party, in a leadership shake-up, chose Paul Martin as a replacement. A very public conflict between the two may have made it difficult for the new leader to maintain continuity of the program. With Martin's loss of the election in 2006 to the opposition Conservative Party, the TCTM became a frequent topic of inquiry to the new prime minister. Once in power, the Conservative government refused to indicate whether they would continue the program. Eventually, the Conservative Party under Stephen Harper organised a few trade missions.

Question 3: In your view, of what value, if any, are trade missions?

Three respondents highlighted the connections that the trade missions afforded participants as the likely benefit. However, two respondents pointed out that the most valuable outcome was forcing Canadians to pay attention to exports. Another respondent highlighted the importance that other countries placed upon the government and the prime minister's involvement as a key factor. One respondent did not see any value in the trade missions except for the opportunities for grandstanding offered to the government. It was encouraging to see that some on the expert panel agreed with the importance of forging connections between the government and the export-oriented business community.

Question 4: In your view, should TCTM be reinstated?

Two respondents indicated that the program should not be continued. However, another two respondents indicated that they should be continued. Five respondents gave qualified approval to the continuation of the trade missions and suggested that various changes needed to be made. With proper monitoring and greater accountability, it seems that the trade missions could be a viable contributing factor to Canada's image as a nation and to its exports.

The responses from the email interviews were minimal. As such, they cannot be taken as indications of broad opinion from the academic establishment. However, the responses added understanding to some of the thought patterns of non-participants regarding the program and trade missions in general. Their value was in the provision of intimations of possible new directions for research on trade missions or the export promotion field.

Chapter 5: Findings

5.1 Introduction

This final chapter provides the findings, although Graham (2011, p. 666) claims it is not appropriate for use with discourse analysis because:

> Discourse analysis informed by Foucauldian or other poststructural theory endeavours to avoid the substitution of one 'truth' for another, recognising that 'there can be no universal truths or absolute ethical positions.'

Additionally, the theoretical and practical implications of the study are outlined, along with information about the contributions of this research to the field of marketing communications and policy, government and business.

5.2 Research Overview

This study was designed to provide an understanding of the kind of power relations that surrounded the TCTM (1994–2005) in terms of who the major groups were, the manner in which they sought to deploy their power and the different meanings they brought to their view of the TCTM under Liberal prime ministers Chrétien and Martin. No nation has unlimited resources, so it is not unreasonable for citizens and concerned interest groups to do what they can to keep their governments accountable by questioning practices that could be considered to be wasteful or detrimental to the progress of the nation and its citizens. The deployment of critical voices is a healthy part of the democratic process. The government of Canada has a responsibility to steward the resources of the nation and to do so without bias unless there is a good reason to favour one group, such as might be the case in giving First Nations people special considerations in an effort to right past wrongs. Therefore, it was legitimate for critics of the TCTM program to raise their voices to question the necessity of the trade missions and to question the program's value to the nation.

5.3 Qualitative Research: In Search of Meaning

This study used the Scheurich–O'Connor policy archaeology framework, which was based on Foucault's theories (1972) and thematic analysis as modes of enquiry to examine a series of events in recent history and the discourse surrounding it. A qualitative approach to doing this research was useful. Creswell (2007, p. 48) argued that qualitative research is conducted because there is a need to explore a particular issue or problem and that such 'exploration is needed, in turn, because of the need to study a group or population, identify variables that cannot be easily measured, or hear silenced voices.' Although many people living in a democracy might suppose that they are autonomous, self-constituting subjects, Foucault contended that the subject is 'a product of regimes of power/knowledge' (Bevir 1999, p. 65). The use of discourse analysis allows the researcher to interpret what they encounter, whether through seeing, hearing or understanding (Creswell 2007). These findings are not presented as the definitive truth about trade missions, but as strands of meaning, which can challenge others to examine their assumptions about trade missions and the TCTM program.

5.4 Main Research Findings: Power Relations and Discourses Surrounding the TCTMs

What power relations and discourses surrounded the TCTM?

This thesis set out to answer the research question—what power relations and discourses surrounded the TCTM?—in light of the confusion that appeared to grip Canadians from the business, political and other viewpoints regarding the value of continuing with the TCTM. The power of the Canadian federal government is the power of the purse, by which it is able to incentivise the various provinces to do what the federal government presumes is in the national interest.

Team Canada Trade Missions Driven by the Centrality of Trade to Canada's Existence

From the inception of the Liberal government's regime under Prime Minister Jean Chrétien, eliminating the deficit and putting the government in the black was a key policy goal. To achieve this, the government saw an opening in focusing upon exports. With the Team Canada Trade Missions having started in 1994, by 2000, the government could report that, 'Exports account for 43 percent of Canada's gross domestic product, compared with 25 percent 10 years ago' (Trade key factor in our prosperity, 2000, p.

B7). In *Canada's Trade Agenda* (2014), 'trade accounts for more than 60 per cent of Canada's annual income (GDP) and one in five Canadian jobs is linked to exports' (Fast Canada's State of Trade Update 2014). Considering how big a part exports are and were to Canada's survival, the logic underpinning Chrétien's initiation, participation and support of the TCTM might have been unassailable. It appears that Chrétien believed that he was doing what was right for the country and saw criticisms of policies such as the TCTM program as baseless attacks that undermined the government's efforts. Some viewed the benefits of Team Canada in terms of the profits it could bring to Canada and the signals that it sent. For example, Eaves and Kara (2004, p. 89) stated that 'the TCTM that began in the 1990s offer concrete evidence of how the federal and provincial governments can work together on the world stage.' From the government's side, the strength of the discourse on the centrality of trade to Canada continued throughout the Liberal government's leadership under Chrétien and Martin.

Team Canada Trade Missions Became a Lightning Rod for Raising Anti-Poverty Issues

The critics also appeared to be sincere about demanding accountability from a government that only seemed to care only about businesses. Various interest groups such as anti-poverty activists saw the government's seemingly inordinate focus on the business community as a zero-sum equation without commensurate government attention on the issues they cared about. While the purpose of the TCTM was business, there was a perception of unfairness that the business constituency appeared to have near-total control of the government in a way that other constituencies did not. Activists and anti-poverty groups were insistent on the point that the government was supposed to be the servant of all, not just the business community. For some critics, such as author, activist and National Chairperson of the Council of Canada, Maude Barlow, having the business community fully attended to while others languished, demonstrated that the policy process could create 'winners and losers' (Mayers 2005, p. 2). It is true that the trade missions were meant for business, although critics did not seem to think that the government of Canada belonged only to the business community.

Confusion Persisted about the Value of TCTMs

Despite billions of dollars in deals apparently signed on trade missions over the years, questions lingered over their value. In one parliamentary meeting, Mr. Roy Culpepper, President of the North-South Institute think tank commented:

> *The Economist* [the magazine] said about a year ago that it's very doubtful that trade missions—and they weren't singling Canada out, by any means—accomplished very much, that there are costs and perhaps benefits…The benefits are often deals that have been reached prior to the mission and the mission is simply a signing ceremony. (Parliament of Canada 1998, p. 4)

Conversely, one participant in a trade mission to South Korea in 1997, Rita Egizii, president of Calgary-based Chromacolour (North America) Ltd., believed that the mission was necessary to close a deal involving exclusive European and North American distribution rights to a Korean-made plexiglass animation disc. Rita Egizii claimed that 'this accord represents and binds the strengths of both our companies—it is an honour to have the event recognised in such a prestigious manner' (Jackson 1997, p. 1).

With one group of Canadians saying that the TCTM were virtually worthless and another group of businesspeople and government officials claiming the opposite, it appeared that there was a clear gap in perceptions. The gap was not in the goal of the missions, which was to help Canadian businesses increase their exports and help Canada boost its revenues, but rather in whether the trade missions were the best means of achieving that goal and if the government had to be so closely involved.

Speaking Truth to Power

On the question of 'what power relations and discourses surrounded the TCTM?,' it appeared that the government under Chrétien saw it as their duty to use the program to fulfil an economic agenda aimed at job creation. In that sense, the government felt that it had the mandate and the power to do what it saw fit and that there was no need to accede to the challenges of critics as to whether the trade missions were working. As far as the government was concerned, it seemed that as long as the participants in the trade missions felt that their needs were being met and that they were making the deals that they expected, there was no need to answer to the larger population.

To put these power relations in perspective, the critics were not a highly organised group assailing the government through an orchestrated discourse as a people under siege might do to emancipate themselves. Rather, they were a disparate group of individual citizens, politicians and interest groups that felt the need to make their voices heard regarding what they believed was the government's misguided approach. However, that the TCTM ran almost every year between 1994 and 2005 meant there was ample opportunity for critics to make their voices heard. The critics of TCTM were in line with Foucault's thinking that 'power manifests itself at all levels of society' (Ali 2002, p. 235) and that 'the workings of power/knowledge can be transformed even by the disempowered' (Ali 2002, p. 235). In a democracy, everyone is supposed to have a voice. However, it also appeared that the continual attempts to challenge the government was tied to a lack of trust in the political establishment. This was evident from the fact that even though the government produced numbers in support of its claims that businesses participating in the TCTM program met with success, critics put no faith in these numbers, calling them puffery, inflated or lies. Challenging the government's data might be seen as an attempt to undermine its power, knowing that the more such numbers were challenged, the more Canadians were apt to withdraw their trust in the government. This is part of the power of discourse to shape perceptions, in which 'discourse analysis can demonstrate how apparently rational processes are contestable, unstable and discursively constructed' (Phillips & Hardy 2002, p. 41).

Perception of Lack of Fair Play

For the critics, a government that appeared to be inordinately interested in the success of the business community, apparently to the exclusion of other groups in society, was not a government that played fair. However, to just say that the government was not playing fair might not be the most powerful form of discourse. After all, the government, with its myriad programs, could always point to some area in which it made a difference to the lives of Canadians. For the most part, the two groups, the Government and the Critics, appeared to talk at each other or past each other with very little attempt to address the concerns or points raised by the other. It appeared that some of the criticisms were more about asserting power and highlighting what appeared to be an imbalance in how various groups were able to influence government.

Perception of Government Waste

From the perspective of critics, the charge that the government was wasting taxpayers' money was something that most citizens could rally around. In this respect, just as the government's figures were thrown in doubt, the critics found no need to prove that their attacks had any basis in truth. To them, the onus was on the government to prove that the TCTM were successful, but the word of the government was not enough. The government's attempts to prove that the trade missions were successful were published in government publications, which did not attract widespread attention. For example, through Team Canada, Inc., the government monitored its efforts at boosting trade in Canada. For instance, Team Canada Inc.'s Annual Report (2002, p. 9) reported that there was a GDP growth of 1.5 per cent, which was the tenth year in which there had been export growth in Canada. In fact:

> Following real growth of 2.9 percent in the fourth quarter of 2001, our economy grew at a robust annual rate of six percent in the first quarter of 2002. During the first five months of 2002, Canada also posted the strongest employment gains in almost a decade.

While some critics disagreed with the government's claims of successful deals done through TCTM, others believed that it was in spite of the government, not because of them.

Critics: Disparate Perceptions from Disparate Camps

As Mayers (2005, p. 3) explained, in any given society, people are apt to evaluate the positions of others relative to their own. These are the stakeholders in a society, that is, 'those who have rights or interests in a system … Stakeholders can be individuals, communities, social groups, or organisations.' Critics of the TCTM program did not come from one or two well-organised blocks of interest groups but rather an assortment of stakeholders, some with clear political intent as members of the opposition and others, such as individual citizens, NPOs and think tanks, with a concern for good governance and fairness.

While for Swimmer (1997, p. 121), 'Team Canada is very much the answer to the Liberal Party's election pledge of "jobs, jobs, jobs",' perhaps the voices of the critics did not go totally unheeded as far as government spending was concerned. Swimmer (1997, p. 122) explained:

> The annual budget for trade missions and trade fairs sponsored by DFAIT has declined to $20m in 1996-97, from $34 million in 1994-95 … More radical proposals have involved the partial or wholesale participation of DFAIT's Trade Commissioner Service, in keeping with models developed in countries such as Germany and Switzerland.

Critics were within their rights to raise questions about the government's involvement in trade missions if they believed that some groups in society benefited to the detriment of others. One of the most vocal critics of the Chrétien government was Maude Barlow, who contended that Chrétien had crafted his policies to fit the rules of globalisation and free trade. She was incensed that while the budget for 1995 had been cut, funds for the agency responsible for foreign trade and DFAIT had doubled. She accused the TCTM program of taking advantage of local politicians to promote the interests of Canadian business around the world (Barlow 2011). Barlow did not see the involvement of politicians in the affairs of foreign trade as a positive development. Rather, she saw the government's growing support of the business community as taking something away from other deserving groups in Canada.

Conversely, groups such as the Conference Board of Canada saw globalisation as the prevailing business model and one that Canada ignored at its peril. Muzyka and Hodgson (2015) argued that the choice that lay before Canadians was whether to futilely fight against globalisation or to embrace it and adapt to the country's inevitable prosperity. Each side saw the rightness of its cause, with very little effort to see merit in the other.

Another group that did not readily embrace globalisation was the labour unions. There was the fear that for those involved in labour-intensive work, the ease with which employers could shift their attention to low wage countries would spell the downfall of this group or heighten 'increased wage inequality and a cause of job loss at the bottom of the labour market' (van Bergeijk et al. 2011, p. 382). Globalisation opened up new avenues for Canadian companies to make their products, in which the increasing power differential between businesses and the labour unions allowed for the expansion of the non-unionised labour pool. For example, Peters (2002, p. 3) drew a link between globalisation and the increasingly depressing plight of unions in Canada:

> Why are Canadian unions in such trouble? And why are unions around the world increasingly vulnerable? One of the reasons is intensified globalisation—the explosion of freer and greater international trade, transnational production and investment, as well as financial globalisation.

The ostensible reason for the TCTM was to expand trade, so there is no record of any direct attacks from the union and labour sector against trade missions *per se*, but the recognition that Canada's acceptance of globalisation had freed capital to become more flexible (Broad 1995) meant that ordinary workers were in a weakened position against the captains of industry.

Critics' Lack of Distinction between Big Business and Small Business

Business was seen as a powerful group that should not need any coddling or handholding by the government. However, critics might have ignored that many of the TCTM participants were small Canadian businesses that did not have as much clout or knowledge to compete on a global scale as one might have supposed. Industry Canada (2011) revealed:

> In 2009, about 86 per cent of Canadian exporters were small businesses compared with 87 per cent in 1999. They were responsible for $68 billion (25 per cent) of the total value of exported goods, with an average value of $2 million per firm. Medium-sized businesses accounted for $51 billion (18 per cent) of the total value of exports, while large businesses accounted for $157 billion (57 per cent).

Longenecker et al. (2019) cite the example of a small business owner, Albert Bohemier of Survival Systems Limited, which participated in various Team Canada trade missions over a three-year period: 'The company benefited not only during the missions but also in the long term. For example, a $400,000 contract for delivery of a system to Malaysia was negotiated, four years after the initial contract during a trade mission' (p. 217). From the foregoing, it is clear that these trade missions were not a quick-fix for ailing companies but for those who had the patience to take advantage of the full panoply of government resources, there was potential for success.

In fact, 'Bohemier credits government services such as Export Development Corporation, which provides insurance, and Canadian trade commissioners, which facilitate client contacts, with easing his company's entry into the international arena' (p. 217). Also, a Montreal Gazette report on the 1997 Team Canada trade missions by Julian Beltrame on Nov 12, 1997, highlighted the extent to which small businesses featured in the TCTM program. As Beltrame writes, 'What is different about this mission that begins today is its size, the fact that all the participants are heads or executives of small and medium-sized businesses, and that they are all women, representing women-owned firms from every province except Prince Edward Island.' Even so, the big businesses that were associated with the TCTMs were often the target of critical ire, as in the comments of prominent Canadian women's rights activist, Maude Barlow, who writes with Tony Clarke, that, 'The Team Canada Trade Missions demonstrate the extent to which the Canadian government, through its Department of Foreign Affairs and International Trade, has become a tool of big business to promote its interests' (2001, p. 102).

Leaders' Own Uncertainty Surrounding Trade Missions

Criticisms of the Team Canada Trade Missions seemed to have come to a crescendo by the time Jean Chrétien was about to leave office in 2003. His successor, Paul Martin, did not give a clear indication as to whether he would continue with them. As a spokesperson for Paul Martin, Scott Reid, said at the time, 'Mr. Martin will insist on creative ways to promote international trade and to attract investment...Whether Team Canada missions will continue to be an aspect of that effort is a decision that will be taken in due course' (Dunfield 2003). In fact, 'In an effort to differentiate himself from his predecessor, Paul Martin abandoned the large-scale "Team Canada" trade missions prioritised by Jean Chrétien' (Cao & Paltiel 2015, p. 136). When he acceded to the leadership, Prime Minister Martin went to China at the same time as trade mission participants led by Minister of International Trade, Jim Peterson (Cao & Paltiel 2015). He ended up supporting trade missions and the 'whole-of-government' approach to assisting Canadian corporate expansion in East Asia, South Asia, and Latin America' (Klassen 2014, p. 205).

Likewise, Paul Martin's successor, Stephen Harper, whose party, the Conservative Party, had been a strong critic of the trade missions, held back for a number of years from indicating whether or not he would participate in trade missions but eventually did go on a number of trade missions (Fekete 2012) and is said to have pursued the trade mission agenda 'with even more tenacity' (Klassen 2014, p. 205). Charges of waste that were levelled at the Chrétien government were also levelled at Harper when it emerged that the government covered expenses such as local transportation and accommodation for executives of some of Canada's biggest corporations. As a representative of one of the most persistent critics of trade missions,

The Canadian Taxpayers Federation stated, 'I think most Canadians would be scandalised to learn that they're paying the expenses of a CEO of a large corporation to promote their company on a junket like this' (Ditchburn 2013). In 2013, Prime Minister Stephen Harper 'went on a four-day Latin American trade mission' (Berthiaume 2013), accompanied by representatives 'from a number of major Canadian companies and industry associations (Berthiaume 2013).

In 2015, the tables turned when the Liberals took over the reins of government, with Prime Minister Justin Trudeau embracing trade missions after a period of uncertainty. When Prime Minister Justin Trudeau went on a trade mission to India in 2018, a Conservative critic, James Bezan, wrote that the prime minister was mocked for wearing an Indian traditional attire and that, 'Conservatives understand the importance of trade missions, the value of Canada's international reputation, and the immense responsibility that comes with the spending of tax dollars' (Bezan 2018, p. 7). It seems that Canadian leaders cannot have an honest conversation about trade missions, choosing to use trade missions when it suits them and especially, with the Conservatives and Libertarians, condemning them when the trade missions are being spearheaded by the opposition. With so much confusion surrounding the utility of trade missions, not surprisingly, a six-day trade mission undertaken by the Ontario government to India in 2019, for example, was not made public until it was over. While provincial government leaders insisted that the trade mission had not been a photo-op, critics were quick to condemn the lack of transparency (Artuso 2019). Finally, in a twist of irony, former Prime Minister Stephen Harper, who delayed going on trade missions for two years after taking office, has, in his post-leadership years, become a consultant on exports, who uses among other tools, trade missions to help his clients boost their exports (Hunter 2019).

The power relations or struggles that surrounded the TCTM did not cease with the passing of the Liberal government under Chrétien. As of 2016, the Liberal Party of Canada, had regained control of the government under Justin Trudeau. Fife (2016, p. 1) argued that:

Prime Minister Justin Trudeau intends to play an activist role in promoting Canadian business and investment with a major trade mission to China and India and a keynote address to the World Economic Forum in Switzerland.

Critics can get the attention of the government because of the sheer volume of avenues by which people can make themselves heard, including radio, television interviews, blogs, newspaper articles and podcasts. Just as the government's discourse has the power to seep into public consciousness, the efforts of the critics were not futile. Even when concerns were repeatedly dismissed by the government, criticisms sowed the seeds of concern in the public square about the notion of fairness and equality. The critics also sent the message that the government did not have a monopoly on truth, which was a signal that each citizen can make a difference if they are willing to raise their voices. A responsive government will take concerns raised by citizens seriously and attempt to address them. It is notable that since the days of Chrétien, when prime ministers have participated in trade missions, they have made it a relatively low-key affair, with nothing of the pageantry and bluster that surrounded the eleven-year run of TCTM largely under Chrétien.

5.5 Ancillary Questions: Criteria for Success -- Government and TCTM Participants

1) How did the government and business participants define the criteria for success of the TCTM program?

A close examination of the marketing communications of the TCTM program and the indicators of success cited by the participants demonstrated that the Canadian government and businesspeople who sought to benefit from the trade missions had a broader view and definition of success than some of the critics who sought to measure success strictly on the basis of dollars in and dollars out. Within the two analysed policy documents, several differences, contrasts, challenges, contradictions and tensions emerged. The government emphasised trade, of which the trade missions served as a cornerstone. Some of the discourses implored Canada not to forget the US in favour of greater trade with other countries. Additionally, the government's push for greater trade with some of the newly influential countries such as China clashed with discourse that pushed for the primacy of human rights considerations. Other issues that dominated at various times between 1994 and 2005 included pushback discourses from environmental groups, which questioned the government's apparent one-sided focus on business and economic prosperity. If the discourse from opposing groups was repeated long enough, it is understandable how the government's own discourse could lose some of its power and credibility. From the discourse of the government and the TCTM organisers, the purported benefits of participating in the trade missions can be summarised into the following five Ps:

Figure 9. The Five Ps of Trade Mission Benefits

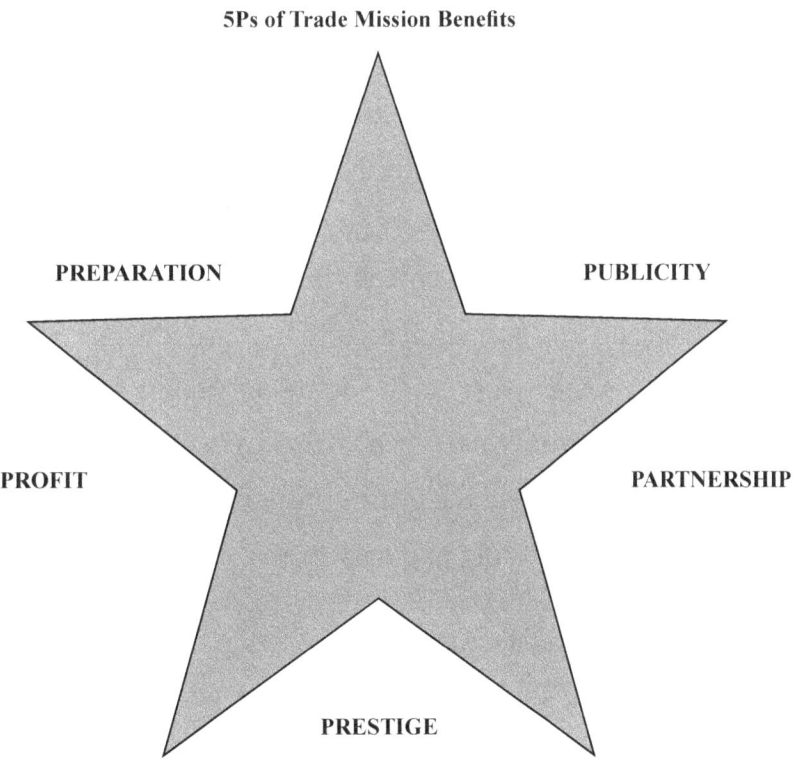

A) PREPARATION—Participating in the trade missions forced some businesspeople to do the kind of homework necessary to get the most out of their experience. Some undertook research on the internet or bought books about the country they were going to visit. Such preparation helped to expand their horizons and had potential benefits beyond the immediate participation in the trade mission. Prior to the trade missions, potential participants were exposed to a plethora of information on the TCTM website regarding the experiences of previous participants and the range of export-related information that could facilitate the process of market entry. The TCTM website, which had links to various other government support systems, helped to prepare businesses planning to embark on a trade mission. The extent to which companies took advantage of these resources was unclear.

B) PUBLICITY—Globalisation may have opened up new markets, although not every businessperson knew how to tap into these new markets by themselves. Some were fearful of not having the necessary language skills or knowledge of the foreign markets, so handholding by government officials was perceived as being positive by many businesspeople without much experience of international trade. The newspaper accounts that surrounded the trade missions, ubiquitous as they were, made some participating companies more widely known within Canada. Such 'free' exposure was the kind of opportunity that might have been too expensive if the companies had sought to pay their way to such exposure with advertising expenditures.

C) PROFIT—Signed deals and expanded markets meant more money in the hands of Canadian businesses. Many companies testified to having signed lucrative deals that they might not otherwise have been able to do. Newspapers touted in big, bold headlines the billions of dollars the trade missions generated for participating businesses and by extension, contributed to the Canadian economy.

D) PARTNERSHIP—Participants in the trade missions expanded connections and got to know some of their Canadian leaders and foreign leaders in the political and business arenas. In addition, some of the participants came to know one another, which may have led to business deals or friendships. This extension of personal and business networks may not have had any immediate tangible benefit but could prove useful in the long run. Of course, the stated goal was to build partnerships with foreign companies, which many participating businesses claimed the TCTM helped them accomplish.

E) PRESTIGE—In some countries, particularly in Asia, government ministers are highly respected. Canadian businesspeople participating in trade missions to such countries could bask in the reflected glory of Canadian ministers or the prime minister and gain access to foreign government and business leaders that could not have been accessed if they had gone to these foreign countries by themselves.

It was evident from the discourse emanating from the government and the trade mission participants that financial benefits formed only one part of the spectrum of benefits accrued to business and to Canada. The whole spectrum of benefits beyond the financial appeared no less important to organisations that participated in the TCTM.

5.6 Ancillary Questions: Criteria for Success -- Critics
2) How did critics define criteria for success of the TCTM program?

Increase in Country's Export Figures, Not Individual Company Success
Critics of the TCTM focused on an increase in export dollars to Canada as the key criterion for success. This meant that even if individual businesspeople and companies were successful in making deals, it did not matter unless there was a net gain for Canada in terms of export volume and income. For much of Canada's history, economic protectionism had been the norm (Bickerton & Gagnon 2014), but, during the Chrétien era, free trade had become a part of the Canadian reality in the form of the North American Free Trade Agreement. Even with this, traces of Canada's mercantilist

past lingered in that despite the inclusion of the free movement of workers in the document there were exceptions for some professionals along with inspections and delays at the Canada-US border that appeared 'contrary to the spirit and letter of the free trade agreement' (Bickerton & Gagnon 2014, p. 447). This focus on increased earnings was part of the government's criteria, which falls under 'Profit' in the five Ps discussed earlier. However, it emerged that the government's figures were not trusted by the critics because these figures were often described as inflated. At the same time that some critics claimed that the trade missions were not making enough money, others considered the practice to focus too much on money to the exclusion of other matters of importance to Canadians, such as human rights. One report insisted with regards to the trade missions:

> While they serve the public relations needs of politicians and participating firms, they have not translated into greatly increased trade …. They have, however, led to a downplay of environmental security, human rights and democracy. (Hibler & Beamish 1998, p. 10)

If this gap in perception of facts was purely objective, one might say that having independent studies on the benefits of the trade missions would be enough to settle the question. The gap that exists in the criteria for judging the success of the trade missions—between the government's and participants' perceptions and those of the critics—appeared so large that it may be challenging to come to an agreement regarding what may be a fair measure. Some critics believed that the trade missions had no benefit, which is why words like 'junket' were used to describe politicians and their involvement in the missions.

Head and Ries (2010) concluded that the TCTM program did not yield rents in profit for Canada. However, this conclusion has not ended the debate regarding whether the program ought to continue. Prime Minister Harper, who had refused to signal his intentions regarding participation in trade missions, embarked on one to Brazil (Chase 2011), which undermined the contention that the trade missions were a useless project of the Liberal government that had come before him. With each new leader, the question is asked: will there be trade missions? Therefore, the discourse on this subject is unlikely to end soon. From the email survey, some respondents sided with the critics in expressing the idea that there did not seem to be enough justification for the trade missions.

5.7 Ancillary Questions: Divergences and Convergences

3a) Where, how and why do these diverge

Figure 10. Major Points of Divergence

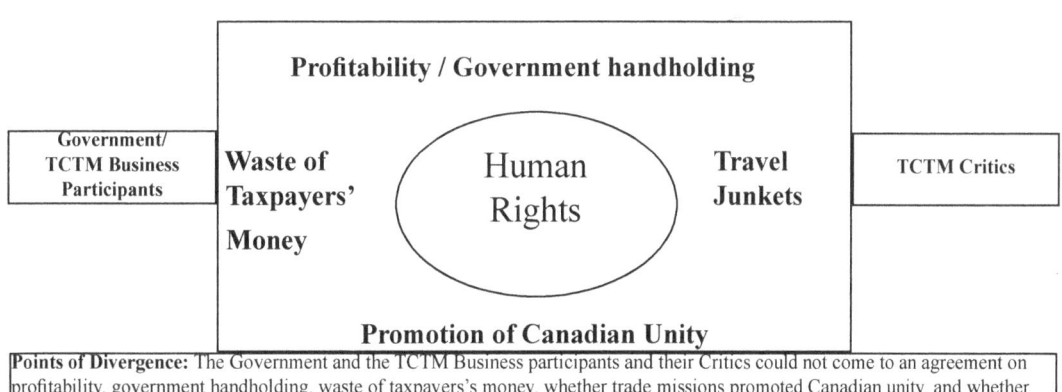

Points of Divergence: The Government and the TCTM Business participants and their Critics could not come to an agreement on profitability, government handholding, waste of taxpayers's money, whether trade missions promoted Canadian unity, and whether the trade missions were just junkets for the benefit of government leaders and their business 'cronies'.

Profitability

The Government and the TCTM participants never wavered on their belief that the trade missions were profitable. This was manifested in individual testimonials of participating businesses and government records of signed contracts with values appended. But these held no meaning for Critics either because they did not trust the government's figures or that they believed the criteria for measurement was flawed.

No Government Handholding for Businesspeople

Canada had a deficit in 1993, which the government vowed to eliminate upon coming to power. In the Liberal Red Book, the government in waiting also promised to make job creation a central plank of their platform. The energy with which the prime minister threw himself into the trade missions and the wide scope, involving as it did the potential for provincial premiers to participate, signified the symbolism and the substance that were attached to the effort. The fact that the prime minister led almost all the trade missions further cemented the importance that the government attached to the new endeavour. Therefore, on the point of the irrelevance of the TCTM, the government found no common ground with its critics. The individual accounts of success of the participants and the figures that were available to the government, convinced it that it was on the right track. In addition, the government and participants understood from the beginning that even though job creation and export growth were at the heart of the effort, there were other intangible benefits that may not be measurable in terms of dollars and cents, including the recreation of Canada's image from a resource haven to a technological powerhouse. Such a change of image was not expected to come after one or two trade missions. In addition, the opportunity that the prime minister had to commune with provincial premiers and for the premiers to be with one another was an invaluable opportunity for the chance at unity, the value of which was incalculable.

From the critics' point of view, businesspeople ought to be equipped to handle their own export transactions. There was no need for any government handholding, especially since the attention of government leaders was not owned by the business community. Therefore, the amount of money that the government spent on the trade missions, whether this was recovered or not, did not appear to make any difference.

Waste of Taxpayers' Money

A substantial part of the resources that government expends come from the contributions of taxpayers. So, taxpayers have a right to know how the government is using those resources. Taxpayers certainly do not want their money being used on activities that hold no benefit for the society as a whole, either from a moral or other necessity. When businesses are given subsidies that they do not appear to need, this can rub critics the wrong way.

Travel junkets

The cost of hotels, taxis, and other expenses associated with the trade missions seemed, at least on the surface, not a matter just of business but of pleasure. The knowledge or perception that government officials and their business counterparts were staying in three-, four-, or five-star hotels, and that the bills were being footed by the government, was totally unacceptable to some Critics.

Promotion of Canadian Unity

When Canadian leaders went abroad, they were able to present a façade of unity. Within Canada itself, there were numerous disagreements among provincial premiers and between premiers and the prime minister. Some Critics felt that painting a picture of apparent unity to the world when this was not the reality at home was deceptive.

3b) Where, how and why do these converge?

Figure 11. Points of Convergence

Human Rights: Not divorcing human rights from trade was the only major point of eventual agreement between the Government and the Critics. It was a change that came gradually.

Eventual Agreement on Human Rights

When activists raised the question of human rights or the need to protect children from labour exploitation around the world, the government dragged its feet on these issues at first, but eventually came to side with the Critics. The government acknowledged that these were legitimate concerns and that it was concerned about such issues. The prime minister was always willing to listen to these concerns, as he did in meeting a 13-year-old anti-child labour activist or in responding that the time was always right to raise human rights concerns in Indonesia regarding the abuses in East Timor.

By the late 1990s, after the question of human rights had come up again and again, the prime minister became emboldened and delivered a speech in China, in which he asserted the importance of human rights. The government also continued to raise the issue of a Canadian who had been jailed in China for being a member of Falun Gong. There was fundamentally no disagreement between the critics and the government when it came to human rights concerns. The point of contention was whether these human rights questions were so important that Canada should forego potential economic interests it could garner from trade in the interest of upholding its values. In this regard, the government felt that by engaging with China and other countries under the cloud of human rights suspicions, the government could make some impact. This approach was supported by various business groups and investors, such as the Bata group, which had business interests in Indonesia and saw no benefit to depriving its thousands of workers of their livelihood in the quest for human rights for their cousins in East Timor. Although the government's approach to dealing with human rights appeared timid, there was some agreement that it was an issue of importance to the government and its critics.

5.8 Results of Email Survey of Expert Panel

While the email survey was not meant to provide definitive answers, it emerged from responses that rather than abandoning the program, the government should do a better job of indicating the extent to which the program was successful through the use of objective data, rather than the self-reports of participants and government officials from DFAIT. They also pointed out the potential need to modify aspects of the trade missions to make them relevant to the Canadian people. Given that experts are apt to disagree, perhaps additional researchers from diverse backgrounds should be invited to analyse the trade missions and determine whether the government's role served the needs of Canadians. From myriad disparate studies, some form of consensus could potentially emerge, which will not be based on the superiority of one study over another, but on the preponderance of evidence from various studies in favour of one viewpoint over another.

5.9 Conclusions

People in government are charged with the responsibility of serving the needs of the people and often have at their disposal financial resources, along with other markers of power such as the police, the military, experts and statistics. Because of this wealth of resources at the government's disposal, many have come to think of governments as inhabiting the realm of power. However, Foucault explained power in terms of relationships and was positive about the possibility for the rearrangement of social relations and the power relations that accompany them. Such knowledge should make us realise that society is not locked into inevitability and despair. Foucauldian analysis acknowledges that 'every power formation can be interrupted and restyled' (Perkins 2008, p. 7). The choices that governments make and for which it tries to impose its ideas through discourse, need not be a *fait accompli*. When people are determined to disrupt, contradict, delay or even reverse ideas or actions that they do not agree with, it is possible to do so through the effective deployment of discourse. Such disruptions should be based on facts rather than opinions or a dislike of the government in power.

Even though the Canadian government under Prime Ministers Chrétien and Martin had at its disposal the power of the media and used news releases, press bulletins, websites and press conferences to assert the benefits of the trade missions, this effort was continually undermined by sceptics who argued that there was no empirical basis for their claims. To some extent, images of government ministers and businesspeople in exotic locales may have reinforced the perception that politicians were looking out for themselves. It may also be that the government did not do enough to demonstrate links between the supposed benefits of trade missions and the lives of Canadians. The government did not appeal to the public to support a program that was considered to benefit only a few people in the business community and drained resources away from others. In addition, it was possible that the overt focus on business success may have clashed with some Canadians' perceptions of the need for modesty. One of the most disturbing charges was that, through its inordinate focus on trade at all costs, Canada had ignored human rights concerns, which were an important part of Canadian values for a long time.[17] This contention does not directly challenge the probable financial benefits of participating in the TCTM program. Rather, critics argued

---

[17] The current Prime Minister of Canada, Justin Trudeau, has raised concerns regarding human rights and trade with some countries, including China and Saudi Arabia.

that money was not the only important thing but that principles were important. Steven Harper, while in opposition commented that:

> I think Canadians want us to promote our trade relations worldwide and we do that, but I don't think Canadians want us to sell out important Canadian values … They don't want to sell that out to the almighty dollar. (MacKinnon 2013)

In this respect, one might argue that where Canada benefits from an improved image rather than an increase in its financial coffers, this could count as success. No one attempted to put a value on the goodwill and publicity generated in favour of Canada during the trade missions. However, having a good reputation around the world cannot be harmful when it comes to forging trade relationships.

The use of money as a measure of success is a long-standing tradition in business. Without such scorekeeping, businesses cannot hope to survive over the long haul. However, a focus on the bottom line cannot be enough because the perceptions that people have of a business or a country need to be managed with an eye on future concerns. The trade missions may have contributed to nurturing this perception of Canada as a vibrant, technologically advanced nation with a unified leadership, which cared about their country and the success of other countries around the world. This was a powerful message that might serve to benefit Canada and Canadians and their image around the world. It appeared that with each uncertain curtailment of the program, Canada may have lost an important weapon in its arsenal as it sought to convince the world that it was a modern, advanced democracy and a force to reckon with. The trade missions may have promoted businesses, but they brought into scope a country that was a beacon of freedom, fairness, human rights and equity. The TCTM, along with the accompanying publicity and marketing discourse, fit with a government agenda that sought to promote a high-profile image for Canada on the world stage. The critical discourses that emerged against the program contributed an opposite discursive formation that cast doubt on the government's message of unbridled success of the missions over time. Perkins (2008, p. 6) asserted:

> Individuals come to understand themselves within the frames provided by their culture's discursive paradigm, its cultural and social production. Subjects do not exist apart from these discourses; rather, they come into being through them.

Continued criticisms in the absence of robust, credible counterclaims may have eroded some of the publicity gains the government and the TCTM team made. It could also have made those responsible for the trade missions more cognisant of the danger of overhyping the financial benefits gained from trade missions. Additionally, from a discourse analysis point of view, the government may have underestimated the power of the voices of disagreement. Although the government had a long stream of discourse in support of TCTM program, it did not appear to have a strategy to deal with discordant voices. The result was that other voices eventually gained a measure of ascendancy. From the comments of the expert panel, it appeared that a revamped TCTM program that had objective accountability, clearly eschewed waste, made limited use of the prime minister's involvement, provided verifiable financial claims, allowed the voices of beneficiaries to seep into popular media and demonstrated how the benefits were good for all Canadians, could be enough to negate the claims of those who contended that the program was not useful.

When people talk past each other, it is difficult for them to grasp the essence of the other's meaning. Critics of the trade missions assumed that the business community had hijacked the government for their own ends while neglecting the needs of other Canadians. However, the comments of Chrétien's top policy adviser, Bartleman (2011, p. 208) is telling in its candour when he claimed:

> Team Canada was the prime minister's chosen instrument to compensate for generations of political neglect. Between 1994 and 1998, three missions would be launched into the Asia–Pacific. The goals were political—to use a 'mother of all trade missions' approach to blast awareness of the world outside North America into the consciousness of Canadians and to expose Asians to Canada.

Although the financial benefits were more often touted, there was an equally strong penchant for portraying Canada as a peaceful, unified, high-technology haven with open arms to the world.

5.10 Implications of the Research

Foucault warned about making facile cause-and-effect connections between events. One of the few studies conducted on the TCTM (Head & Ries, 2010) focused solely on financial benefits to the country, in a search for a significant measure of increase in exports as a result of the program. Elements such as the increased knowledge of participants, newly created partnerships and greater knowledge of foreign markets were not accounted for over the long term. However, the net effect of the discourses surrounding the trade missions may have favoured those who were sceptical about its benefits, whether this was justified or not. In the world of discourse, truth is not necessarily always the winner, but perceptions of credibility can be critical. The implications of the findings from the analysis of policy documents and the surrounding discourses of the time have important implications for government and for business, which are discussed in the following sections.

5.10.1 From a Policy Perspective

Need to uncouple the image of trade missions from political party affiliations

The TCTM may have been too closely linked with the Liberal Party under Chrétien. His flamboyant style of running the trade missions may have been a turnoff, which triggered some criticisms, for instance, that, the trade missions were big trade junkets (Kercher 2019; Potter 2009, p. 183). If these had been seen as a government program rather than being tied so closely to the prime minister, the governments of Martin and Harper could have seamlessly continued with the program without taking a break, pauses which raised doubts about the value they placed on the trade missions. Since Martin, Harper and Trudeau eventually continued with the trade missions (Cao 2015, p. 136; Lunn 2014; Rabson 2018), it can be assumed that they saw merit in the program. However, some of the old criticisms will remain unless Canadian governments can determine what it is about the trade missions that ignite the negative passions of critics and address those concerns.

Need to Portray a Serious Image

It might seem like a minor point, but image counted as much as the substance of what was supposed to be occurring. Government ministers should have used discretion and not have allowed themselves to be photographed in exotic places having so much fun. When it appears that government officials are just on the trips to waste taxpayers' money or to enjoy themselves, this breeds a lot of cynicism. All the governments that have participated in trade missions since Chrétien have, with the possible exception of Paul Martin, who eschewed Chrétien's brand of 'high-profile mission' (Potter 2009, p.183), received criticisms that they were wasting taxpayers' money and that the image they were portraying was more reflective of personal pleasure than sober attention to business. For example, 'it cost taxpayers $1.2-million in cancellation fees when the Prime Minister [Jean Chrétien] aborted a trade mission to Australia in 1998' (Cernetig 2000), and in 2000, with another cancellation of a trade mission to China looming, the question was raised as to how much the cancellation was going to cost taxpayers considering that over 600 rooms had been booked 'at a cost of more than $85,000 a night' (Cernetig 2000).

Need for ongoing independent evaluations of government-backed trade missions

Independent, empirical and qualitative reports on TCTM (Dana 2012, p. 124) could have helped to clarify how useful this government and business partnership was. The benefits of the trade missions to constituencies other than businesses should have been articulated and the government should have developed a strategy to consistently counter the voices of critics. The government should also have heeded the voices that called for objective or independent assessments of the value of the trade missions. Whereas reporters who travel with the government on trade missions are billed for the expenses the government incurred on their behalf, 'The Public Accounts of Canada show that between 2006 and 2011, [Prime Minister Stephen Harper's] wife Laureen Harper – and for many years his personal stylist Michelle Muntean – were the most common add-ons to the government tab' (Ditchburn 2013). And, Prime Minister Justin Trudeau was criticised on his trip to India for using Canadians' money 'to wine and dine…an attempted murderer and to fly a celebrity chef halfway around the world so Trudeau and his friends would have someone to cook for them' (Bezan 2018).

5.10.2 From a Business Perspective
Need for a clear, logical narrative

The business community could have shared their discourse of how increased profitability contributed to taxes and helped other sectors of Canadian society. This may have led to buy-in from groups that viewed the government's support of business as being harmful to their cause. Perhaps, rather than 'hijacking' the government and having the prime minister and key ministers serve the needs of businesspeople, the government could designate a special business envoy from the ranks of government who accompanied businesspeople to foreign lands and served as the government figurehead expected by potential foreign partners. However, such a move would need to be based on solid evidence that it was useful and not also a waste of taxpayers' money.

Public relations: Of what worth?

Most companies and organisations consider public relations and the promotion of a good image to be important, as it helps to preserve reputation (Watson & Noble 2007, p. 45). Waddington (2015) captures the challenge many nations face when he writes that, 'As distasteful as applying branding to a nation may be, it is not difficult to argue that in the highly competitive modern world, a country wishing to succeed may have little choice but to improve its brand image' (Waddington 2015, p. 255). However, critics of the TCTM program did not appear to want to accord importance to the public relations benefit of the trade missions. While the program was running, there were other concurrent trade missions. The difference was that they were organised either by provinces or by business groups. Although these trade missions were not the focus of this research, information about them was continually within this researcher's purview and it did not appear that criticisms were directed at those programs. When it came to non-TCTM trade missions, there appeared to be an assumption that whatever benefits or losses might be incurred was not the concern of the Canadian taxpayer because it did not involve the time and attention of the prime minister or other government ministers. It seems that the participation of the prime minister in the TCTM program was one of the main triggers for criticism. However, if public relations are of any worth, critics might have recognised that there was some public relations benefit from having Canadian leaders and businesspeople travel together in a show of unity.

5.11 Strengths of the Research

Comprehensive approach

What little research there has been on trade missions has mostly been quantitative in nature, which satisfies the worldview that privileges measurement, along with 'cause-and-effect thinking' (Creswell & Plano-Clark 2007). Further, Creswell and Plano-Clark (2007, p. 13) claimed that 'the complexity of our research problems calls for answers beyond simple numbers in a quantitative sense or words in a qualitative sense.'. These are useful sentiments, although sometimes miss elements behind the data that might only be uncovered when the participants have the opportunity to express themselves.

The use of Foucault's (1972) *Archaeology of Knowledge*, channelled through the Scheurich–O'Connor framework, allowed the researcher to explore the context within which the TCTM came into being. Although the time frame of 11 years was shorter than what Foucault was wont to consider, other researchers (e.g., O'Connor 2005; Scheurich 1997) focused on events of relatively short duration and analysed them using Foucault's methodology. The use of thematic analysis to tease out the different strands of thought, on the side of the government and participating businesses as well as the side of critics, was illuminating.

Need to understand context

Without an understanding of background factors, our understanding of almost any phenomenon falls short. Therefore, a key strength of this research was in the provision of a repository of the voices of the individuals, NPOs, anti-poverty advocates, media, think tanks and others who criticised the TCTM and the government and business participants, so that Canadians interested in having their government do what is right can enter the debate with a much deeper knowledge base.

5.12 Contributions to Knowledge

First use of discourse analysis to analyse trade missions

While Ries and Head (2010) undertook a quantitative study of TCTM, this was the first study that used discourse analysis to examine the Canadian government's export-oriented assistance program. This study highlighted the power of discourse and how messages can interact or clash to shape public perceptions and actions. In addition, it highlighted the power of interest groups to challenge the government using new tools such as the internet and sustained criticism to shift perceptions in society.

Need to consider all stakeholders in achieving successful marketing communications

This study also suggested that marketing and promotion of an idea need not focus only on potential 'buyers', but that messages should be directed to those who oppose the message. Not adequately countering such discordant voices means that society become more influenced by these countervailing messages. Marketing should enlist the assistance of credible actors to contribute to the discourse, especially in cultures in which the government's voice is frequently suspect. If the discourse of the government and the export-oriented business community were regarded as lacking credibility, the government could have explored whose support of the trade missions might have added greater credibility to the claims that the trade missions were successful. This might simply have meant calling for an independent assessment.

Need to use objective criteria to silence critics

The use of objective sources to back up TCTM discourse could have been useful to make a strong case for the government's efforts. The Canadian government runs Statistics Canada, which business and government alike rely upon for accurate information. Therefore, the government could have mandated Statistics Canada to use its experts to gather relevant information pertaining to the TCTM program. It is possible that information supplied by Statistics Canada might have come across as being more believable than that produced by the TCTM promotion group.

If the program was successful and had to be continually defended, it might be understood as a cautionary tale to those with responsibility for marketing to ensure that they make use of the proper techniques, which will get the message to consumers and have the messages become part of the lore of customers' lives. Having to repeatedly respond to attacks that have no basis in reality is a waste of time and is potentially debilitating for the product in question and the entity that stands behind the product. Discourse has power to change society, for good or ill and knowing how to deploy discourse, knowing how to defend one's discourse, can make the difference in whether one's 'truth' survives or thrives through the cacophony of voices that are an everyday part of any society.

Respectful engagement with opponents

Chrétien had a reputation for being abrasive; as Bashevki (2002, p. 54), explained, 'as the federal party leader, Chrétien was a pragmatic populist, a scrappy veteran of the flexible middle.' If critics felt that the prime minister was genuinely interested in addressing their concerns, the two sides could have worked out a way in which criticisms could be addressed to the benefit of the country. However, the back and forth did not seem to yield much fruit other than to allow the two sides to continue to criticise each other.

Greater emphasis on commercial and cultural diplomacy

By always making a direct correlation between the TCTM and export growth, the government invited scrutiny because many stakeholders, including the media and citizens, considered it their duty to ensure that they received the truth from their government. It was difficult to draw a straight through-line between trade mission activities and export growth, despite the claims of individual companies that they were benefiting greatly, which meant that the emphasis on billions of dollars in benefit should not have been the primary angle for promoting the TCTM. If the government had emphasised the benefits of its commercial and cultural diplomacy, in terms of helping to brand Canada and to let the world know about the country's changing face in terms of its multicultural bona fides and its increasingly high-technology capabilities, there might have been less pushback. Nobody asks how much revenue a nation's diplomats directly generate for the country, understanding that the benefits such efforts engender—peaceful relationships, the creation of a good image for the country (Naray & Bezençon 2017), the attraction of investments and the attraction of foreign students into the country—are difficult to isolate in terms of their monetary contribution to the nation.

5.13 Limitations of the Research

Non-generalisability

The problem of globalisation that triggered the Chrétien government's response in initiating the TCTM can be placed in the timeline of recent history. It is impossible to claim that a similar constellation of events or context would emerge in the future in ways that would parallel the events, discourse and practices detailed in this research. Therefore, the results are not presented with any suggestion for generalisability.

No concrete solution to the issue of objective criterion acceptable to all

No matter what criteria one side uses to judge the success of trade missions, there will be critics who question its motives, methods and merits. Therefore, if the Canadian government sees merit in the trade missions, whether for public relations purposes or something more concrete, civil society, including academia, should be invited to participate in developing objective criteria. Further, academics ought to refrain from letting partisan preferences influence their judgement on such matters.

Sample size of email responses

An ample research size is necessary for research to convey results that betoken credibility. In this case, although hundreds of potential respondents were contacted, most indicated that they were not familiar with the subject or that they had not paid enough attention to the issue to make an informed contribution. However, the people who responded had clear perspectives on the subject that were illuminating, although there were not enough responses to assume that the views had exceeded the point of saturation. This is a limitation on the potential for triangulation in this research.

5.14 Suggestions for Future Research

One study is insufficient to move people to change long-held notions. Additional research on various aspects of trade missions will increase the likelihood that what passes for truth would emerge. Although TCTM received the bulk of the attention, likely because of the involvement of the prime minister, Canada has several regionally based trade missions that run continuously with limited scrutiny. It is possible that there may be a similar state of affairs in other countries, in which locally based trade missions are not studied. However, to understand trade missions in terms of participation, effects and impact, studies on trade missions ought to be comprehensive and include research at the national and regional or local levels.

Comparative studies of the experiences, perceptions and results of trade missions organised in different countries would illuminate the extent to which cultural or national factors play a role in the success of trade missions. This is because different countries may have different priorities or emphases, which could affect outcomes. More research into what constitutes objective criteria in measuring the benefits of trade missions would be useful for stakeholders. As things stand, 'commercial diplomats try to present the success of trade missions in more objective terms, but evaluations are still rather subjective' (Ruel 2019, p. 23). Much of the confusion that surrounds trade missions and whether they are successful stem from the lack of universally acceptable criteria. More research into this area, possibly using a multidisciplinary approach, could be useful.

Case studies of individual companies that participated in trade missions can help to build a body of knowledge that provides insight into benefits at the micro-level. This is crucial because it may also help establish parameters for successful participation in trade missions. Reading through the success stories from participants of the TCTM program and the continual insistence of critics that the trade missions were useless, raised the question of whether the critics thought that these businesses were lying for the government and that they were willing to take time out of their business to visit far-off countries and risk damaging their reputations, in addition to the loss of sponsorship fees and time invested in the trips, some of which lasted several weeks. Further, despite the insistence of participating companies that the benefit of the trade missions was not for immediate financial gain but the contacts and the relationships, some critics seemed unwilling to accept such claims.

Ruel's (2019, p. 28) suggestion for a three-stage approach to trade missions is sound. Although trade mission sponsoring organisations might claim that they follow a three-step approach of preparing participants, performing the trade mission and effecting some kind of follow-up, it appears that Ruel (2019) advocated a more robust approach of engaging in a multi-step preparation process, which might weed out those who are unlikely to fully benefit from a particular trade mission experience. It would also be illuminating to learn from participants what their experiences of trade missions were, including aspects such as matchmaking, meetings, seminars, hotels and other elements pertaining to the experience.

Longitudinal research that follows several companies involved in trade missions and attempts to tease out how companies feel about different potential benefits to be accrued could be useful. For example, at the beginning of the trade mission, a company might not be concerned about the financial returns and be focused on establishing contacts, but after three or four years, there might be a change in priorities, in which more attention is given to monetary gain. Further, it would be enlightening to acquire additional personal accounts regarding trade missions. There are official statements released by organisers regarding seminars held, deals signed and new contacts made. However, how do participants experience trade missions? Do they have an opportunity to experience the countries they visit in ways that influence their perception of the usefulness of trade missions? Once again, interviewing participants in a trade mission, either as a cohort or over a succession of trade missions and learning about their experiences from multiple perspectives can help to establish a larger body of knowledge regarding trade missions.

Finally, it is important to understand Canadian trade missions from different dimensions. It would be useful to understand trade missions from the perspective of government officials who administer these trade missions, so a quantitative or qualitative survey of a wide range of government officials involved in different aspects of trade mission organisation, administration, and follow-up will be useful.

References

Aarts, D 2011, 'Trade mission truths', *Profit*, vol. 30, no. 4, p. 75.

Abramson, NR and Ai, J 1999, 'Canadian companies doing business in China: Key success factors', *Management International Review*, vol. 39, no. 1, pp. 7-35.

About Canada Trade Missions. Government of Canada. https://international.gc.ca/trade-commerce/trade_events-evenements_commerciaux/trade_missions-missions_commerciales/about-a_propos.aspx?lang=eng.

A dialogue on foreign policy: Report to Canadians 2003, Minister of Foreign Affairs, Ottawa, Ontario.

'*A Guide to Commercial Diplomacy*' 2019. Geneva, Switzerland: International Trade Centre (WTO/UN).

Al-Amoudi, I 2000, *The economy of power. An analytical reading of Michel Foucault,* viewed 20 August 2009, <http://www.csun.edu/~hfspc002/foucault1.pdf>.

Alberts, S 1999, 'PM pushes high-tech goods despite word that Japan's recession will continue', *National Post*, 5 Sep, p. A7.

Albo, G 2002, 'Neoliberalism, the State, and the Left: A Canadian Perspective', *Monthly Review*, vol. 54, no. 1, pp. 46-55.

Ahmed, Z, Johnson, JP, Mohamad, O, & Leong, ME 2002, 'Export promotion programs of Malaysian firms: An international marketing perspective', Journal of Business Research, vol. 55, no. 10, pp. 831-843.

Allen, S 2018 'Justin Trudeau to meet Narendra Modi tomorrow amid Khalistan controversy', *University Wire/The Acorn*, 23 February, n/a.

Ali, A 2002, 'The convergence of Foucault and feminist psychiatry: Exploring emancipatory knowledge building', *Journal of Gender Studies*, vol. 11, no. 3, pp. 233-242.

Aliber, R Z & Click, R W 1993, *Readings in International Business: A Decision Approach,* MIT Press, USA.

Al-Rodhan, NRF and Stoudmann, G 2006, 'Definitions of globalisation: A comprehensive overview and a proposed definition', *Geneva Centre for Security Policy,* viewed 8 September 2008, <http://www.gcsp.ch/e/publications/Globalisation/index.html>.

Alvarez, R 2004, 'Sources of export success in small- and medium-sized enterprises: The impact of public programmes', *International Business Review*, vol. 13, no. 3, pp. 383-400

Alvesson, M & Kärreman, D 2000, 'Varieties of Discourse: On the Study of Organisations through Discourse Analysis', *Human Relations*, vol. 53, no. 9, pp. 1125-1149.

Anholt, S 2007, *Competitive identity: The new brand management for nations, cities, and regions*, Palgrave Macmillan, N.Y., New York.

Ariff, M 1998, *APEC & Development Co-operation,* Institute of Southeast Asian Studies, Singapore.

Artuso, A 2019, 'Ontario trade mission to India flies under the radar', *Toronto Sun*, 6 May, www.torontosun.com

Assche, A V 2019, 'Global Value Chains & Economic Diplomacy,' *AIB Insights*, vol. 19, no. 1, pp. 16-19.

Audet, J & Marcotte, G 2018, 'Student Trade Missions: An Experiential Learning Opportunity', *American Journal of Business Education*, vol. 11, no. 1, pp. 1-14.

Authier, P 1997a, 'Premiers riled by N.B. pitch to businesses', *Edmonton Journal*, 21 January, p. A3.

Aw, BY and Roberts, MJ 1985, 'The role of imports from the newly-industrialising countries in U.S. production', *The Review of Economics and Statistics*, vol. 67, no. 1, pp. 108-117.

Ayob, A H & Freixanet, J 2014, 'Insights into public export promotion programs in an emerging economy', *Evaluation and Program Planning*, vol. 46, pp. 38-46.

Ball, SJ 1995. 'Intellectuals or technicians? The urgent role of theory in educational studies', *British Journal of Educational Studies*, vol. 43, no. 3, pp. 255-271.

Barlow, M 1998, T*he fight of my life: confessions of an unrepentant Canadian*, HarperCollins Canada, Toronto.

Barlow, M. 2001, *Global Showdown: How the New Activists are Fighting Corporate Rule,* Stoddart, North York.

Barlow, M 2011, *Profit Is Not the Cure*, McClelland & Stewart, Toronto.

Bartleman, J 2011, *Rollercoaster: My hectic years as Jean Chrétien's diplomatic advisor 1994-1998*, McClelland and Stewart, Toronto.

Barry, T. E. 2012, 'The Development of the Hierarchy of Effects: An Historical Perspective', *Current Issues and Research in Advertising*, vol. 10, no. 1-2, pp. 251-295.

Bashevki, SB 2002, *Welfare hot buttons: Women, work, and social policy reform*, University of Toronto Press, Toronto.

Baskerville, RF 2003, 'Hofstede never studied culture', *Accounting, Organisations and Society*, vol. 28, no. 1, pp. 1-14.

Bazeley, P 2013, *Qualitative data analysis: Practical strategies*, Sage, London.

Beauchesne, E 1998, 'The government's Team Canada Trade Missions are...', *CanWest News*, 20 May, p.1.

Belloc, M and Di Maio, M 2011, 'Survey of the literature on successful strategies and practices for export promotion by developing countries', *International Growth Centre Working Paper No. 11/0248*, viewed 19 August 2013, <http://www.theigc.org/wp-content/uploads/2011/06/Belloc-Di-Maio-2011-Working-Paper.pdf >.

Beltrame, J 1997, 'Women executives target U.S.', *Montreal Gazette*, 12 Nov.

'Benefits of globalisation not being enjoyed' 2003, *Bernama*, 11 Nov, p. 1.

Bernard, AB and Jensen, JB 1999, 'Exceptional exporter performance: Cause, effect, or both?', *Journal of International Economics*, vol. 47, pp. 1-25.

Berthiaume, L 2013, 'Harper looks to South American trade mission as senate questions linger', *Postmedia News*, 21 May, https://o.canada.com/national/

Bertsch, AM 2012, 'Validating GLOBE's societal values scales: A test in the U.S.A.', *International Journal of Business and Social Science*, vol. 3, no. 8, pp. 10-23.

Betlem, F 2012, *Business Diplomacy in International Firms*. Master Thesis, University of Twente, The Netherlands, www.essay.utwente.nl

Bevir, M 1999, 'Foucault and critique: Deploying agency against autonomy', *Political Theory*, vol. 27, no. 1, pp. 65-84.

Bezan, J 2018, 'Justin Trudeau embarrasses Canada on world stage', *The Interlake Spectator*, 22 March, p. 7. 1

Bickerton, J & Gagnon, A 2014, *Canadian Politics*, University of Toronto Press, Toronto.

Bolen, M 2013, 'Americans fail to understand Canada', *Huffington Post Canada*, 19 December, viewed 9 December 2014, <www.huffingtonpost.ca>.

Boone, L and Kurtz, D 2013, *Contemporary marketing*, Cengage Learning, London.

Bonaccorsi, A 1992, 'On the relationship between firm size and export intensity', *Journal of International Business Studies*, vol. 23, no. 4, pp. 605-635.

Boromisa, A, Tisma, S & Raditya-Lezaic 2012, 'Commercial Diplomacy of the Republic of Croatia – Why Croatia desperately needs a strong and systematic commercial diplomacy', *Institute for International Relations IMO*, Zagreb.

Boso, N, Ogechi, A, Danso, A, & Assadinia, S 2019, 'The effect of export marketing capabilities on export performance: Moderating role of dysfunctional competition', *Industrial Marketing Management*, vol. 78, pp. 137-145.

Bourke, T & Lidstone, J 2015, 'What is Plan B? Using Foucault's archaeology to enhance policy analysis', *Discourse: Studies in the Cultural Politics of Education*, vol. 36, no. 6, pp. 833-853.

Boyer, J P (ed.) 2003, *Leading in an Upside-Down world: New Canadian Perspectives on Leadership*, Dundurn, Toronto, Ontario.

Brewster, M 2012, 'Harper sets Canada, Thailand on path to free trade agreement', *The Globe and Mail*, 6 September, viewed 18 February 2013, <http://www.theglobeandmail.com/news/politics/harper-sets-canada-thailand-on-path-to-free-trade-agreement/article534105/>.

Broad, D 1995, 'Globalisation, Free Trade, and Canadian Labour', *Critical Sociology*, vol. 21, no. 2, pp. 19-41.

Broek, S 2017 'Explaining trade missions: the role of program characteristics in explaining trade missions' outcomes', Master's Thesis, The University of Twente, viewed 6 September, 2018.

Brooks, A. &Van Biesebroek, J. 2017, 'The impact of export promotion on export market entry', *Journal of International Economics*, vol. 107, pp. 19-33.

Brown, R.C., 2005. *Canada and the First World War: Essays in Honour of Robert Craig Brown*, University of Toronto Press.

Buchanan, J 2008, 'Using Foucauldian critical discourse analysis as a methodology in marketing', Australia and New Zealand Marketing Academy Conference 2008: marketing: shifting the focus from mainstream to offbeat (1-3 December 2008: Sydney).

Buckner, P 2004, *Canada and the End of Empire*, UBC Press, Vancouver.

Budd, JM 2006, 'Discourse analysis and the study of communication in LIS', *Library Trends*, vol. 55, no. 1, pp. 65-82.

Burpitt, WJ and Rondinelli, DA 2000, 'Small firms' motivations for exporting: To earn and learn?', *Journal of Small Business Management*, vol. 38, no. 4, pp. 1-14.

Burton, FN and Schlegelmilch, BB 1987, 'Profile analyses of non-exporters versus exporters grouped by export involvement', *Management International Review*, vol. 27, no. 1, pp. 38-49.

Caemmerer, B 2009, 'The planning and implementation of integrated marketing communications', *Marketing Intelligence and Planning*, vol. 27, no. 4, pp. 524-538.

Calof, JL 1993, 'The impact of size on internationalisation', *Journal of Small Business Management*, vol. 31, no. 4, pp. 60-69.

Calof, JL and Beamish, PW 1995, 'Adapting to foreign markets: explaining internationalisation', *International Business Review*, vol. 4, no. 2, pp. 115-131.

Campbell, B 2003, 'The real Chrétien legacy budget', *Policy Alternatives*, 18 Feb, http://www.policyalternatives.ca

Canada Border Services Agency n/a, *Exporting Goods from Canada: A Handy Guide for Exporters*

https://www.milgram.com/

'Canada leads: Improving international governance' 2006, *Harvard International Review*, vol. 28, no. 3, pp. 66-68.

Canada in the World 1995, Ministry of Foreign Affairs, Ottawa, Ontario, viewed 1 December 2006,

<http://dfait-aeci.canadiana.ca/1 >.

'Canada's Trade Agenda' 2014, viewed 1 May, 2014, <www.actionplan.gc.ca>.

'Canadian farmers promote grain sales in South America' 1970, *The Lethbridge Herald*, 2 October, p. 43.

Canadian Press, The 2013, 'Tax payers paid tab for CEO's on Harper's 2012 China trip', *CBC News: Politics*, 21 January, viewed 30 December 2014,

<http://www.cbc.ca/news/politics/taxpayers-paid-tab-for-ceos-on-harper-s-2012-china-trip-1.1371229>.

'Canadians overall views on Trade Missions' 1997, 3 Feb, viewed 3 November 2007,

http://www.ipsos-na.com/news-polls/pressrelease.aspx?id=947.

'Canadian trade mission heads to Ja, B'dos' 2008, *Kingston Weekly Gleaner*, 24 January, p. E5.

'Canola growers seek increased quota to maintain markets' 1982, *The Drumheller Mail*, 17 February, p. 25.

Cao, H & Paltiel, J 2015, *Facing China as a New Global Superpower: Domestic and International Dynamics from a Multidisciplinary Angle*, Springer, New York.

Cassey, A J, 'The Destination of State Trade Missions', *CESifo Economic Studies*, vol. 62, vol. 3, pp. 547-571.

Castaldi, RM, De Noble, AF and Kantor, J 1992, 'The intermediary requirements of Canadian and American exporters', *International Marketing Review*, vol. 9, no. 2, pp. 21-40.

Castleberry, A & Nolen, A 2018, 'Thematic analysis of qualitative research data: Is it as easy as it sounds?' *Currents in Pharmacy Teaching & Learning*, vol. 10, no. 6, pp. 807-815.

Cavusgil, S T 1993, 'Preparing for export marketing', *International Trade Forum*, no. 2, pp. 16-21.

Caywood, CL 1997, *The handbook of strategic public relations and integrated Communications*, McGraw Hill, Boston.

CBC News 2002, Feb. 22 'PM says Team Canada trade missions will continue', viewed 19 October 2012, <www.cbc.ca>.

CBC 2013, 'Taxpayers paid tab for CEOs on Harper's 2012 China trip', viewed 21 September 21, 2014, <http://www.cbc.ca/news/politics/taxpayers-paid-tab-for-ceos-on-harper-s-2012-china-trip-1.1371229>.

Cellucci, AP 2005. *Unquiet diplomacy*, Key Porter Books, Toronto.

Cernetig, M 2000, 'Taxpayers face trade mission hotel bill', *The Globe and Mail*, 23 Oct. www.theglobeandmail.com

Chaiyapa, W., Esteban, M. & Kameyama, Y 2018, 'Why go green? Discourse analysis of motivation for Thailand's oil and gas companies to invest in renewable energy', *Energy Policy*, vol. 120(C), pp. 448-459.

Chase, S 2011, 'Stephen Harper hopes to woo Brazil for trade deal', *Globe and Mail*, 4 August, viewed 13 April 2013, <http://www.theglobeandmail.com/news/politics/stephen-harper-hopes-to-woo-brazil-for-trade-deal/article599752/>.

Chen, SX, Lam, BCP, Hui, BPH, Ng, JCK, Mak, WWS, Guan, Y, Buchtel, EE, Tang, WCS, Lau, VCY 2015, 'Conceptualizing Psychological Processes in Response to Globalisation: Components, Antecedents, and Consequences of Global orientation, *Journal of Personality and Social Psychology*, vol. 110, no. 2, pp. 302-33.

'Chinese trade' 1965, *Winnipeg Free Press*, 6 May, n/a.

Chrétien, J March/April 1998, 'Remarkable progress', *Presidents and Prime Ministers*, vol. 7, no. 2, pp. 10-12.

Chrétien, J. 2001, 'Canada's goals for the Summit of the Americas', *Canadian Speeches*, vol. 15, no. 1, pp. 11-14.

Chua, RY 2012, 'Building effective business relationships in China', *MIT Sloan Management Review*, vol. 53, no. 4, pp. 27-33.

Chutter, D 1998, 'Exporting Housing', *Building*, vol. 47, no. 6, Jan/Feb, pp. 42-43.

Clarke, D Jul/Aug. 1998, 'On the road with Team Canada', *Canadian Banker*, vol. 105, no. 4, pp. 26-30.

Clarke, V & Braun, V 2017, 'Thematic analysis', *The Journal of Positive Psychology*, vol. 12, no. 3, pp. 297-298.

Clayton, M 1994, 'Canada-China deals draw cheers, boos', *The Christian Science Monitor*, 10 November, viewed 10 January 2007, <http://www.csmonitor.com/1994/1110/10082.html>.

Cody, H 1998, 'A Captive Three Times Over: Preston Manning and the Dilemmas of the Reform Party', *American Review of Canadian Studies*, vol. 28, no. 4, pp. 445-467.

'Commerce Reports: A Weekly Survey of Foreign Trade' 1930. *Bureau of Foreign and Domestic Commerce*, United States, 12 May, no. 19, p. 198.

Communications New Brunswick. 2001, 'Premier leads NB delegation on Team Canada Trade Mission to China', 8 Feb, viewed 9 November 2017, https://www.gnb.ca/cnb/news/pre/2001e0115pr.htm.

Constantinou, P 1998, 'Trade missions: Business or boondoggle?', Economic Development Journal, viewed 19 November 2007, <http://www.ecdevjournal.com/index.php>.

Contractor, FJ 2007, 'Is international business good for companies? The evolutionary or multi-stage theory of internationalisation vs the transaction cost perspective', *Management International Review*, vol. 47, no. 3, pp. 453-475.

Cooper, J 2006, 'Team Canada's changing profile', *CMA Management*, vol. 80, no. 3, pp. 53-54.

Cordon, S 2001, 'More profile than profit; With Team Canada in Beijing yet again, veterans of China trade say long-term gain is hard to come by', *Toronto Star*, 11 February, B05.

Cordrey, JB 1994, 'Targeting international business: Strategies expanding local economies', *Economic Development Review*, vol. 12, no. 2, p. 55.

Costa, E, Lucas, AL & Sousa, JP 2017, 'Institutional networks for supporting the internationalisation of SMEs: the case of industrial business associations', *Journal of Business and Industrial Marketing*, vol. 32, no. 8, pp. 1182-1202.

Courchene, T J, Savoie, D J, & Schwanen, D 2008, *The Art of the State II: Thinking North America*, IRPP, Montreal.

Crandall, RW 1987, 'The effects of U.S. trade protection for autos and steel', *Brookings Papers on Economic Activity*, no. 1, pp. 271-288.

Crane, D 1996, 'Canada can gain from globalisation', *Toronto Star*, 21 May, p. D2.

Creswell, JW 2007, *Qualitative inquiry and research design: Choosing among five approaches*, 2nd edn, Sage Publications, London.

Creswell, JW and Plano Clark, VL 2007, *Designing and conducting mixed methods research*, Sage Publications, London.

Crompton, K 1997, 'Trade mission follow-up begins', *Journal of Business*, vol. 12, no. 8, p. A1.

Cuthbertson, W 2012, *Labour Goes to War: The CIO and the Construction of a New Social Order, 1939-45 (Studies in Canadian Military History)*, UBC Press, Vancouver, BC.

Czinkota, MR 2002, 'Export promotion: A framework for finding opportunity in change', *Thunderbird International Business Review*, vol. 44, no. 3, pp. 315-324.

Czinkota, MR and Johnston, WJ 1983, 'Exporting: Does sales make a difference?' *Journal of International Business*, vol. 14, no. 11, pp. 147-153.

Czinkota, MR, Kotabe, M and Ronkainen, I 2011, *The future of global business: A reader*, Routledge, NY, New York.

Dana, L P 2012, *Global Marketing Co-Operation and Networks*, Routledge, Abingdon, UK.

Das, S 1997, 'Biggest game in town: 10 Steps to Export Success', *Edmonton Journal*, 24 Aug, p. G4.

Das, D 2008, *The Chinese Economic Renaissance: Apocalypse or Cornucopia?* Springer, New York.

Day, G and Schoemaker, PJH Nov 2005, 'Scanning the periphery', *Harvard Business Review*, vol. 83, no. 11, p. 135, viewed 7 October 2007, <http://www.hbr.org/2005/11/scanning-the-periphery>.

'Debates (No. 147)'1997, *Journals (No. 147)*, March 19, Parliament of Canada – Publications, Ottawa.

'Defining Canada's role in the world' 2004, *Toronto Star*, 30 October, p. H06.

De Munnik, D, Jacob, J and Sze, W 2012, 'The evolution of Canada's global export market share', *Working Paper/Document de travail 2012-31*, viewed 2 June 2014, <www.bank-banque-canada.ca>.

Deng, S, Verma, V, & Lendsay, K 1995, 'The satisfactions and frustrations of exporting to Malaysia: A case study of three small Canadian exporters', *Journal of Small Business and Entrepreneurship*, vol. 12, no. 4, pp. 49-64.

Denzin, NK and Lincoln, YS 2000. 'Introduction: The discipline and practice of qualitative research', in NK Denzin and YS Lincoln (eds.), *Handbook of qualitative research*, 2nd edn, Sage, Thousand Oaks, pp. 1-28.

De Wit, H 2009, 'Measuring success in the internationalization of higher education: An introduction', in H. de Wit (ed.), *Measuring success in the internationalization of higher education*, Occasional Paper No. 22, European Association for International Education, Amsterdam, pp. 1-18.

Ditchburn, J 2013, 'Ottawa paid expenses for CEOs travelling with Harper on China trip', *The Globe and Mail*, 11 May. www.theglobeandmail.com

Dobrowolsky, A 2004, 'The Chrétien Legacy and Women: Changing Policy Priorities With Little Cause for Celebration', *Review of Constitutional Studies*, vol. 9, no. 1-2, pp. 171-197.

Dichtl, E, Koeglmayr, H & Mueller, S 1990, 'International orientation as precondition for export success', *Journal of International Business Studies*, vol. 21, no. 1, pp. 23-40.

Dingwall, J 1994, 'The new government's goals', *Dun and Bradstreet Reports*, vol. 43, no. 1, pp. 46-47.

'Do your homework' 1998, *Canadian Business*, 13 March, vol. 71, no. 4, p. S5.

Doudou Sidibé & Raymond Saner 2017, 'Business Diplomacy in Emerging markets: Intersection of Roles between States and Multinationals', in H. Ruel (2017) *International Business Diplomacy, Advance Series in Management*, vol. 18, pp. 115-128, Emerald, Bingley, UK.

Doz, Y, Santos, J and Williamson, P 2004, 'Marketing myopia re-visited: Why every company needs to learn from the world', *Ivey Business Journal*, vol. 68, no. 3, pp. 1-6.

Duckenfield, M 2017, *Battles Over Free Trade*, Volume 4, Routledge, Abingdon-on-Thames, UK.

Dunfield. A 2003, 'Martin will scrap Team Canada: Chrétien aide says', *The Globe and Mail*, 23 October, viewed 7 March 2005, <http://www.theglobeandmail.com/news/national/martin-will-scrap-team-canada-chretien-aide-says/article1168336/>.

Dunne, N 1998, 'Commerce's diplomatic decline: Round the world, embassies are glorified trade missions and governments strive to win export contracts', *Financial Times*, 7 August, p. 14.

Dunning, J. H. 2014, *The Globalisation of Business: The Challenge of the 1990s*, Routledge, London.

Durmaz, A & Eren, M F 2018, 'Export performance: Is it possible through knowledge and capabilities? Evidence from Turkish Manufacturing Firms', *Journal of Global Marketing*, vol. 3, no. 13, pp. 180-196.

Durmusoglu et al. 2012, 'The effect of government-designed export promotion service use on small and medium-sized enterprise goal achievement: A multidimensional view of export performance. *Industrial Marketing Management*, vol. 41, no. 4, pp. 680-691.

Dyer, E. (2018). Trudeau's India mission mixes global business with local politics, 17 Feb, viewed 18 July 2018, www.cbc.ca.

Eagleton, T 1976, *Marxism and Literary Criticism*, University of California Press, Berkeley.

Eaves, D and Kara, N 2004, *From middle power to model power: Recharging Canada's role in the world*, viewed 7 January, 2016, <http://thetyee.ca/Views/2005/01/26/RechargingCanadaRoleinWorld/>.

Eagleton-Pierce, M 2001, 'The internet and the Seattle WTO protests', *Peace Reviews*, vol. 13, no. 3, pp. 331-337.

Eberstadt, N 2006, 'Why poverty doesn't rate', *Washington Post*, 3 September, viewed 4 June 2008, <www.washingtonpost.com>.

Etemad, H. & Wright, R. W. 2003. Internationalisation of SMEs: toward a new paradigm. Small Business Economics, vol. 20, no. 1, pp. 1-4.

Evans, P 2005, *Canada Among nations*, McGill-Queens University Press, Kingston.

Export Controls Handbook 2017, Foreign Affairs, Trade and Development, http://www.exportcontrols.gc.ca

Fairclough, N 2003, *Analysing discourse: Textual analysis for social research,* Routledge, London.

Fairclough, N & Wodak, R 1997, 'Critical Discourse Analysis', In Van Dijk, TA (ed.) *Discourse as Social Interaction*, Sage, Thousand Oaks, California.

Fan, PK and Zigang, ZK 2004, 'Cross-cultural challenges when doing business in China', *Singapore Management Review*, vol. 26, no. 1, pp. 81-90.

Fast, E 2014, Canada's State of Trade: Trade and Investment Update – 2014, https://www.international.gc.ca/economist-economiste/performance/state-point/state_2014_point/index.aspx?lang=eng

Fekete, J 2012, 'Harper ends 'very successful' China trade mission', *Postmedia News*, 11 Feb.

Ferguson, N 2005, 'Sinking globalisation', *Foreign Affairs*, vol. 84, no. 2, pp. 64-77.

Fernández-Mesa, A and Alegre, A 2015, 'Entrepreneurial orientation and export intensity: Examining the interplay of organisational learning and innovation', *International Business Review*, vol. 24, no.1, pp. 148-156.

Fife, Robert. 2016, 'Trudeau sets sights on free-trade deal with China', *The Globe and Mail*, Jan 5, viewed 2 February 2016, <http://www.theglobeandmail.com/news/politics/trudeau-sets-sights-on-free-trade-deal-with-china/article28029612/>.

Flaherty, E 1994, 'China trade mission unity showcase – Klein', *Edmonton Journal*, 29 September, p. A3.

Flanagan, T 2000, *First nations? Second thoughts,* McGill-Queens University Press, Montreal.

Fletcher, R and Melewar, TC 2001, 'The complexities of communicating to customers in emerging markets', *Journal of Communication Management*, vol. 6, no. 1, pp. 9-23.

Foucault, M 1972, *The Archaeology of Knowledge*, Harper and Row, New York.

Foucault, M 1977, *Nietzsche, genealogy, history*, Cornell University Press, New York.

Foucault, M 1980, *Power/knowledge: Selected interviews and other writings, 1972-1977*, Pantheon, New York.

Foucault, M 1982a, *The order of things: An archaeology of the human sciences*, The Harvester Press, Sussex.

Foucault, M 1982b, 'The subject and power', *Critical Inquiry*, vol. 8, no. 4, pp. 777-795.

Fox, N 1993, *Post-modernism, sociology, and health*, Open University Press, Buckingham.

Fraser, G 2001, 'Diplomats are the unsung heroes of trade mission', *Toronto Star*, 25 February, A02.

Freeman, RE, 2010, *Strategic management: A stakeholder approach*, Cambridge University Press, Cambridge.

Freixanet, J 2012, 'Export promotion programs: Their impact on companies' internationalisation, performance and competitiveness', *International Business Review*, vol. 21, pp. 1065-1086.

Funding and support programs, www.tradecommissioner.gc.ca

Galunic, C 2018, 'Sustaining Digitisation Hinges on Culture', *Insead Knowledge,* 11 Apr, https://knowledge.insead.edu/leadership-organisations/sustaining-digitisation-hinges-on-culture-8851

Gamble, D 1999, 'Bouchard defends role in Team Canada mission', *Edmonton Journal*, 13 September, p. A8.

Gamble, D 1999, 'Payette to help Team Canada's Image: Trip to Japan to focus on Canada's high tech', *National Post*, 8 September, p A7.

Gaston, N and Trefler, D 1997, 'The labour market consequences of the Canada-U.S. free trade agreement', *The Canadian Journal of Economics*, vol. 30, no. 1, pp. 18-41.

Gelders, D and Ihlen, O 2010, 'Government communication about potential policies: Public relations, propaganda or both?', *Public Relations Review*, vol. 36, no. 1, pp. 59-62.

Georgevitch, D and Davis, P 2004, 'Benefits of giving testimonials', *The Practical Accountant*, vol. 37, no. 7, p. 12.

Gertz, G 2017, 'Commercial Diplomacy and Political Risk', *Global Economy and Development Working Paper 106*, Brookings Institution, Stanford, CA.

Ghosh, R 2004, 'Globalisation in the North American region: Toward renegotiation of cultural space', *McGill Journal of Education,* vol. 39, no. 1, pp. 87-101.

Goh, A and Sullivan, M 2010, 'The 5 biggest challenges businesses face when they expand to China', *Business Insider: Australia,* 14 Dec, vol. 12, no. 42, p. 1.

Goldenberg, S 1991, *Global pursuit: Canadian business strategies for winning in the borderless world,* McGraw-Hill Ryerson, Toronto.

Gopal, S 2001, 'American anti-globalisation movement: Re-examining Seattle protests, *Economic and Political Weekly*, vol. 36, no. 34, pp. 3226-3232.

Gordon, M., Mintz, J. & Chen, D. 1998, 'Funding Canada's health care system: A tax-based alternate to privatisation', *Canadian Medical Association Journal*, vol. 159, no. 5, pp. 493-496.

Gormley, K 2017, The Discursive Construction of the Concept of Creativity in Australian Education Policy and Practice', Thesis, Ph.D., School of Education, UNSW, Australia, https://www.unsworks.unsw.edu.au/primo-explore/fulldisplay/unsworks_44883/UNSWORKS

Government Communication Network 2011, *Evaluating the financial impact of public sector marketing communication: introduction to payback, return on marketing investment (ROMI), and cost per result*, Central Office of Information, UK, viewed 3 November 2013, <http://adfx.ie/upload/files/1386941894_intro-to-payback-romi-and-cpr.pdf>.

Government of Canada Launches Cultural Trade Program 2001, *CCH Canadian, Canadian Government Programs and Services*, Issue 339, Dec, p. 3.

Graham, L 2005, 'Schooling and 'disorderly' objects: doing discourse analysis using Foucault', Paper presented at Australian Association for Research in Education 2005 Annual Conference, Sydney 27 November - 1 December, viewed 9 December 2012, <http://eprints.qut.edu.au/2806/1/2806.pdf>.

Graham, LJ 2011, 'The Product of Text and 'Other' Statements: Discourse analysis and the critical use of Foucault', *Educational Philosophy and Theory*, vol. 43, no. 6, pp. 663-675.

Grange, M 1996, 'Poverty ignored by Chrétien, bishops charge', *The Globe and Mail*, 8 October, p. A10.

Gray, G 20 01, 'Globalisation: Does Canada have a Future?', viewed 13 March 2009,

<http://globalisation.icaap.org/content/v1.1/gabriellegray.html>.

Groen, A, Cook, G & Van der Sijde, P 2015, *New Technology-Based Firms in the New Millennium*, Emerald Group,

Bingley, UK.

Gronstedt, A 1996, 'Integrating marketing communications and public relations: A stakeholder relations model', in E

Thorsen and J Moore (eds.), *Integrated communication: synergy of persuasive voices*, Routledge, Oxford,

pp. 287-304.

Guba, EG and Lincoln, YS 1994, 'Competing paradigms in qualitative research', *Handbook of qualitative research*,

Sage, Thousand Oaks, pp. 105-117.

Gudjonsson, H 2005, 'Nation branding', *Place Branding*, vol. 1, no. 3, pp. 283-99.

Guest, D 1980, *Emergence of social security in Canada*, University of British Columbia, Vancouver.

Guest, G, Bunce, A, Johnson, L 2006, 'How many interviews are enough? An experiment with data saturation and

variability', *Field Methods*, vol. 18, no. 1, pp. 59-82.

Guiltinan, JP and Paul, GW 1991, *Marketing management: Strategies and programs*, McGraw Hill, New York.

Guthrie, D 1998, 'The declining significance of *guanxi* in China's economic transition', *The China Quarterly*, vol. 154,

pp. 254-282.

Hakanen, M., Kossou, L. & Takala, T 2016, 'Building Interpersonal Trust in Business Networks: Enablers and Roadblocks', *Journal of Business Models*, vol. 4, no. 1, pp. 45-62.

Halabisky, D, Lee, B and Parsley, C 2005, 'Small business exporters: A Canadian profile', *Small Business Policy Branch Industry Canada*, viewed 7 September 2007, <www.strategis.gc.ca/sbexporters_profile>.

Hale, G 2006, *Uneasy partnership: The politics of business and Government in Canada*, Broadview Press, Peterborough.

Hampden-Turner, C and Trompenaars, F 2006, 'Cultural intelligence: Is such a capacity credible?' *Group and Organisation Management*, vol. 31, no. 1, pp. 56-63.

Hampson, F 1997, *Canada Among Nations, 1997: Asia Pacific Face-Off*, McGill-Queen's Press – MQUP, Montreal.

Harper Government Announces Trade mission to the Dominican Republic and Haiti 2012, *Targeted News Service*, 15 August (News release)

Harper, T 2002, 'Premiers ambush PM on climate deal: Klein stuns Chrétien with anti-Kyoto letter', *Toronto Star,* 16 Feb, p. A01.

Hart, M 2002, *A trading nation: Canadian trade policy from colonialism to globalisation*, UBC Press, Vancouver.

Harwood, V 2001, 'Foucault, Narrative and the Subjugated Subject: Doing Research with a Grid of Sensibility', *The Australian Educational Researcher*, vol. 28, no. 3, pp. 141-166.

Head, K and Ries, J C 2010. 'Do trade missions increase trade?' *Canadian Journal of Economics/Revue Canadienne d'economique*, vol. 43, no. 3, pp. 754-775.

Heinbecker, P 2011, *Getting Back in the Game: A Foreign Policy Handbook for Canada*, Key Porter Books, Toronto.

Helgesen, O 2007, 'Drivers of customer satisfaction in business-to-business relationships: A case study of Norwegian fish exporting companies operating globally', *British Food Journal*, vol. 109 no. 10, pp. 819-837, https://doi.org/10.1108/00070700710821359

Heller, M 2016, 'Foucault, Discourse, & the Birth of British Public Relations', *Enterprise & Society*, vol. 17, no. 3, pp. 651-677.

Hennink, M, Kaiser, B N, Marconi, V C 2017, 'Code Saturation versus Meaning Saturation: How Many Interviews are Enough?', *Qualitative Health Research*, vol. 27, no. 4, pp. 591-608.

Herman, LL 1998, 'Settlement of international trade disputes – challenges to sovereignty - a Canadian perspective, *Canada-U.S. Law Journal*, vol. 24, p. 121-144.

Herrington, C 2002, 'Latin America is not a country', *Chief Executive*, no. 175, p. 10, viewed 2 May 2005, <http://chiefexecutive.net/latin-america-is-not-a-country/>.

Hibbert, EP 1995, *The principles of export marketing*, William Heineman, London.

Hibler, M and Beamish, R 1998, *Canadian Development Report 1998: Canadian corporations and social responsibility*, The North-South Institute, Ottawa.

Hofstede, G 2002, 'Dimensions do not exist: A reply to Brendan McSweeney', *Human Relations*, vol. 55, no 11, pp. 1-7.

Hofstede, G 2003, 'What is culture: A reply to Baskerville', *Accounting, Organisations and Society*, vol. 28, no. 7, pp. 811-813.

Holden, M 2008, *Canada's trade policy and economic relationship with China*, International Affairs, Trade, and Finance Division, Ottawa.

Holley, D 1994, 'How 3 U.S. firms solved the Japan enigma', *Los Angeles Times*, 18 April, Sec D, p. 1.

Holley, D 1994, 'How 3 U.S. firms solved the Japan enigma', *LA Times*, 18 April, viewed 30 January 2011, <www.latimes.com>.

Holroyd, C & Coates, KS 1996. *Pacific Partners: The Japanese Presence in Canada*, James Lorimer, Toronto.

Howlett, M and Lindquist, E 2004, 'Teaching policy analysis: Policy styles and implications for training policy analysts', Paper presented to the Annual Meeting of the Canadian Political Science Association, viewed 9 October 2011, <http://www.cpsa-acsp.ca/papers-2004/Howlett-Lindquist.pdf>.

How to Prepare for your Trade Mission http://www.tradecommissioner.gc.ca

Hsieh, H & Shannon, SE 2005, 'Three approaches to Qualitative Content Analysis.' *Qualitative Health Research*, vol. 15, no. 9, pp. 1277-1288.

Hunter, A 2019, 'Saskatchewan hires Stephen Harper to help expand province's trade in Asia', *Canadian Broadcasting Corporation*, 16 Nov, www.cbc.ca

Hurn, BJ 2016, 'The role of cultural diplomacy in nation branding', *Industrial and Commercial Training*, vol. 48, no. 2, pp. 80-85.

Hutchings, K and Murray, G 2002, 'Australian expatriates experiences in working behind the bamboo curtain: An examination of *guanxi* in post-communist China', *Asian Business and Management*, vol. 1, no. 3, pp. 373-393.

Iftody, D 1997, 'Team Canada: promoting Canada abroad to create jobs at home', *The Carillon*, 10 Feb, p. 5A.

Ihlstrom, C & Nilsson, M 2011, 'E-Business Adoption by SMEs – Prerequisites and Attitudes of SMEs in a Swedish Network', *Journal of Organisational Computing and Electronic Commerce*, vol. 13, no. 4, pp. 211-233.

Industry Canada 2011, 'Canadian small business exporters: Special edition – key small business statistics', viewed 17 July 2013, <www.bdc.ca/EN/Documents/Other/KSBS_June2011.pdf>.

'Infrastructure program called major success: Chrétien taunts Manning' 1996, *Daily Commercial News and Construction Record*, 7 June, vol. 69, no. 112, p. B1.

Ingalsbe, S 1974, Canada now courting Latins, says Gillespie, *Winnipeg Free Press*, 22 June, p. 63.

Innovation, Science and Economic Development Canada 2016, *Archived – 1998-99 estimates – report on plans and priorities*, Government of Canada, viewed 1 February 2016, <https://www.ic.gc.ca/eic/site/017.nsf/eng/00470.html>.

'International Trade' 1999, *Canadian Business*, vol. 72, no. 18, 12 November, pp. 37-42.

Inwood, G J, Johns, C, & O'Reilly, P 2011, *Intergovernmental Policy Capacity in Canada: Inside the Worlds of Finance, Environment, Trade, and Health*, McGill-Queen's Press – MQUP, Montreal.

Ismael, T 1985, *Canada and the Arab World*, The University of Alberta Press, Canada.

Jack, I 1999, 'Liberals cancel Australian visit as Team Canada members balk: No export benefits: Three premiers say trip not worth their while', *National Post*, 1 September, p. A7.

Jackson, W 1997, 'News', *Animation World Magazine*, vol. 2, no. 1, p. 1.

Jacobs, K 2006, 'Discourse analysis and its utility for urban policy research', *Urban Policy and Research*, vol. 24, no. 1, pp. 39-52.

Janigan, M 2001, 'Mission critical: Team Canada sets off for China amid doubts about Ottawa's trade road shows', *Maclean's*, vol. 114, no. 6, pp. 30-32.

Jansen, H 2010, 'The Logic of Qualitative Survey Research and its Position in the Field of Social Research Methods' *Forum: Qualitative Social Research*, vol. 11, no. 2, pp. 1-21, http://www.qualitativeresearch.net/index.php/fqs/article/view/1450

Jansen, I Sep – Dec 2008, 'Discourse analysis and Foucault's 'Archaeology of Knowledge'', *International Journal of Caring Sciences*, vol. 1, no. 3, pp. 107-111.

Jiang, K, Lee, HL and Seifert, RW June 2006, 'Satisfying customer preferences via mass customisation and mass production', *IIE Transactions*, vol. 38, no. 1, pp. 25-38.

Jiwani, I 2000, 'Globalisation at the level of the nation-state: The case of Canada's third sector', *Innovations: A Journal of Politics*, vol. 3, pp. 27-46.

Johnston, DJ 2007, 'Globalisation: Canada tomorrow', *Canadian Business Magazine*, Oct 17, viewed 9 July 2008, <http://www.canadianbusiness.com/lifestyle/globalisation-canada-tomorrow/>.

Jones, K 2000, 'Canada's Liberal government embraces the tax-cutting agenda of big business', March 4, viewed 9 October 2007, <http://www.wsws.org/en/articles/2000/03/can-m04.html>.

Jørgensen, MW and Phillips, LJ 2002, *Discourse analysis as theory and method*, Sage, London.

Kahn, KB (ed) 2013, *The PDMA handbook of new product development*, 3rd edn, Wiley, Hoboken, NJ.

Kaplan, AM. and Haenlein, M 2009, 'The increasing importance of public marketing: Explanations, applications and limits of marketing within public administration', *European Management Journal*, vol. 27, no. 3, pp. 197-212.

Kärreman, D & Alvesson, M 2009, 'Resisting resistance: Counter-resistance, consent and compliance in a consultancy firm', *Human Relations*, vol. 62, no. 8, pp. 1115-1144.

Kärreman, D & Levay, C 2017, 'The interplay of text, meaning and practice: methodological considerations on discourse analysis in medical education', *Medical Education*, vol. 51, no. 1, pp. 72-80.

Katsikeas, CS, Deng, SL, and Wortzel, LH 1997, 'Perceived export success factors of small and medium-sized Canadian firms', *Journal of International Marketing*, vol. 5 no. 4, pp. 53-72.

Keengwe, J 2018, *Handbook of Research on Virtual Training and Mentoring of Online Instructors*, Information Science Reference, Hershey, PA.

Kellner, D 2002, 'Theorising globalisation', *Sociological Theory*, vol. 20, no. 3, pp. 285-305.

Kendall, G and Wickham, G 1999, *Using Foucault's Methods*, Sage, London.

Kennedy, C 1989, 'Corporate Canada goes for the big time', *Director*, vol. 42, no. 12, pp. 85-88.

Kennedy, K 1975, 'Alberta Export Industry Booms', *Brandon Sun*, 8 May, p. 16.

Kercher, A 2019, *Canada and the World since 1867*, Bloomsbury Publishing, New York.

'Key Small Business Statistics' July 2012, viewed on 19 August 2013, https://www.ic.gc.ca/eic/site/061.nsf/vwapj/KSBS-PSRPE_July-Juillet2012_eng.pdf/$FILE/KSBS-PSRPE_July-Juillet2012_eng.pdf.

'Key Small Business Statistics' 2013, viewed on 7 November 2015, <https://www.ic.gc.ca/eic/site/061.nsf/vwapj/KSBS-PSRPE_August-Aout2013_eng.pdf/$FILE/KSBS-PSRPE_August-Aout2013_eng.pdf>.

Kinnucan, H W & Zhang, D 2004, 'Incidence of the 1996 Canada-U.S. Softwood Lumber Agreement and the Optimal Export Tax', *Canadian Journal of Agricultural Economics*, vol. 52, no. 1, pp. 73-88.

Kitchen, PJ, Brignell, J, Li, T and Jones, GS 2004b, 'The emergence of IMC: A theoretical perspective', *Journal of Advertising Research*, vol. 44, no. 1, pp. 19-30.

Kitchen, PJ, Schultz, DE, Kim, I, Han, D, and Li, T 2004a, 'Will agencies ever "get" IMC?', *European Journal of Marketing*, vol. 38, no. 11/12, pp. 1417-1436.

Klassen, J 2014, *Joining Empire: The Political Economy of the New Canadian Foreign Policy*, University of Toronto Press, Toronto.

Korenovska, S 2008, 'Benefits of globalisation questioned', *Washington Times*, Feb 7, p. 15.

Kosteki, M & Naray, O 2007, 'Commercial Diplomacy and International Business', Netherlands Institute of International Relations 'Clingendael', pp. 1-141, <https://www.clingendael.org/sites/default/files/pdfs/20070400_cdsp_diplomacy_kostecki_naray.pdf>.

Knight, GA and Cavusgill, ST 2004, 'Innovation, organisational capabilities and the born-global firm', *Journal of International Business Studies*, vol. 35, no. 2, pp. 124-141.

Kotler, P & Armstrong, G 1997, *Marketing: An introduction*, Prentice Hall, Upper Saddle River, NJ.

Kotler, P & Armstrong, G 2011, *Principles of marketing*, Prentice Hall, Upper Saddle River, NJ.

Kotler, P & Keller, KL 2012, *Marketing management*, Prentice Hall, Upper Saddle River, NJ.

Kotler, P & Lee, N 2007, *Marketing in the public sector: A roadmap for improved performance*, Prentice Hall, Upper Saddle River, NJ.

Kotler, P., Haider, D., & Rein, I. (1994). 'There's no place like our place! The marketing of cities, and nations', *Public Management*, vol. 76, no. 2, p. 15.

Kramer, J K G 2002, *High and Low Erucic Acid in Rapeseed Oils: Production, Usage, Chemistry and Toxicological Evaluation*, Academic Press, Cambridge, Massachusetts.

Krauss, C 2002, 'Canada's leader plans more social spending after years of cuts', *New York Times*, 3 October, p. A.5

Kufeldt, K, Este, D, McKenzie, B, and Wharf, B 2011, 'Critical issues in child welfare', in K Kufeldt and B McKenzie (eds.), *Child Welfare: Connecting Research Policy and Practice*, 2nd edn, Wilfrid Laurier University Press, Waterloo, pp. 395-428.

Lauckner, H, Paterson, M, & Krupa, T 2012, 'Using Constructivist Case Study Methodology to Understand Community Development Processes: Proposed Methodological Questions to Guide the Research Process', *The Qualitative Report*, vol. 17, no. 13, pp. 1-22.

Lazar, H 1998, *Canada: The State of the Federation 1997 Non-constitutional Renewal*, Institute of Intergovernmental Relations, Kingston, ON.

Leclerc, R 2006 'Mission South America: Team Textile Canada does it again', *Canadian Textile Journal*, vol. 12, no. 1, pp. 46-50.

Lederman, D, Olarreaga, M, & Payton, L 2006, 'Export promotion agencies: What works and what doesn't', *World Bank*, viewed 18 October 2007, <http://siteresources.worldbank.org/EXTEXPCOMNET/Resources/2463593-_1213887855468/41_Export_Promotion_Agenices_What_Works_and_What_Doesnt.pdf>.

Levinson, M 2013, 'Why grocers like Tesco find trouble in the U.S. market', *BloombergView*, 3 April, viewed 7 June 2014, <www.bloomberg.com>.

Levitt, T 1983, 'The globalisation of markets', *Harvard Business Review*, May-June, pp. 92-102.

Ley, D 2010, *Millionaire Migrants: Trans-Pacific Life Lines*, Wiley Blackwell, Chichester.

Leyton-Brown, D 2000, *Canadian annual review of politics and public affairs*, University of Toronto, Toronto.

Liberal Party of Canada 1993, *Creating Opportunity: The Liberal Plan for Canada*, The Liberal Party of Canada, Ottawa.

Lin, AC, 1998, 'Bridging positivist and interpretivist approaches to qualitative methods', *Policy Studies Journal*, vol. 26, no 1, pp. 162-180.

Lincoln, YS 2001, 'An emerging new bricoleur: promises and possibilities – a reaction to Joe Kincheloe's 'Describing the bricoleur", *Qualitative Inquiry,* vol. 7, no. 6, pp. 693-705.

Lincoln, YS & Guba, EG 2001, *The Constructivist Credo*, Routledge, Philadelphia.

London, M 1999, *Principled Leadership and Business Diplomacy: Values-based strategies for management development,* Quorum Books, Westport, Connecticut.

Longenecker, J, Petty, B W, Palich, L E 2019, *Small Business Management: Launching and Growing New Ventures,* Cengage Learning, Boston, Massachusetts.

Longmuir, F 2019, 'Resistant leadership: countering dominant paradigms in school improvement', *Journal of Educational Administration and History,* vol. 53, no. 3, pp. 256-272.

Luke, A 2002, *Beyond science and ideology critique: Developments in critical discourse analysis,* Cambridge University Press, Cambridge.

Lunn, S 2014, 'Stephen Harper heads to China to 'reanimate' trade relations', *CBC News,* 05 Nov, www.cbc.ca/

MacCharles, T 2012, 'Harper in China: Team Canada without the label', 6 Feb, viewed March 8, 2014, <www.thestar.com>.

MacInnis, P 1998, 'Chrétien unveils feds e-commerce strategy', *Technology in Government,* vol. 5, no. 11, p. 1, 8.

MacKinnon, M 2013, 'How Harper's foreign policy focus evolved from human rights to the "almighty dollar", *The Globe and Mail,* 27 November, viewed 11 October 2015, <http://www.theglobeandmail.com/news/world/how-harpers-foreign-policy-focus-evolved-from-human-rights-to-the-almighty-dollar/article15631389/>.

Mackinnon, M & Marotte B 2001, 'Bombardier ties with Ottawa run deep', *The Globe and Mail*, 13 January, www.theglobeandmail.com

'Marchi defends value of Team Canada' 1998, *Ottawa Letter*, vol. 24, no. 10, n/a.

Martin, J 1993, 'Going international', *Business Quarterly*, vol. 57, no. 4, p. 72.

Martin, P Feb 2003, 'Coming to terms with Uncle Sam: Managing Canada-US bilateral relationships after September 11', *Policy Options*, viewed 1 January 2010, <http://www.irpp.org/po/archive/feb03/martin.pdf>.

Martincus, CV and Carballo, J 2008, 'Is export promotion effective in developing countries? Firm-level evidence of the intensive and the extensive margins of exports', *Journal of International Economics*, vol. 76, no. 1, pp. 89-106.

Maskell, P, Bathett, H and Malinberg, A 2006, 'Building global knowledge: The role of temporary clusters', *European Planning Studies*, vol. 14, no. 8, pp. 997-1013.

Mawhinney, HE 1995, 'Towards an archaeology of policy that challenges conventional framing of the problem of violence in schools', *Canadian Journal of Educational Administration and Policy*, vol. 2, pp. 1-9, <https://journalhosting.ucalgary.ca/index.php/cjeap/article/view/42658>.

Mayers, J 2005, *Stakeholder power analysis*, International Institute for Environment and Development, London.

Mayo, A 2003, 'Culture: The mother of all hurdles', *Training Journal*, p. 36.

McCarthy, S 1997, 'Trade mission focuses on jobs', *Toronto Star*, 05 Jan, p. A2.

McCullough, M 2011, 'Business without borders: All for one, none for all?', *Canadian Business*, 8 April, viewed 18 February 2013, <http://www.canadianbusiness.com/business-strategy/business-without-borders-all-for-one-none-for-all/>.

McMahon, RO and Gottko, J 1989, *Export marketing activities of small-firm lumber manufacturers*, College of Business (Corvalis), Oregon State University.

McNeil, M and Pedigo, K 2001, 'Western Australian managers tell their stories: Ethical challenges in international business operations', *Journal of Business Ethics*, vol. 30, no. 4, pp. 305-317.

Menezes, RSS & de Oliveira, J L 2013, 'Discourse analysis of "women in business" associated to business professional women', *Revista de Gestão*, vol. 20, no. 4, viewed 6 February 2007, http://www.revistas.usp.br/rege/article/view/99932.

Menzies, H 1996, *Whose Brave New World?: The Information Highway and the New Economy*, Between the Lines, Toronto.

Mika, J 1970, 'Exploit China Trade, Canada Advised', *Winnipeg Free Press*, 12 November, p. 35.

Milic, J, Palang, KA & Webster, E 2017, Entering Global Value Chains: Do Trade Missions Work? *Working Paper Series 1/17*, Centre for Transformative Innovation, viewed 5 September 2018, http://www.swinburne.edu.au/media/swinburneeduau/research/research-centres/cti/working-papers/CTI-Working-Paper-1-17-Entering-Global-Production-Chains.pdf.

Mitchell, D 2010, 'Where have all the policy-makers gone?', *The Globe and Mail*, 16 Feb, p. A21.

Moons, SJV & van Bergeijk, PAG 2016, 'Does Economic Diplomacy Work? A Meta-analysis of Its Impact on Trade and Investment', The World Economy, pp. 1-33, viewed 7 March 2018, doi: 10.1111/twec.12392.

Morgan, NA, Katsikeas, CS, and Vorhies, DW 2012, Export marketing strategy implementation, export marketing capabilities, and export venture performance. *Journal of the Academy of Marketing Science*, vol. 40, no. 2, pp. 271-289.

Morris, P, 1996, 'Asia's four little tigers: A comparison of the role of education in their development', *Comparative Education*, vol. 32, no. 1, pp. 95-109.

Motion, J 2005, 'Participative public relations: Power to the people or legitimacy for government discourse?', *Public Relations Review*, 31, pp. 505-512.

Motion, J & Leitch, SR 2007, 'A toolbox for public relations: The oeuvre of Michel Foucault', *Public Relations Review*, vol. 33, no. 3, pp. 263-268.

Murphy, R Apr 23, 2007, 'Good times roll on: Luxury watch sales reach record heights', *Women's Wear Daily*, vol. 193, no. 85, pp. 1-13.

'Must export more and import less' 1962, *Winnipeg Free Press*, 21 June, p. 15.

Muzyka, D & Hodgson, G 2015, 'What Canada needs to succeed in a changing, globalised world', *The Globe and Mail*, 28 September, p. B4.

Nakata, C and Sivakumar, K 2001, 'Instituting the marketing concept in a multinational setting: The role of national culture', *Journal of the Academy of Marketing Science*, vol. 29, no. 3, pp. 255-276.

Naray, O & Bezençon, V 2017, 'Management and Business Research on Commercial Diplomacy: Examining Trends and Themes', *The International Trade Journal*, vol. 31, no. 4, pp. 332-359.

Nimijean, R. 2014, 'Domestic brand politics and the modern publicity state', in K Kozolanka (ed.), *Publicity and the Canadian state: Critical communication*, University of Toronto Press, Toronto, pp. 172-194.

Noumoff, S 2001, 'Globalisation and the marginalised', *Labour, Capital and Society*, vol. 34, no. 1, pp. 50-91.

Nowell, LS, Norris, JM, White, DEC & Moules, NJ 2017, 'Thematic Analysis: Striving to Meet the Trustworthiness Criteria', *International Journal of Qualitative Methods*, vol. 16, no. 1, pp. 1-13.

Nummela, N, Saarenketo, S and Puumalainen, K 2004, 'A global mindset — a prerequisite for successful internationalisation?' *Canadian Journal of Administrative Sciences*, vol. 21, no. 1, pp. 51-64.

O'Connor, MK 2005, 'Policy archaeology: A qualitative approach to policy analysis', viewed 1 October 2008, <http://www.gptsw.net/wp-content/uploads/Oconner3.pdf>.

O'Connor, MK & Netting, FE. 2008, 'Teaching policy analysis as research: consideration and extension of options,' *Journal of Social Work Education, Journal of social Work Education,* vol. 44 no. *3, pp. 159-172.*

O'Connor, MK and Netting, FE 2011, *Analysing social policy: Multiple perspectives for critically understanding and evaluating policy*, John Wiley and Sons, Oxford.

OECD 2004, 'OECD environmental performance reviews: Canada 2004', viewed 3 January 2006, <http://www.keepeek.com/Digital-Asset-Management/oecd/environment/oecd-environmental-performance-reviews-canada-2004_9789264107786-en#page3>.

O'Grady, S and Lane, HW 1997, 'Culture: An unnoticed barrier to Canadian retail performance in the USA', *Journal of Retailing and Consumer Services*, vol. 4, no. 3, pp. 159-170.

Ogunmokun, G and Ng, S 2004, 'Factors influencing export performance in international marketing: A study of Australian firms', *International Journal of Management*, vol. 21, no. 2, pp. 172-185.

O'Neil, MO 2001, 'Globalisation: Is Canada ready?', viewed 10 March 2009, <http://www.globalenvision.org/library/3/1502>.

Ordeix-Rigo, E & Duarte, J 2009, 'From Public Diplomacy to Corporate Diplomacy: Increasing Corporation's Legitimacy and Influence', *American Behavioural Scientist,* vol. 53, no. 4, pp. 549-564.

Organisations that can help you export http://www.canadabusiness.ca

O'Rourke, KH 2001, 'Globalisation and inequality: Historical trends', paper presented at the Annual World Bank Conference on Development Economics, 1-2 May, 2001, viewed 30 December 2012, <http://www.tcd.ie/Economics/TEP/2001_papers/TEPNo9KO21.pdf>.

Osei-Bonsu, N 2016, 'Discourse analysis of cross-cultural competencies in international business management', *European Scientific Journal*, vol. 12, no. 22, pp. 359-379.

Osterland, A 2019, 'Federal Chairman Sink Stock Market', Entrepreneur Index Finishes Down', *Entrepreneur*, 1 May, www.entrepreneur.com.

Oudalov, N 2013, 'How Trade Missions Work: An Exploratory Study', Master's Thesis, The University of Twente, viewed 6 September, 2018. <https://essay.utwente.nl/63014/1/Master_Thesis_BA_Nikolai_Oudalov.pdf>.

'Our Trade Offices Around the World' (n.d.), *Foreign Affairs and International Trade Canada,* viewed 8 August 2009, <http://www.tradecommissioner.gc.ca/eng/trade-offices.jsp>.

Padgett, DK 2008, *Qualitative methods in social work research*, 2nd edn, Sage Publications, Thousand Oaks.

Parliament of Canada 1998, 'Standing committee on foreign affairs and international Trade', viewed 7 May 2009, <http://www.parl.gc.ca/HousePublications/Publication.aspx?Language=eandMode=1andParl=36andSes=1andDocId=1038868>.

Pearlstein, S 2000, 'O Canada, a national swan song?' *Washington Post Foreign Service,* viewed 1 September 2013,

<http://www.fcpp.org/publication.php/364>.

Pechter, K 1992, 'Trade: Mission possible', *International Business*, vol. 5, no. 10, pp. 58-62.

Perkins, J 2008, *Roman imperial identities in the early Christian era*, Routledge, New York.

Peters, J 2002, *A Fine Balance: Canadian Unions Confront Globalisation*, Centre for Policy Alternatives, Ottawa.

Petersen, B, Welch, LS, Liesch, PW 2002, 'The internet and foreign market expansion by firms', *Management International Review*, vol. 42, no. 2, pp. 207-221.

Pettigrew, P 2000, 'Why globalisation works', *Canadian Business*, 21 October, vol. 73, no. 18, p. 107.

Phelps, JE, Harris, TE & Johnson, E 1996, Exploring decision-making approaches and responsibility for developing marketing communications strategy, *Journal of Business Research*, vol. 37, no. 3, p. 217.

Phillips, N and Hardy, C 2002, *Discourse analysis – investigating processes of social construction*, Sage, Thousand Oaks.

Phillips, R 2002, 'Canadian foreign policy in the American millennium', *Peace Magazine*, viewed 27 January 2013, <www.peacemagazine.org/archive/v18n2p06.htm>.

Pigman, GA 2010, *Contemporary Diplomacy: Representation and Communication in a Globalised World*, Polity Press, Malden, MA, USA.

Pigman, GA 2012, 'Public diplomacy, place branding and investment promotion in ambiguous sovereignty situations: the Cook Islands as a best practice case', *Place Branding and Public Diplomacy*, vol. 8, no. 1, pp. 17-29.

Pigman, GA 2016, Trade *Diplomacy Transformed: Why trade matters for global prosperity,* 2nd edition, Lulu Publishing, N. Carolina, USA.

Pinker, S 2007, 'The evolutionary social psychology of off-record indirect speech acts', *Intercultural Pragmatics*, vol. 4, no. 4, pp. 437-461.

Plamondon, B 2017, 'Canada's most conservation Prime Minister? It's not who you think', *Ottawa Citizen*, 18 Dec, viewed 7 January 2018, <https://ottawacitizen.com/opinion/columnists/plamondon-canadas-most-conservative-prime-minister-its-not-who-you-think>.

Porter, M E 1990, 'The Competitive Advantage of Nations', *Harvard Business Review*, pp. 73-91, www.economie.ens.fr

Potter, EH 2002/2003 (Winter), 'Canada and the new public diplomacy', *International Journal*, vol. 58, no. 1, pp. 43-64.

Potter, EH 2004, 'Branding Canada: The renaissance of Canada's commercial diplomacy', *International Studies Perspectives*, vol. 5, no. 1, pp. 55-60.

Potter, E H 2009, *Branding Canada: Projecting Canada's Soft Power Through Diplomacy*, McGill-Queens Press, Montreal, Quebec.

Potter, EH, 2009. *Branding Canada: Projecting Canada's soft power through public diplomacy*, McGill-Queen's Press-MQUP, Montreal.

Powers, P 2013, 'Rawlinson's Three Axes of Structural Analysis: A Useful Framework for a Foucauldian Discourse Analysis', *Aporia*, vol. 5, no. 1, pp. 6-12.

Poy, V and Cao, H 2009, *The China challenge: Sino-Canadian relations in the 21st century*, University of Ottawa Press, Ontario.

Price, J 2007, '"Orienting" the empire: Mackenzie King and the aftermath of the 1907 race riots', *BC Studies*, no. 156/157, pp. 53-81.

Punch, KF 1998, *Introduction to social research*, Sage, London.

Rabson, M 2018, 'Trudeau. Takes wing on trade mission to India, where Sikh politics loom', *The Canadian Press*, 16 Feb.

Ray, M, Sawyer, AG, Rothschild, ML, Heeler, Rm, Strong, EC & Reed, JB 1973, 'Marketing Communication and the Hierarchy-Of-Effects, Working Paper No. 180', viewed 5 May 2016, <www.gsb.stanford.edu>,

Rethinking Canada's international priorities' 2010, viewed 12 September 2013, <http://cips.uottawa.ca/eng/documents/Priorities_Report.pdf>.

Richards, J 2004, 'The reign of Jean Chrétien', *Inroads: a Journal of Opinion,* vol. 14, no. 4, viewed 7 November 2006, <https://www.highbeam.com/doc/1G1-127058117.html>.

Riege, A and Lindsay, N 2006, 'Knowledge management in the public sector: Stakeholder partnerships in the public policy development', *Journal of Knowledge Management,* vol. 10, no. 3, pp. 24-39.

Riordan, S 2014, *Business Diplomacy: Shaping the firm's geopolitical risk environment,* Clingendael, The Netherlands Institute of International Relations, pp. 1-7. www.clingendael.org

Roberts, M J & Tybout, J R 1997, 'What Makes Exports Boom?' *World Bank Publications,* Washington DC.

Robertson, L 1996, 'It was another day of handshakes and another day of human rights issues for Team Canada's trade mission in Asia', *CTV National News,* 17 January.

Rochlin, J 2014, 'A golden opportunity: Canada's human rights impact assessment and the free trade agreement with Colombia', *The International Journal of Human Rights,* vol. 18, no. 4-5, pp. 545-566.

Rogers, R, Malancharuvil-Berkes, E, Mosley, M, Hui, D and Joseph, GO 2005, 'Critical Discourse Analysis in Education: A Review of the Literature', *Review of Educational Research,* vol. 75, no. 3, pp. 365-416.

Rondinelli, DA 1993, 'Resolving US-China trade conflicts: Conditions for trade and investment expansion in the 1990s', *Columbia Journal of World Business,* vol. 28, no. 2, pp. 66-81.

Rose, AK 2007, 'The foreign service and foreign trade: Embassies as export promotion', *The World Economy,* vol. 30, no. 1, pp. 22-38.

Ruel, H 2019, *Making Trade Missions Work: A Best Practice Guide to International Business and Commercial Diplomacy*, Emerald, Bingley, UK.

Ruel, HJM 2013, 'Diplomacy means business', Windesheim reeks Kennis en Onderzoek, nr. 46, viewed 6 September, 2018, https://www.windesheim.nl/~/media/files/.../13444_diplomacymeansbusiness.pdf.

Ruel, HJM, Lee, D, Visser, R 2013, 'Commercial diplomacy and international business: Inseparable twins?', *AIB Insights*, vol. 13, no. 1, pp. 14-17.

Ruel, JMH 2012, 'The Effectiveness of Commercial Diplomacy: a survey among Dutch Embassies & Consulates', *Discussion Papers in Diplomacy*, No. 123, Netherlands Institute of International Relations 'Clingendael', www.clingendael.nl/cdsp/publications/diplomacy-papers

Salkind, NJ (ed.) 2010, 'Path Analysis', *Encyclopedia of Research Design*, Sage, UK.

Saner, R 2001, 'Globalisation and its impact on leadership qualification in public administration', *International Review of Administrative Sciences*, vol. 67, pp. 649-661.

Saner, R (2009), 'Trade Policy Governance through Inter-Ministerial Coordination: A source book for trade officials and development experts', *Republic of Letters*, Dordrecht. *http://www.diplomacydialogue.org/images/files/20181215-book_saner-trade_1.pdf*

Saner, R, Michalun, V (Eds) (2009), "State actor versus Non-State Actor Negotiations", *Republic of Letters*, The Hague, NL. http://www.diplomacydialogue.org/images/files/20181215-full%20version.pdf

Saner, R, Yiu, L, Sondergaard, M 2000, 'Business diplomacy management: a core competency for global companies', *Academy of Management Executive*, vol. 14, no.1, pp. 80-92.

http://www.diplomacydialogue.org/images/files/20110409- Business%20Diplomacy%20Management.pdf

Sato, M 1999, 'Ottawa to stress high-tech trade: Trade mission targets First World economies', *National Post*, 28 July, p. C6.

Schaeffer, M 2012, 'Promoting Commodity Exports through Government-Led Trade Missions: Governors' Permissible (and WTO Permissible) Role of Exporter-in-Chief, *Proceedings of the Annual Meeting (American Society of International Law)*, vol. 106, pp. 273-278.

Scheurich, JJ 1994, 'Policy archaeology: a new policy studies methodology', *Journal of Education Policy*, vol. 9, no. 4, pp. 297-316.

Scheurich, JJ 1995, 'A postmodern critique of research interviewing', *Journal of Qualitative Studies in Education*, vol. 8, no. 3, pp. 239–252.

Scheurich, JJ 1997, *Research method in the postmodern*, Routledge, UK.

Schiller, B 2008, 'Miller declares China mission 'an eye-opener'', *Star.com*, 20 April, viewed 6 October 2010, <http://www.thestar.com/News/World/article/416357>.

Schmidt, D 2018, 'Stock market rumors and credibility', Review of Financial Studies, Forthcoming, *HEC Paris Research Paper No. FIN-2019-1331*, <https://papers.ssrn.com/sol3/papers.cfm?abstract_id=3329650>.

Schnietz, KE and Schüller, DA 1999. 'Much ado about nothing? The economic impact of US foreign trade mission participation', *Business and Politics*, vol. 1, no. 2, pp. 155-178.

Schultz, DE and Block, MP 2003, 'Moving marketing communication measurement inside', *Singapore Nanyang Business Review*, vol. 2, no. 1, pp. 48-60.

Schultz, DE and Kitchen, PJ 2000, *Communicating globally: An integrated marketing approach,* McGraw Hill, London.

Schwartz, SH 1994 'Beyond individualism/collectivism: new cultural dimensions of value', in Kim, U, Triandis, HC, Kagitcibasi, C, Choi, SC and Yoon, G (eds.), *Individualism and collectivism: Theory, method and applications*, Sage, Thousand Oaks, pp. 85-119.

Sclater, SD 2017, *The Uses of Narrative: Explorations in Sociology, Psychology and Cultural Studies (Memory and Narrative)*, Routledge, Abingdon-on-Thames, UK.

Scoffield, H 2000, 'Team Canada juggles trade, human rights in mission to China', *The Globe and Mail*, 13 January, p. B5, www.theglobeandmail.com

Seguin, R 1997, 'Smaller firms cash in on trade mission: Canadian group opens doors for businesses seeking opportunities in S. Korea, Thailand, the Philippines', *The Globe and Mail*, 13 January, B 3.

Sengupta, J, 2007, 'Economic Relations between the US and Two Asian Giants', In *The New Asian Power Dynamic*, Rasgotra, M, ed., Sage Publications, India.

Seringhaus, FHR 1987, 'Promoting exports: what role do government programs play?', *Business Quarterly*, vol. 52, no. 1, pp. 57-61.

Seringhaus, FHR 1989, 'Trade missions in exporting: State of the art', *Management International Review*, vol. 29. no. 2, pp. 5-16.

Seringhaus, FHR and Botschen, G 1991, 'Cross-national comparison of export promotion services: The views of Canadian and Austrian companies', *Journal of International Business Studies*, vol. 22, no. 1, pp. 115-133.

Seringhaus, FHR and Mayer, CS 1988, 'Different approaches to foreign market entry between users and non-users of trade missions', *European Journal of Marketing*, vol. 22, no. 10, pp. 7-18.

Seringhaus, FHR and Rosson, PJ 2001, 'Firm experience and international trade fairs', *Journal of Marketing Management*, vol. 17, no. 7/8, pp. 877-901.

Seringhaus, FHR and Rosson, PJ 2001, *Government export promotion: A global perspective*. Routledge, Abingdon-on-Thames, UK.

Shankar, A, Cherrier, H, Canniford, R 2006, 'Consumer empowerment: A Foucauldian interpretation', *European Journal of Marketing*, vol. 40, no. 9/10, pp. 1013-1030.

Sharp, E and Richardson, T 2001, 'Reflections on Foucauldian discourse analysis in planning and environmental policy research', *Journal of Environmental Policy and Planning*, vol. 3, no. 3, pp. 193-209.

Sheehan, KB and Doherty, C 2001, 'Re-weaving the web: Integrating print and online communications', *Journal of Interactive Marketing*, vol. 15, no. 2, pp. 47-59.

Sheikh, F 2003, 'Missions possible', *Profit: the magazine for Canadian entrepreneurs*, vol. 22, no. 6, p. 10.

Shi, X & Wang, J 2011, 'Interpreting Hofstede model and GLOBE model: Which way to go for cross-cultural research?', *International Journal of Business and Management*, vol. 6, no. 5, pp. 93-99.

Skalen, P 2010, 'A discourse analytical approach to qualitative research', *Qualitative Market Research*, vol. 13, no. 2, pp. 103-109.

Sokoll, S 2011, 'The relationship between GLOBE's future orientation cultural dimension and servant leadership endorsement', *Emerging Leadership Journeys*, vol. 4, no. 1, pp. 141-153.

Spence, MM 2003, 'Evaluating export promotion programmes: UK overseas trade missions and export performance', *Small Business Economics*, vol. 20, no 1, pp. 83-103.

Spence, MM and Crick, D 2001, 'An investigation into UK firms' use of trade missions', *Marketing Intelligence and Planning*, vol. 19, nos. 6/7, pp. 464-474.

Spence, M and Crick, D 2004, 'Acquiring relevant knowledge for foreign market entry: the role of overseas trade missions', *Strategic Change*, vol. 13, no. 5, pp. 283-292.

Spriggs, J & Isaac, G 2001, *Food Safety and International Competitiveness: The Case of Beef*, CABI, Oxfordshire, England.

Steenkamp, JEM 2001, 'The role of national culture in international marketing research', *International Marketing Review*, vol. 18, no. 1, pp. 30-44.

Stevenson, C and Cutcliffe, J 2006, 'Problematising special observation in psychiatry: Foucault, archaeology, genealogy, discourse and power/knowledge', *Journal of Psychiatric and Mental Health Nursing*, vol. 13, no. 6, pp. 713-721.

Stevenson, S 2001, 'The rise and decline of state-funded community information centres: A textually oriented discourse analysis', *The Canadian Journal of Information and Library Science*, vol. 26, no. 2/3, pp. 51-75.

Stiglitz, JE 2002, *Globalisation and its discontents*, WW Norton and Company, New York.

Stoddard, E 2016, 'Tough times, shifting roles: examining the EU's commercial diplomacy in foreign energy markets', *Journal of European Public Policy*, vol. 24, no. 7, pp. 1048-1068.

Stollery, R 1989, 'How to manage change in an age of uncertainty', *Financial Executive*, vol. 5, no. 1, pp. 56-61.

Suarez, JL 2015, The business of culture, *Ivey Business Journal Online*, viewed 1 February 2016, <http://iveybusinessjournal.com/the-business-of-culture/>.

Svensson, G 2001, 'Glocalisation of business activities: A "glocal strategy" approach', *Management Decision*, vol. 39, no. 1, pp. 6-18.

Swimmer, G 1997, *How Ottawa Spends, 1997-1998: Seeing Red: A Liberal Report Card*, McGill-Queen's Press – MQUP, Montreal.

Szondi, G 2008, 'Public diplomacy and nation branding: Conceptual similarities and differences', *Discussion Papers in Diplomacy,* The Netherlands Institute of International Relations 'Clingendael', The Hague, pp. 1-49, viewed 21 March 2009, <http://www.peacepalacelibrary.nl/ebooks/files/Clingendael_20081022_pap_in_dip_nation_branding.pdf>.

Taber, J 2009, 'Chrétien betting on resort-casino in Vietnam', *The Globe and Mail,* 16 April, viewed 9 September 2010, <http://www.theglobeandmail.com/news/national/chretien-betting-on-resort-casino-in-vietnam/article1196257/>.

'Talking trade and human rights in Asia' 1996, *Toronto Star*, 7 January, p. F2.

Team Canada Inc. – Annual Report 2002, viewed 16 May, 2018, <www.exportsource.ca>.

Team Canada Inc. – Annual Report 2004, viewed 6 September, 2018, http://publications.gc.ca/collections/collection_2007/exportsource/Iu1-7-2004E.pdf.

'Team Canada Trade Missions – Archive',[18] <http://www.international.gc.ca/trade-missions-commerciale/previous-missions-precedentes.aspx?lang=eng>.

---

[18]The Team Canada Trade Missions archive has moved from website to website. The site used by Head and Ries (2010) www.tcm-mec.gc.ca is non-operational. Also, the Library and Archives Canada site — http://www.bac-lac.gc.ca/eng/Pages/home.aspx appears defunct.

'Team Canada trade missions of little value', says economist' 1998, *Edmonton Journal*, April 26, p. E11.

"Team Canada' 1997: Taking on the World', Canadian Business, vol. 70, no. 3, pp. S1-9,

<https://business.highbeam.com/5274/article-1G1-19345003/team-canada-1997-taking-world>.

Teddlie, C and Tashakkori, A 2009, *Foundations of mixed methods research: Integrating quantitative and qualitative approaches in the social and behavioural sciences*, Sage, London.

'The Canadian Taxpayers Federation 1997, 'Let's Talk Taxes', *The Star & Times*, 30 April, 4A.

'The Government of Canada Helps Farmers and Agri-Food Exporters Develop New Markets' 2010, *Marketwire*, 4 August.

'The Team Canada trade mission to Japan' 1999, *CTV National News – CTV Television*, 8 Sep, n/a.

Thorelli, HB and Glowacka, AE 1995, 'Willingness of American industrial buyers to source internationally', *Journal of Business Research*, vol. 32, no. 1, pp. 21-30.

Thyer, B 2012, *Quasi-Experimental Research Designs*, Oxford University Press, UK.

'Trade key factor in our prosperity 2000', *The Lethbridge Herald*, 20 April, p. B7.

'Trade mission is 'off to good start'' 1962, *The Russell Banner*, 8 November, p. 6.

'Trade missions swap, to boost Canada sales' 1965, *The Winnipeg Tribune*, 30 Jan, p. 31.

'Trade mission to scale the Great Wall' 2000, *Transportation & Distribution*, vol. 41, no. 1, p. 12.

Trompenaars, F 1993, *Riding the waves of culture: Understanding cultural diversity in business*, The Economist Books, London.

Tunnicliffe, J 2004, 'Canada and the Human Rights Framework', *Historiographical Trends*, vol. 12, no. 10, pp. 807-817.

Twiss, J 2019, Buckle up, we're in for a wild ride', *Shellbrook Chronicle*, 9 May, p. 4.

United States Bureau of International Commerce 1974, *Trade Mission: A Handbook for Trade Mission Members*, vol. 57, no. 67.

Valls, J 2010, 'What is left of the country brand?' *Paradigmes*, no. 5, pp. 34-65, viewed 29 March 2014, <http://www.raco.cat/index.php/Paradigmes/article/viewFile/219018/299415>.

van Bergeijk, PAG, Fortanier, F, Garretsen, H, de Groot, HLF & Moons, SJV 2011, 'Productivity and Internationalisation: A Micro-Data Approach', De Economist, vol. 159, pp. 381-388. https://doi.org/10.1007/s10645-011-9175-4

van Bergeijk, PAG & Moons, S 2009, 'Economic Diplomacy and Economic Security', in Carla Guapo Costa, (ed). *New Frontiers for Economic Diplomacy*. Lisboa: Instituto Superior de Ciéncias Sociais e Politicas, pp. 37-54, https://ssrn.com/abstract=1436584.

van Biesebroeck, J., Yu, E., and Chen, S. Sep 2011, 'The impact of trade promotion services on Canadian exporter performance', viewed 6 April 2015, <http://www.international.gc.ca/economist-economiste/assets/pdfs/research/_tpr_2010/chapter5-eng.pdf>, pp. 145-190>.

van Ham, P 2001, 'The rise of the brand state: The postmodern politics of image and reputation', *Foreign Affairs*, vol. 80, no. 5, pp. 2-6.

Vitell, SJ and Festervand, TA 1987, 'Business ethics: Conflicts, practices and beliefs of industrial executives' *Journal of Business Ethics*, vol. 6 no. 2, pp. 111-122.

Waddington, S 2015, *Chartered Public Relations: Lessons from Expert Practitioners*, Kogan Page, London, UK.

Wadhva, CD & Woo, YP (eds.) 2005, *Asian Regionalism, Canadian and Indian Perspectives*, APH Publishing Corp., Delhi, India.

Walker, H 2013, *A Genealogy of equality: The curriculum of social education and training*, Routledge, Abingdon-on-Thames, UK.

Walsh, K 1994, 'Marketing and public sector management', *European Journal of Marketing*, vol. 28, no. 3, pp. 63-71.

Wandell, T 2001, 'The Power of discourse: Michel Foucault and critical theory', *Cultural Values*, vol. 5, no. 3, pp. 368-382.

Watson, T & Noble, P 2007, *Evaluating Public Relations: A Best Practice Guide to Public Relations Planning, Research & Evaluation*, Kogan Page, London, UK.

Webb, C & Wood, B 2009, 'Barbarian invasions: Canadian immigration and the dynamics of global migration', *Canadian Dimension*, vol. 43, no. 5, pp. 24-27.

Weiss, JW 2006, *Business ethics: A stakeholder and issues management approach*, 4th edn, Thomson/South-Western, Mason, OH.

Welch, L S, Benito, G R G, & Peterson, B.2008, *Foreign Operation Methods: Theory, Analysis, Strategy*, Edward Elgar Publishing, Cheltenham, UK.

Welch, LS & Luostarinen, R 1988, 'Internationalisation: Evolution of a concept', *Journal of General Management*, vol. 14, no. 2, pp. 34-55.

'Welcome to Canada: We take care of business', *Government of Canada*, viewed 7 August 2011, <http://publications.gc.ca/site/eng/9.651962/publication.html>.

Wetherell, M, Taylor, S and Yates, S 2001, *Discourse theory and practice: A reader*, Sage, London, UK.

White, SK 1986, 'Foucault's challenge to critical theory', *American Political Science Review*, vol. 80, no. 2, pp. 419-432.

Wijaya, BS 2012, 'The Development of Hierarchy of Effects Model in Advertising', *International Research Model in Advertising*, vol. 5, no. 1, pp. 73-85.

Wilkinson, T and Brouthers, LE 2006, 'Trade promotion and SME export performance', *International Business Review*, vol. 15, no. 3, pp. 233-252.

Willson, K & Howard, J 2000, *Missing Links: The Effects of Health Care Privatisation on Women in Manitoba & Saskatchewan*, Prairie Women's Health Centre of Excellence, Winnipeg, MB.

Wilson-Smith, A 1994. 'A Slippery Slope (Canada's relationship with China on trade and human rights issues)', *Maclean's*, vol. 107, no. 15, p. 20, http://link.galegroup.com/apps/doc/A15111475/UHIC?u=csudh&sid=UHIC&xid=6f55b8b.

Wolf, G 2013, 'Trade missions', *Alaska Business Monthly*, vol. 29, no. 2, p. 24.

Yazdannik, A, Yousefy, A & Mohammadi, S 2017, 'Discourse analysis: A useful methodology for health-care system researches', *Journal of Education and Health Promotion*, vol. 6, p. 111. https://www.ncbi.nlm.nih.gov/pmc/articles/PMC5747223/

Young, S 1996, 'Ontario launches trade missions: Delegations sent to Texas, California to promote investment', *The Globe and Mail*, 04 Sep, p. B4.

Zuidema, L and Ruel, H 2012, 'The effectiveness of commercial diplomacy: A survey among embassies and consulates', in Ruel, H (ed.), *Commercial diplomacy and international business: A conceptual and empirical exploration (advanced series in management, volume 9)*, Emerald Group Publishing, Bingley, UK, pp. 105-140.

Appendix 1: Newspaper Articles & Team Canada Trade Missions Archive Sources for Thematic Analysis

Bibliography

Alberts, S 1999, 'PM pushes high-tech goods despite word that Japan's recession will continue', *National Post*, 5 Sep, p. A7.

Alberts, S 1999, 'China's show of pique', *Toronto Star*, 04 Dec, p. A22.

Anonymous 1998, 'Do your homework', *Canadian Business*, vol. 71, no. 4, p. S5.

Anonymous 1998, 'Team Canada Fosters Teamwork', *Canadian Business*, vol. 7, no. 4, p. S4.

Anonymous 2011, 'Team Canada a winning idea', *Toronto Star*, 02 Aug, p. A18.

'A team divided: Canadian politicians on trade mission in Germany/Russia', 2002, *Maclean's*, 4 Mar, p. 16.

'Attending: Keith Peiris (student joins Team Canada 2001 trip' 2001, *Maclean's*, 15 Jan, p. 9, viewed 18 August, 2011, <http://link.galegroup.com/apps/doc/A69075876/AONE?u=csudh&sid=AONE&xid=89c01851>.

Aubry, J 2000, 'Premiers slowly warming up to February trade mission: Only Klein likely to say no', *National Post*, 27 Dec, p. A4.

Aubry, J 2000, 'Team Canada – brought to you by...Corporate sponsorships for upcoming trade missions', *Star-Phoenix*, 4 Aug, p. A7.

Banch, H 2005, 'Former PM's wife handpicked trinkets for trade missions, inquiry told', *CanWest News*, 05 May, p. 1.

Barlow, M & Clarke, T 2002, 'Taking to the streets {Global Showdown: how the new activists are fighting corporate rule}', *Our Times*, vol 21, no. 3, pp. 35, 37.

Baxter, J 2002, 'The Chrétien government plans to push for...', *CanWest News*, 3 Sep, p. 1.

Baxter, J & Gamble, D 2002, 'Prime Minister Jean Chrétien is warning developed nations to be prepared for peacekeeping missions like East Timor even though Canadians troops will...', *CanWest News*, 16 Sep, p. 1.

Beauchesne, E 1998, 'The government is now in better financial...' *CanWest News*, 12 July, p. 1.

Beauchesne, E 1998, 'The government's Team Canada trade missions are...', *CanWest News*, 20 May, p. 1.

Beltrame, J 1994, 'Human rights activists are calling on Canada....', *CanWest News*, 06 Dec, p. 1.

Blanchfield, M 2002, 'Prime Minister Jean Chrétien may want to...', *CanWest News*, 09 Feb, p. 1.

Branswell, H 1998, 'Executives defend presence of MPs', *The Medicine Hat News*, 22 May, p. 22.

Brown, J 2000, 'Sponsorship questioned', *Brandon Sun*, 4 Aug, p. 4.

Bryden, J 2001, 'Prime Minister Jean Chrétien blasted the unit', *CanWest News*, 01 Sep, p. 1.

Bryden, J 2001, 'With Prime Minister Jean Chrétien poised to...', *CanWest News*, 17 July, p. 1.

'Buchard joins team Canada' 1997, *Panama City News Herald*, 08 Jan, p. 14.

Calleja, D 2004, 'Jean's help: priceless', *Canadian Business*, vol. 77, no. 4, p. 10.

'Canadian leader to head trade mission to China' 1994, *Los Angeles Times*, 3 Nov, vol. 113, p. D5.

Carmichael, K 1999, 'Free trade debate cooled, not quelled', *Medicine Hat News*, 02 Jan, p. 11.

Chetauti, V 1998, 'Small is big news in exporting!', *Maclean's*, vol. 111, no. 11, pp. SS1-SS2.

Cernetig, M 1999, 'China likes Canada, but is that enough?' The Globe and Mail, 13 April, p. A1, p. A12.

Chapnick, A 2008-09, 'The Golden Age: A Canadian foreign policy paradox', *International Journal*, p. 205.

Cheadle, B 1998, 'Team Canada Trae Figures try to fudge facts', *Brandon Sun*, 23 Jan, p. 16.

Cheadle, B 1998, 'PM plugs Pan Am Games at stop in Brazilian mall', *Winnipeg Free Press*, 18 Jan, p. 6.

'Chrétien defends European trade mission' 2002, *Medicine Hat News*, 20 Feb, p. 24.

'Chrétien in Europe' 1998, *Maclean's*, 1 June, vol. 111, no. 3, p. 32.

Chrétien, J 'Poverty and corruption seen as more world-threatening than Iraq', *Canadian Speeches*, vol. 16, no. 5, p. 36-39.

Chrétien, J 2003, 'Canada poised to take its place as a world leader', *Canadian Speeches*, vol. 16, no. 6, p. 42-47.

'Chrétien leads trade mission to China' 1996, *Panama City News Herald*, 09 Jan, p. 19.

'Chrétien meets with young activist' 1996, *Medicine Hat News*, 16 Jan, p. A10.

'Chrétien stresses that he is still the boss' 2002, *CTV News*, 22 Aug, p. n/a.

'Chrétien to lead western premiers on southern U.S. trade trip' 2001, *Brandon Sun*, 24 Nov, p. A7.

'Chrétien's team reminded about human rights' 1996, *Medicine Hat News*, 08 Jan, p. A10.

Clarke, D 1998, 'On the road with Team Canada', *Canadian Banker*, vol. 105, no. 4, pp. 26-29.

Clayton, M 1996, 'When political winds blow cold in Canada, try travel (PM Jean Chrétien on trade mission to Asia)', *The Christian Science Monitor*, vol. 88, no. 32, p. 7.

Cooper, AF 2012, 'Canada's engagement with the Americas in comparative perspective: Between declaratory thickness and operational thinness', *International Journal*, p. 685-701.

Corcoran, T 2001, 'Falling Trade, Photo-op Dragon', *National Post*, 8 Feb, p. C18.

'Corporate actions abroad win institute's praise: Team Canada trade missions criticised [1998 report from North-South Institute]', *Daily Commercial News & Construction News*, vol. 71, no. 101, p. B1.

'Corporate sponsorship of Team Canada Trade mission questioned' 2000, *Expositor*, 04 Aug, p. A8.

Cosh, C 2002, 'The Ugly Canadian (Jean Chrétien & the trade mission to Germany), *Report Newsmagazine* (Alberta Edition), 18 Mar, vol. 29, no. 6, p. 4.

Cox, B 1994, 'Team Canada's score elusive', *Winnipeg Free Press*, 13 Nov, p. 16.

Cox, B 1996, 'Businesses helping young could receive tax breaks', *Medicine Hat News*, 15 July, p. A10.

Cox, B 1996, 'Cabinet shuffle next for Chrétien, *Brandon Sun*, 20 Jan, p. 6.

Cox, W 1996, 'Young people now a Liberal cause celebre', *Brandon Sun*, 17 July, p. 12.

Cox, W 1996, 'Liberals focusing on Generation X', *Winnipeg Free Press*, 17 July, p. A3.

Crane, D 1997, 'Another high-tech winner in CAE', *Toronto Star*, 13 Apr, p. E2.

Crane, D 2000, 'Chrétien and G8 leaders ignore real issues', *Toronto Star*, p. E02.

Curren, R 1998, 'Manning defends international jaunt', *Medicine Hat News,* 21 July, p. A9.

Curry, B 2003, 'A key architect of Jean Chrétien's proposed aboriginal policies in the 1993 Liberal Red Book says the prime minister's 10 years in power have left a legacy of 'betrayal and broken promises' for Canada's First Nations', *CanWest News*, 10 July, p. 1.

Dugas, D 1997, 'Chrétien leads Team Canada to Asia', *Brandon Sun*, 8 Jan, p. 4.

Edison, S 1999, 'Canadian business boasts $409 million in Japan deals; But mission can't make up losses in overall trade with ailing nation', *Toronto Star*, 17 Sep, p. 1.

'Election results please labour' 1995, *Shelbrook Chronicles*, 27 June, p. 5.

Ferguson, J 1996, 'Bay St. applauds shuffle of cabinet. Says best news is that Martin stays in Finance', *Toronto Star*, 26 Jan, p. C1.

Fife, R 2002, 'Putin jumps gun with $1B trade announcement: Upstages Chrétien: Canada must increase pace of investment, Russian leader says', *National Post*, 15 Feb, p. A10.

Fife, R 2000, 'U.S. ambassador criticises missions by Team Canada: Better for Business to visit Southern U.S., Griffin says', *National Post*, 24 May, p. A4.

Foster, P 2001, 'Child labour is OK if you're the CEO', *National Post*, 10 Jan, p. C15.

Francis, D 2002, 'Russian follies', *Sudbury Star*, 29 April, p. A6.

Francis, D 2002, 'Team Canada trade mission are really photo-ops', *CanWest News*, 28 April, p. 1.

'Free trade deal sought for countries of Western Hemisphere' 1998, *The Toronto Star*, 14 April, p. C4.

Fulton, EK 1996, 'Mixed signals: The Liberals' Throne Speech – issues a call for a new domestic Team Canada', *Maclean's*, 11 Mar, vol. 109, no. 11, p. 22.

Gamble, D 1999, 'Money, not sovereignty, will motivate Bouchard: Pettigrew', *National Post*, 10 Sep, p. A7.

Gamble, D 1999, 'The Japanese frenzy for snack food now....', *CanWest News*, 14 Sep, p. 1.

Gamble, D 1999, 'Payette to help Team Canada's image: Trip to Japan to focus on Canada's high-technology aerospace expertise', *National Post*, p. A7.

Gamble, D 1999, 'Prime Minister Jean Chrétien's Team Canada trade...', *CanWest News*, 16 Sep, p. 1.

Gamble, D 1999, 'Quebec Premier Lucien Bouchard , says he's united', *CanWest News*, 12 Sep, p. 1.

Geffen, GD, 2000, 'Ambassador is a team player', *National Post*, 27 May, p. B11.

Gherson, G 1997, 'Jean Chrétien's Team Canada trade mission', *CanWest News*, 09 Jan, p. 1.

Goar, C 2011, 'Anti-poverty success airbrushed out', *Toronto Star*, 12 Jan, . A17.

Grallz, P 2001, 'Keeping Kids Off Streets', 7 May, www.eweek.com.

'Great expectations: PM off to Beijing' 1994, *The Lethbridge Herald*, 4 Nov, p. 4.

Hunter, J 1998, 'Trade deal snaps', *The Medicine Hat News*, 19 Jan, p. 1.

Iftody, D 1995, 'Keeping the commitment to small business', *The Carillon*, 6 Dec., p. 5A.

Iftody, D 1997, 'Team Canada: promoting Canada abroad to create jobs at home', *The Carillon*, 10 Feb, p. 5A.

Iftody, D 1996, 'The liberal government at work for Canadian youth', *The Carillon*, 14 Aug, p. 5.

Ivison, J 2016, 'Chinese trade deal could boost exports by nearly half: study', *The Windsor Star*, 02 Jan, p. 4.

Israelson, D 1996, 'Jobs linked to trade missions; would be worse without trips, Eggleton says', *Toronto Star*, 06 July, p. F3.

Jack, I 1999, 'Pettigrew vows to link social issues with trade', *National Post*, 10 Sep, p. C08.

Janigan, M 2001, 'Mission Critical: Team Canada sets off for China amid doubts about Ottawa's trade road shows', *Maclean's*, 5 Feb, p. 30.

Janigan, M 2004, 'The New Road Show', *Maclean's*, vol. 117, no. 48, p. 18.

'Japan: Chrétien meets up with Team Canada', 1999, *Asahi Shimbun*, 14 Sep, p. ASAH7220973.

'Jeans maker to sew up deal?' PM's trade trip may ease tough sale' 1997, *Winnipeg Free Press*, 6 Jan, p. B3.

Johnstone, B 1998, 'Saskatchewan exporters heavy hitters on Team Canada', *Saskatchewan Sterling Network*, 13 Jan, p. C4.

Keenan, K 2010, 'Canadian Mining: Still unacceptable', *NACLA Report on the Americas*, p. 29-34.

Kennedy, M 2003, 'Paul Martin: A politician who defies definition, and inspires great expectations', *CanWest News*, 15 Nov, p. 1.

Kilgour, D 2002, 'The 'Asianification' of Canada', *National Post*, 31 July, p. FP15.

'Klein's timing suddenly not so impressive' 2002, *Brandon Sun*, 17 Feb, p. A4.

Kuxhaus, D 1998, 'Chrétien joining the team. Brazil, Canada sign pledge of more human-rights protection' *Winnipeg Free Press*, 16 Jan, p. 13.

Lalonde, K 1998, 'No reason to laud trade mission', *The Carillon*, 26 Jun, p. 7A.

Lalonde, K 1998, 'Liberal lack business skills', *Stonewall Argus & Teulon Times*, 1 June, p. 5.

Laxar, J 1993, 'Chrétien must show he can restore real government', *Toronto Star*, 02 Sep, p. B3.

Laxar, J 1995, "'Populist' Chrétien implements big business agenda', *Toronto Star*, 01 Oct, p. D3.

'Let's help Mexico boost smaller firms' 1998, *Toronto Star*, 24 June, p. 1.

Lett, D 1997, 'Axworthy's Cuban gamble', *Winnipeg Free Press*, 26 Jan, p. 5.

Libin, K 2009, 'Maybe they should stay home', *Financial Post Magazine*, Dec, p. 21.

'Look ahead' 2003, *National Post*, 24 Mar, p. FP2.

MacDonald, J 1996, 'Klein absence hurt Alberta', 22 Jan, *Medicine Hat News*, p. A6.

MacLeod, S 1998, 'Travel bug is malady of all prime ministers', *Brandon Sun*, 9 June, p.4 6.

MacLeod, S 1996, 'Do Big Corporations have souls', *Brandon Sun*, 15 March, p. 4.

MacQueen, K 1996, 'Speech long on security, short on hope', *Medicine Hat News*, 28 Feb, p. 12.

Manning, P 2007, 'As Canadian as possible under the circumstances', *Winnipeg Free Press*, 12 Sep, p. A3.

Manthorpe, J 1994, 'Prime Minister Jean Chrétien said today his...', *CanWest News*, 17 Nov, p. 1.

Markusoff, KM 2018, 'Alberta's best frenemy', *Maclean's*, 1 June, p. 1.

Marotte, B 1994, 'Big trade missions won't always work: China made 'Team Canada' trip unique, members say', *Toronto Star*, 29 Nov, p. C5.

McGovern, P 2000, 'Go, Team Canada', *National Post*, 06 Aug, p. A19.

McKie, P 2001, 'Trade missions: more wheel than deal?' *Winnipeg Free Press*, 18 Feb, p. 4.

McMurdy, D 1996, 'Mission Impossible: group tours may be fun, but the economic benefits of trade missions are questionable', *Maclean's*, 15 Jan, vol. 109, no. 3, p. 32.

McNeil, M 2002, 'Student realises dream trip to Asia', *Winnipeg Free Press*, 2 Aug, p. B4.

Mertl, S 2002, 'Asia-Pacific region is still important to Canada, says David Kilgour', *Canadian Press Newswire*, 14 Nov, p. n/a.

Mihychuk, M 2003, 'Trade missions made money', *Brandon Sun*, 17 Jan, p. 4.

'Mission in Asia' 1996, *Maclean's*, 15 Jan, vol. 109, no. 3, p. 15.

Moore, T 1996, 'Mining Indonesian gold', *Winnipeg Free Press*, 13 Dec, p. A16.

Mosher, J 1996, 'Business urged to eye export markets', *The Interlake Spectator*, 16 Sep, p. 12.
Mosher, J 1996, 'Business urged to embrace exports', *The Selkirk Journal*, 16 Sep, p. 11.

Nankivell, N 1999, 'Overlooking Australia a mistake – Team Canada missing chance to foster proven trade relationship', *National Post*, 09 Sep, p. C07.

O'Neil, J 1998, 'Economic turmoil in Russia have prompted the…' *CanWest News*, 08 Oct, p. 1.

Ortman, D 1997, 'Double standards: the Canadian government talks trade and whispers human rights everywhere in the world except Cuba', *Briarpatch*, vol. 26, no. 2, p. 32.

Panetta, A 2003, 'Chrétien says China still needs rights work', *Winnipeg Free Press*, 24 Oct, p. A20.

Panetta, A 2003, 'Team Canada missions bound for scrap heap?', *Winnipeg Free Press*, 24 Oct, p. 21.

'PM, business officials embark on Asian mission' 1996, *Winnipeg Free Press*, 09 Jan, p. 45.

'PM speaks to city politicians' 1996, *The Medicine Hat News*, 03 Jun, p. 2.

'Promoting Canada: The prime minister travels the world looking for deals' 1996, *The Lethbridge Herald*, p. 33.

Robertson, B 1997, 'Trade pact opens doors for exporters', *Winnipeg Free Press*, 1 Feb, p. 27.

Ross, DA 1996/1997, 'Canada and the world at risk: depression, war and isolationism for the 21st century? *International Journal*, vol. 52 no. 1, p. 1.

'Russian turmoil likely won't stop Team Canada's trade mission', *The Lethbridge Herald*, 29 Aug, p. A6.

Samyn, P 2001, 'Power deals on tap?', *Winnipeg Free Press*, 27 Jun, p. 20.

Sato, M 1999, 'Ottawa to stress high-tech trade: Trade mission targets First World economies', *National Post*, 28 July, p. C6.

'Scold S. Korea, PM told: Push worker rights, trade mission urged', 1997, *Winnipeg Free Press*, 09 Jan, p. 18.

Sebastianelli, P 2002, Review of 'Taking to the Streets: Global Showdown; How the New Activists are Fighting Corporate Rule; By Maude Barlow & Tony Clarke', *Our Times*, vol. 21, no. 3, p. 35.

Seguin, R 1997, 'Smaller firms cash in on trade mission – Canadian group opens doors for businesses seeking opportunities in S. Korea, Thailand & the Philippines', *The Globe and Mail*, p. B3.

Sheppard, R 1994, 'Chrétien should let Parizeau stay home', *Brandon Sun*, 8 Oct, p. 34.

Simpson, J 2010, 'Canadian Foreign Policy: Time for a Revolution', *Queen's Quarterly*, vol. 117, no. 1, p. 56.

Speirs, R 1996, 'What is this nation's foreign policy anyway?' *Brandon Sun*, 16 Dec, p. 4.

Stevens, G 1001, 'Why Chrétien may not get chance to lose an election', *Toronto Star*, 01 Dec, p. B3.

Stock, P 2002, 'Chrétien's ethical blind spots', *The Report Newsmagazine*, 18 Nov, p. 27.

Sumi, C 1996, 'While Prime Minister Jean Chrétien is quick...' *CanWest News*, 19 June, p. 1.

Sutel, S 1996, 'Economic growth leaves many behind: report', *Medicine Hat News*, 15 July, p. A10.

Taber, J 1999, 'Talking tough about trade', *The Ottawa Citizen*, 09 Jan, p. B3.

'Talking trade and rights in Asia' 1996, *Toronto Star*, 07 Jan, p. F2.

'Team Canada begins trade mission to Asia', 1996, *The Lethbridge Herald*, 9 Jan, p. A5.

'Team Canada descends on China' 2001, *Maclean's*, 19 Feb, p. 43.

'Team Canada off to Asia' 1997, *The Medicine Hat News*, 08 Jan, p. A10.

'Team Canada trade missions' 2004, *National Post*, 01 Jan, p. 13.

'Team Canada trade mission and panel discussion', 1997, *Sunday Report-CBC Television*, Jan 12.

'Team Canada trade missions stalled' 2000, *The Lethbridge Herald*, 24 Oct, p. A4.

'The Bottom Line: More Exporters, More deals', *Canadian Business*, vol. 71, no. 4, p. S8.

Thompson, A 2000, ' 'Team Africa' to boost trade; 200 officials seek business links', *Toronto Star*, 05 May, p. E04.

'Top-level trade mission means business – Jean Chrétien leads group of entrepreneurs in bid to forge commercial partnerships with Hong Kong companies' 2001, *South China Morning Post*, 16 Feb, p. SCMP15185199.

Toulin, A 2001, 'Business opposes call for Timor sanctions. Inappropriate response; Would just hurt Indonesia workers, Bata warns', *National Post*, 4 Sep, p. B3.

Toulin, A 2001, 'Foreign investment, training key to promises: Research and development', *National Post*, 31 Jan, p. A9.

'Trade key factor in our prosperity' 2000, *The Lethbridge Herald*, 20 April.

'Trade missions unearth export opportunities for Canada' 1997, *The Lethbridge Herald*, 6 Jan, p. B4.

Trickey, M 2002, 'Prime Minister Jean Chrétien May Want to...', *CanWest News*, 09 Feb, p. 1.

Urquhart, J 1998, 'Canada reports GDP rise of 3.8% on strong exports', *Wall Street Journal*, Eastern Edition, 03 March, p. C15.

'US focus hurts trade with Asia' 2002, *Winnipeg Free Press*, 15 Nov, p. 34.

Veldhuis, N & Clemens, J 2016, 'Why Waste a Budget? Trudeau Should Learn from Chrétien and Martin', 18 March, <www.fraserinstitute.org>.

Warren, P 1997, 'Country of Origin tag should be mandatory', *The Russell Banner*, Aug 19, p. 6.

Wilson-Smith, A 1996, 'Bonding in the air (Team Canada's January 1996 Asian tour)', *Maclean's*, vol. 109, no. 4, p. 12.

Wilson-Smith, A 1996, 'Dealing in goodwill', *Maclean's*, vol. 109, no. 5, 29 Jan, p. 10-12.

Wilson-Smith, A 1996, 'On the road: Team Canada tries to score business and political points', *Maclean's*, vol. 109, no. 4, 29 Jan, p. 10.

Wilson-Smith, A 1996, 'The China deal', *Maclean's*, vol. 107, no. 47, 21 Nov, p. 14.

Wood, N 2003, 'Talking up the team', *Maclean's*, 02 Aug, vol. 106, no. 31, p. 14.

Yaffe, B 1998, 'Chrétien quite good at globetrotting', *Medicine Hat News*, 17 April, p. 23.

Young, S 1996, 'Ontario launches trade missions: Delegations sent to Texas, California to promote investment', *The Globe and Mail*, 04 Sep, p. B4.

Yuen, PW 2000, 'Canada playing catch-up in Asia', *National Post Business*, 1 Feb, p. C7.

Appendix 2: Thematic Analysis (Primary Codes)

2.1 TCTM PARTICIPANTS

- Important to get out there and be seen.
- Be patient.
- It takes time to establish customers in other countries.
- Market is tough in the U.S. but not in other parts of the world.
- Consulting in conjunction with local counterparts.
- Helped establish more than 3,500 micro-enterprises headed by women.
- Placed more than 100 young Canadians in challenging internships.
- Involved in the social needs of the communities where it operates.
- 1700 employees there enjoy one of the best health-and-safety benefits packages in the country.
- Helping to solve the growing global problem of harmful exhaust emissions.
- Won a $15 million contract to treat municipal waste water and sewer overflows during storms in Jefferson County, Alabama.
- Joined forces to form a formidable consortium offering expertise found in very few places in the world.
- Serve as cultural ambassadors.
- Over the past two years, the company's exports have tripled and now account for 93 percent of total revenue.
- Exports account for 85 percent of income – performed more than 800 times in 200 cities worldwide.
- Ensures that logistics are made as seamless as possible for clients.
- Donate a portion of its profit to the Seagull Foundation.
- Provide hundreds of jobs to summer students and seasonal workers.
- Formed alliances with key international players in the financial, processing and payment engine industries.
- Global relationships help build export capabilities to enter large markets in the U.S., Europe and Asia.
- Serving clients in more than 70 countries around the world.

- Governments around the world depend on company's market-leading security solutions.
- Has more than 2000 clients in some 40 countries.
- Company's solutions are now used by more than 300 financial institutions around the world.
- Export about 40 percent of their production to distributors in the U.S. and 20 percent to markets in Europe, Australia, the Pacific Rim countries, and even Africa.
- Over the past five years, the company's sales have risen dramatically, due in part to its international activities.
- Most effective means of promotion is word of mouth.
- Do considerable business through e-commerce.
- A key component in the company's exporting strategy...is attending international trade shows.
- Canadian snowboards have an excellent reputation worldwide.
- Company's components are used around the world in all kinds of winter sports gear.
- Had to find new clients in other parts of the world.
- First sale of $800 000 worth...was followed by further projects.
- Our approach is to work with local organisations rather than set up an office abroad.
- About 90 percent of sales is generated b exports worldwide – primarily to Russia.
- Exports more than 85 percent of its production.
- Canada is at the forefront of this technology.
- Developing and closing prospects typically takes up to two years.
- Company is already setting up distributorship arrangements in Russia.
- We are known as the best in the world in what we do.
- TCTM will help us connect with people we would not have access to.
- Highly specialised so we have no competition from Germany or Europe.

- Fully 95 percent of sales are generated by exports to the U.S., Europe, Australia, Japan, and Taiwan.
- Products are battle-proven by customers all over the world.
- Looking to secure new distribution channels.
- Among the best – won medals at four competitions.
- Repeat participant, signed a distribution deal in Hong Kong; doors opened to negotiations in mainland China.
- Joined TCTM to Moscow in order to meet with government officials.
- With the help of local agents and Canadian embassy staff, began a massive promotional campaign.
- 2002 – signed a memorandum of understanding worth $200,000 for the sale of 25,000 bottles of wine in Germany.
- Approximately 32 percent of annual production is exported to more than 40 countries on five continents.
- Already has a presence in Russia and participated in the Team Canada mission to Moscow to gain a better understanding of the market.
- By joining TCTM, we can develop our network of contacts.
- Company well-established in Russian participated in TCTM to highlight the potential for Russia/Canadian cooperation in agriculture and agri-food.
- To explore or seal new trade relations in India.
- About 98 percent of the company's sales are generated by exports – mainly to the United States.
- Team Canada opened doors / excellent opportunity to gain additional market credibility.
- Still capitalising on the contacts made through the TCTM.
- Meeting the political and private-sector elite in other countries is not only important for export success – it is essential.
- Team Canada is the best way to get the job done (meeting political and private-sector elite).

- From contacts developed through TCTM 1996, opened a Global Development Centre in India.
- TC showcased technology opportunities in India / allowed us to establish significantly more contacts there than we would have been able to generate on our own.
- TCTM provide a well-organised opportunity to make valuable contacts within the country.
- Firms in exploration mode looking for business opportunities benefit from association with other business people by discussing best business practices and forging business ties.
- We have a couple of contacts in India with whom we will be discussing strategic alliances to distribute our products.
- Participated in the Team Canada West trade mission / agreement was signed to supply ceramic paint to a North Hollywood-based franchiser.
- Renowned clients include Disney, Warner Bros. and DreamWorks.
- Sold over $15 million in equipment to India since the Team Canada 199 trade mission
- Signed a partnership agreement.
- Established a number of new business contacts.
- Joining upcoming TCTM to increase opportunities / to gain more exposure.
- Canada's Trade Commissioners consistently provide very useful contacts and advice.
- The greatest potential for growth rests in overseas markets.
- Canada is way ahead of the competition in mining industry technologies.
- Enthusiastic participant in several Team Canada trade missions.
- Company's objective was simply to establish its credibility.
- Team Canada has helped us achieve our goal and more.
- Several promising contacts established.
- Upcoming trade mission will help to forge agreements for new and expansion projects.

- These trips are very useful…They provide us with a larger profile and open many high-level doors.
- Company's leading edge technology is already helping law enforcement agencies in more than 26 countries worldwide.
- Participation in the trade mission will help speed up negotiations.
- Commercial attaché staff have always been available when we needed them
- Results varied for participants.
- Biggest advantage – profile.
- Cynicism can be fueled by announcements that fizzle.
- Trade mission was essential for closing the deal.
- Memorandum of understanding helped move the deal along.
- Needed to understand cultural and business differences.
- Cost of TCTM participant - $10,000 (considered a bargain).
- Signing contracts with premiers around generated excitement among foreign distributors.
- TCTM gives credibility.
- Some deals fell through.
- Signed $1.5 million agreement for distribution network in Latin America; will create 30 new jobs.
- You've got to be prepared before you go.
- Premiers/Prime Minister set the stage: business have to make them pay off.
- You learn from those who have been there, done that.
- Will make a deal for $5 million to $10 million with Japanese partners at a TCTM ceremony in Tokyo.
- If you come with the Prime minister, the red carpet is out and you meet the right people and that's good P.R..
- Having our leaders standing on stage with us, as one unified group, speaks very powerfully. It saved us maybe six to nine months of confidence building.
- The whole idea of a locker room atmosphere that gest developed when you get outside the country and the camaraderie and those things are every much here.

- Advice from 3X participant in TCTM: start by networking in Canada. Talk or meet with experienced exporters that do business in your target country. Their knowledge and experience can help you avoid common pitfalls or costly ventures.
- You need to be aware of the risks before you can reap the benefits of exporting.

2.2 MEDIA REPORTS

- Canadian government signed bilateral agreement with Brazil to deal with human rights (poor children).
- TCTM a key part in attracting foreign investment.
- 1990s - Chrétien unable to comment on China's human rights / By 2003, able to comment freely on Human Rights in China.
- Prime Minister Chrétien gave speech on Human Rights in Beijing University.
- Canadian justices consulting with Chinese judges for judicial reform in China.
- 12 day trip (Malaysia, Indonesia); $8.7 billion in agreements.
- Education has become a big part of Team Canada.
- Real potential for education to sell around the world.
- 1989-99 Canadian universities hosted 35,000 foreign students; Canadian colleges hosted 17,000 students.
- Canada has criticised Cuba's human rights record / Supported UN Resolution 1994/1995/1996.
- Youth should be included in TCTM.
- New England and Atlantic Trade missions generated an estimated $50 million in direct contacts and follow-up sales.
- Negotiations often begin before the trade mission.
- TCTM strengthens the social/working relationships of the Prime Minister and premiers.
- TCTM are affordable for small businesses.
- TCTM signed 27 pacts worth $7.5 million Canadian (if they all come to fruition).
- Deals to be signed: environmental products, telecommunications, and infrastructure supplies.
- 1998 – 300 business deals worth $ 2 billion Canadian in contracts.
- 1998 – Trade between Canada and China went up.
- TC for national image building abroad.
- Potentially thousands of jobs created from TCTM.
- TCTMs – highly, visible, public relations.

- TCTMs has an important role but is' not the prime role; the work has to be done by the companies.
- Participants are highly enthusiastic.
- Optics necessary to make an impression in Asia.
- Canada needs more trade with Asia to reduce dependence on U.S..
- Need for free trade with Asian countries (87% of Canada's trade is with U.S. / only 5% across Pacific).
- Image of Canada – nice holiday destination.
- We have to do more to persuade people that we're a high tech advanced industrial economy.
- Need for corporate sponsorship of youth to join TCTMs / nurture the next generation
- German image of Canada is quaint.
- Canadians can provide state of the art equipment and technology, not just metals, logs, and other unrefined resources.
- Canada is trying to diversify.
- 200 Canadian companies sponsored Junior Team Canada trade missions to China and the Philippines.
- In 2000, 56% of students studying in Canada come from the Asia-Pacific area
- China releases *Falun gong* member connected to Canada.
- Boycott of production in which child labour had been used is misguided; led to children being put out of the factory and into less desirable occupations such as prostitution.
- TC meant to impress.
- Government and corporate heavyweights on display.
- 1998: Mission to Latin America saw a record 306 deals valued at $1.78 billion signed by more than 140 companies.
- The latest mission has paid diplomatic dividends.
- SMEs stole the show (Mexico, Brazil, Argentina, Chile); $3.3 billion of Canada's exports in 1996.

- 80% of the 532 businesspeople were SMEs.
- Canadian banks handle more than 2,000 transactions worth $800 million from the 4 countries visited.
- Mission to Latin America had the largest representation of Canadian universities and schools.
- During the last TC trip to Latin America, the Bank of Nova Scotia purchased Banco Quilmes in Argentina for US$57 million.
- NorthStar Finance signed 19 loans ($180 million) to SME exporters.
- The political presence helped TCC to seal deals to supply both Brazil and Mexico with 40,000 TELE translators, devices that automatically provide Spanish subtitles for English news and television shows.
- Somewhat stagy but tried and true TC approach.
- Of the 75 business deals signed in South Korea by 51 businesses and government organisations, half were by small businesses employing fewer than 100 people.
- SMEs have become an important part of the equation in Canada's export trade.
- On TM trip – At various times, the premiers, either individually or as a group, broached subjects with the prime minister.
- The Prime Minister, who turned 62 during the trip, often appeared tired by the grueling pace of 15-hour days.
- In Indonesia, Chrétien raised concerns about East Timor (1996).
- Although much of the legwork on potential contracts is done well before Team Canada arrives business leaders are unanimous in their opinion that showing up with the prime minister always helps close a deal.
- The federal government has insisted that bringing along a large contingent of MPs of Italian descent, Canada has been getting noticed.
- One of the objectives of the current trip is reversing the imbalance in trade between the two countries, currently running two-to-one in Italy's favour.
- 1996 – The human rights aspects have had a higher profile in recent days.

- Canada, which exports more than one-third of what it produces, is now in the big leagues of trade promotion, joining such countries as Germany, France and Japan in sending delegates of businesspeople and politicians abroad.
- Canadian-made clothing enjoys a good reputation in Asia, which is beginning to import luxury goods not available at home.
- The $10,000 TCTM participation fee is a bargain; jeans manufacturing company with 60 people.
- The benefits from TC are more than just contacts abroad. The trade mission also helped to build new business relationships among Canadian companies.
- The image of Canada that still springs to mind for most Chinese is that of the happy homeland of Dr. Norman Bethune, with big mountains, giant trees and sky-high taxes.
- Business consultant: There's no doubt that everybody in China likes Canada. But I'm not sure they care about Canada. And I'm not sure they really know what we're about these days.
- The Chinese pay a lot of attention to political seniority. Doors open to a Prime Minister that would not open to a premier or cabinet minister.
- Centralised authorities approve power sector decision in China. And [TCTM participant] believes it will be far easier to meet those authorities when he is tagging along with PM Jean Chrétien.
- TCTM has become Ottawa's key weapon to pry open doors for timid Canadian exporters.

2.3 MEDIA CRITIQUE OF TEAM CANADA TRADE MISSIONS
- The large delegations sent on TCTM may be a sign of incompetence.
- TCTM signing ceremony merely ceremonial, not impressive.
- Some deals falls through.
- Canadian mining operations in Mexico violate human rights.
- Rich countries like Canada are less willing to share their wealth with the world's poor.
- Progress on debt relief very slow.
- G8 has good goals but provide no funding.
- Jean Chrétien's flying circus, aka Team Canada.
- Team Canada junket.
- 1997 – in last 5 years, Canadian trade to the U.S. doubled (81%).
- Market share in the rest of the world falling.
- Of the five countries Chrétien led trade missions to, five actually bought less from Canada in the first ten months of 1996 than they did in the same period of 1995.
- Overall record of TCTMs may not be all that positive.
- There's great photo-ops.
- Deals already in the can (by the time the trade mission takes place).
- Optics are important: It's about looking like you're creating jobs as much as creating them.
- There are a lot of memorandums that won't be realised.
- Politicians may not be all that good at pitching Canada's business.
- TCTMs backfire – we began importing more products from countries targeted by trade missions.
- Leaving the prime minister and his front bench at home won't hurt a bit.
- Feds obligated to tell businesses about pitfalls in Russia.
- TCTM : photo-ops for the Liberals.
- PM has led TCTM to dangerous places (e.g. Russia) / irresponsible / shakedowns, bribery.
- Japan's images of Canada are the Rockies and polar bears.

- Principal sponsors pay $50,000 to participate in TCTMs – fear that payment will give privileged access to government.
- Bank of Montreal and Canada Post paid $50,000 to be named premier sponsors.
- Top level sponsorships offer high-profile place on the mission's website and promo material plus access to top-level bureaucrats.
- Two top sponsors get a seat on Prime Minister's plane plus full page ad in the tour guide.
- You almost get the feeling that small business need not apply.
- Trade mission cancelled because too many premiers dropped out – Chrétien considered their presence essential to his TC concept.
- The focus should be solely on commerce, rather than being blurred by the complexities of Canadian federal-provincial relations.
- New PM (Chrétien' successor Martin) likely to ground TC in favour of more effective measures.
- Since 1995, exports to visited overseas nations have declined by 14%.
- Army of corporate executives, favour-seekers and hangers-on searching for investment and trade deals.
- 1994 deal announcements worth $8.6 billion / actual statistics never lived up to box office claims.
- Canada's exports to China dropped even lower after 1995, from $3.4 billion to $2.5 billion in each of the following three years.
- Despite hype about technology, most Canadian shipments to China are resource products (pulp, grains, raw materials, fertiliser) / For this we need trade missions?
- The only thing booming is China's record exports of higher-level manufacturing goods to Canada.
- Three sponsors of TCTMs are government corporations.
- TCTM delegates include hundreds – low-budget bureaucrats, government dependents and officials from corporations receiving government assistance to enter China.

- Bunch of premiers jockeying for photo-ops.
- "business delegation" includes Algonquin and Lakeshore Catholic School District of Napanee, Ontario.
- Why the fixation with China?
- China: Human and property rights don't exist.
- China: laws and regulations are arbitrary and randomly enforced.
- China has the largest total official debt outstanding to Canada, $2.4 billion.
- Canada sends more foreign aid to China than to any other country - $103 million in 1998-99, with the occasional exception of Bangladesh.
- The entire aid and subsidy operations may well exceed the trade and investment activity.
- In Japan, there's a traditional stereotypical image of Canada: a provider of coal, Anne of Green Gables.
- 1995 – Canadian exports to Japan fell by 25% to $8.6 billion due to economic upheavals in Japan.
- Child labour is okay as long as you claim to be a CEO; Keith Paris, 12-year-old joining Team Canada trade missions.
- Has it occurred to anybody at TC that what they are taking along to China is a child labourer?
- Many deals had been in the works before the media and politicians showed up for the signing ceremonies.
- Prime Minister is actually subverting Canadian values abroad with its aggressive and unqualified promotion of trade.
- TCTM serve the public relations needs of politicians and participating firms; they have not translated into greatly increased trade.
- TCTMs have led to a downplaying of environmental, security, human rights and democracy.
- The Liberals are not only failing to export Canadian values, they're importing antidemocratic values, such as pepper-spraying protesters.

- Canadian International Development Agency and Export Development Corporation place few restrictions on Canadian firms receiving taxpayer help.
- It seems that Prime Minister Chrétien has spent a highly-impressive $12.2 million on travel since assuming office in 1993.
- Despite Mr. Chrétien's much-touted Team Canada trade missions to drum up business, Canadian exports to China have been dropping dramatically (1999). Last year, they totaled $2.145 billion, compared with almost $3 billion in 1996. China's exports to Canada, meanwhile, are soaring - $7.65 billion last year versus $4.92 billion in 1996.
- Asked in the House of Commons just why Canada had agreed to suspend its own environmental assessment rules to facilitate a $4 billion nuclear reactor sale to China, Axworthy said, "When we sell abroad, we abide by the rules abroad.'
- TCTMs – has government-inflated trade figures.

2.4 CANADIAN GOVERNMENT

- Chrétien: Worked from 7 am to 11 pm while on TCTM.
- Premiers from smaller provinces want more trade missions.
- Premiers have a sense of unity while travelling abroad.
- Trumpeting Manitoba's hydroelectricity rates to U.S. companies.
- 1997 – Human rights problems are being resolved.
- Team Canada Director responds to notion of sponsorship being unsavory:
  - Sponsorships started in 1994.
  - Sponsorships follow Treasure Board guidelines.
  - TCTM conducted on a cost-recovery basis.
  - Companies pay their way.
  - Sponsorships help to minimise public expenditure.
  - Sponsorships subsidise cost for smaller companies to participate in Team Canada Trade Missions.
  - Six levels of sponsorship available depending on size.
- Prime Minister Chrétien: We're competing with other countries / We have to fight.
- Asia-Pacific has been a priority.
- Trade has become the engine driving Canada's economy.
- Exports account for 37% of Canada's GDP.
- Canadian companies must be made aware of opportunities.
- Focus on youth, tech, and trade.
- Promoting Canadian products to encourage job creation at home.
- TCTM promote Canadian products with expertise.
- Canada is well established as a trading nation.
- Canada needs to be aggressive.
- Canadians should discard the modesty that so typifies our approach to challenge us.
- Economic policy and social policy are linked.
- Government works closely with the provinces.

- Need for continued dialogue and trade ties with repressive regimes.
- Engagement is better than non-engagement.
- Chrétien will push for improved human rights when he goes to China.
- Canada has advanced technology (Japan).
- Business seminars help trade mission participants.
- Goal is to expose small and medium-sized enterprise (SMEs) to export markets.
- Nearly 3/4s of the mission participants are SMEs.
- Premier of Nova Scotia – needs to examine whether there's merit to Nova Scotian taxpayers for premier to take time away from government to participate in TCTMs.
- Trade missions to boost exports.
- Team Canada mission yields $8.6 billion in deals; although 70% are mere agreements in principle.
- 1999 – focus of TC to Japan is high technology and aerospace technology.
- Team Canada TM success can't be measured only by the value of the deals signed.
- Team Canada is more than just contracts; it's about raising profile and creating opportunities for Canadian firms and establishing a long-term business presence.
- We're trying to underscore high technology and innovation as Canadian capabilities.
- Trade Minister: It's the smaller companies that can really benefit from these missions.
- Foreign Minister: We had to kick trade into high gear, and thank God we did.
- Trade Minister: Exports now account for 43% of Canada's GDP (Year 2000).
- Because small business creates most of the jobs in Canada, we are helping them to get financing, to use technology and t export to new market so they can grow and hire people.
- PM Chrétien: People who are together for two weeks do a lot of business among themselves.

- Canadian ambassador to China: What I'm trying to do is change our image from a clean and pretty country with Norman Bethune to one that offers some of the best technologies in the world.
- Canadian ambassador to China: We don't get a lot of profile in the China Daily.
- PM Jean Chrétien: For us, what is important is not the amount of money; it's the number of contracts we have signed.

2.5 LABOUR UNION
- Canadian Labour Congress president Bob White – urged Chrétien to speak out against South Korea law.

2.6 THINK TANKS

- **Asia Pacific Foundation**: more trade deals with Asia needed to reduce dependence on the U.S..
- 87% of Canadian exports go to the U.S.; only 5% crosses the Pacific.
- **Council of Canadians:** Maude Barlow – sovereign governments are being rendered powerless by multinational agreements.
- **Council of Canadians** – Urging Prime Minister to make human rights and especially Mexico's treatment of Mayan Indians a key issue.
- **Council of Canadians** – Maude Barlow: Multinationals take advantage of deregulation – 'these powerful organisations show disregard for human welfare.'
- **Council of Canadians** – Maude Barlow: cheap labour rules countries try to attract business by lowering wages and ditching human rights.
- Canadian Chamber of Commerce: Need partnership between the private sector and government.
- Canadian companies pressure foreign governments, e.g., Kristine Fernandez.
- **Asia Pacific Foundation** – trade mission to corrupt country is irresponsible.
- **Asia Pacific Foundation** – Canada is becoming important to Asia.
- **North-South Institute** – TCTMs are morally and commercially bankrupt ventures that undermine Canadian values abroad while adding nothing to the economy's bottom line.
- **North-South Institute** – foreign investment has now supplanted foreign aid as a source of development funds and that it can be used as a lever to encourage human rights and democratic reforms.
- **North-South Institute** – It's hard for a high profile mission headed by senior politicians to bring up issues such as human rights in a public way that will embarrass their hosts and themselves.
- **North-South Institute** – Canada gets zero benefits from the trip / nobody in their right minds except the airlines would defend the trade mission.
- **North-South Institute** – Canada's trade with the fastest growing markets has been declining as a share both of our total exports and of their total imports.

- **North-South Institute** – Canada's trade dependence on the U.S. continues to grow.
- **North-South Institute** – It's more the failure of the politicians to promote Canadian values on human rights, democracy, and the environment … that bothers the institute.
- **North-South Institute – 1994** – TC members avoided virtually any mention of human rights. Environmental considerations were set aside in the signing of deals to participate in China's Three Gorges Dam project and in preparation for the sale of CANDU reactors.
- **Canadian Federation of Independent Business** – On high sponsorship fees – It does sort of perpetuate the perception that big bucks from big corporations leads to big political contacts.

2.7 NPOS

- **East Timor Alert Network** (human rights advocacy group) – Canadian government should impose military and economic sanctions against Indonesia.
- **East Timor Alert Network** – wants the TCTM to encourage Japan, Indonesia's largest donor, to cut its economic aid.
- Business groups, e.g., Bata, reject the call for economic sanctions
- **Free the Children**: Thirteen-year-old activist Craig Kielburger dogs mission, draws attention to child labour abuse; Kielburger asked PM Chrétien not to forget about the exploitation of Asian children after the TCTM is over.
- **Free the Children** – made up on young people between nine and 16, sent half a dozen of its youthful members to Pearson Airport to remind Chrétien's business team about concerns over child labour.

2.8 BUSINESS GROUPS

- **Canadian Federation of Independent Business** – ironic that Ottawa and the provinces appeared to work so well together in Asia but can't agree on binging down all interprovincial trade barriers back home.
- **Canadian Federation of Independent Business -** $50,000 sponsorship – You almost get the feeling that small business need not apply.
- **Saskatchewan Trade and Export Partnership (STEP)** – TCTM gives you a fairly high profile very quickly.
- **CEO of Norex**: - Chrétien leading sheep to slaughter.
- Tim Reid – **Canadian Chamber of Commerce** – a large delegation to Latin America is not useful because the state does not play as big a role in the economy.
- 85,000 SMEs can't even expand to next-door provinces.
- North American Congress on Latin America (NACLA): Canadian mining operations in Latin America cause significant environment damage, social disruption, generate conflict with and among local communities (Guatemala/El Salvador).

2.9 ACADEMICS

- Professor / policy : Big hit to China useful because 'economy is controlled by the government.'
- 'You really do need as many Canadian government officials as you can get.'
- There's a role for government to assist Canadian business.
- Professor – unfair to ask companies to take on the role of international bodies and institutions in making countries respect human rights.

2.10 CITIZENS

- Skeptical of loan granted by Canada to China: Will it be paid back?
- Need for stricter post-mortems after Team Canada Trade Missions.
- Canada lent money to China to buy Canadian reactors; if they don't pay back, Canadian taxpayers on the hook.
- Potential loans to Romania (Canada subsidising governments of other countries).
- Canadian government lacks business sense.
- The only benefit of TM is to large corporations, not Canadian citizens.
- Canadian banks are being used for overseas corporate expansion (Export Development Bank loans to business - $1.5 billion).
- Loans to Asian countries to buy Canadian products // Asian crisis – if they don't pay?
- Corporate profits are replacing human values.

2.11 GOVERNMENT OPPOSITION

- I have always been concerned that the TC mission are a boon for lobbyists and companies seeking access to government decision makers.
- TC is wasteful.
- Of the 15 countries targeted by TC missions eleven actually saw reduced purchases of Canadian goods and services in the year following the missions.
- The Reform Party has slammed Prime Minister Chrétien for running up a $12 million foreign travel bill since he took office (1993-1998 figures).

2.12 US AMBASSADOR TO CANADA

- Team Canada missions have been a success.
- TC should send a mission to southern U.S. states.

Appendix 3: Email Survey Letter to Expert Panel of Canadian Business/Management/Economics Academics

September 1, 2012

Attention:

Subject: Expert Panel View on Criteria for Judgment of the Success of Trade Missions
Name of project: A Discourse Analysis Approach to Examining the Canadian Government's Support of Export-Oriented Canadian Companies in a period of Global Transformation.

My name is Everett Ofori, and I am a Canadian citizen. I am conducting research as part of my Doctorate in Business Administration (DBA) at Southern Cross University, through distance studies. While the bulk of the research has been completed additional guidance from experts like you is needed for triangulation purposes.

Questions:
1) What do you think are/were the criteria for success of the Team Canada Trade Missions (1994-2005)?
2) Why do you think the Team Canada Trade Missions were curtailed in 2005?
3) In your view, of what value, if any, are trade missions?
4) In your view, should Team Canada Trade Missions be reinstated?

As the researcher it will be my responsibility to analyse all the information received from participants and to uncover any patterns that can extend the knowledge of the research community, policy makers, and the business community regarding this important phase of Canadian business history. This research has been approved on an expedited basis because it does not pose any risks to participants, who are of course, completely free to determine the amount of information they want to include. All information obtained will be held in the strictest confidence and no names of individuals or companies will be divulged in the final reports unless you give your permission for identifying information to be published or disclosed. The results obtained from this research will first be presented in a doctoral thesis and subsequently presented in book form for the benefit of a wider audience. If you so desire, a copy of any reports arising from this research will be made available to you. Thanks in anticipation.

Everett Ofori, MBA

Mailing address: Takarazuka University of Art and Design, Tokyo Campus Building 1F, Suite 123 (MBE), 7-11-1 Nishi Shinjuku, Shinjuku-ku, Tokyo, Japan 160-0023.
Tel: 81-80-6683-6262

Email address: **everettofori@gmail.com (Kindly respond to my email address)**

Inquiries

The ethical aspects of this study have been approved by the Southern Cross University Human Research Ethics Committee. The Approval Number is ECN-09-010. If you have any complaints or reservations about any ethical aspect of your participation in this research, you may contact the Committee through the Ethics Complaints Officer, Neroli Sheldon, (telephone (07) 55069230, email: ethics.tweed@scu.edu.au). Any complaint you make will be treated in confidence and investigated, and you will be informed of the outcome. Alternatively, you may write to the following address if you have concerns about the **ethical conduct** of the research, the following procedure should occur.

Write to the following: The Ethics Complaints Officer, Southern Cross University, PO Box 157, Lismore, NSW 2480

ethics.tweed@scu.edu.au / All information is confidential and will be handled as soon as possible.

Appendix 4: Raw Responses from Expert Panel involved in Email Interview

R = Respondent

	Question 1: What do you think are/were the criteria for success of the Team Canada Trade Missions?
R 1	Frankly, I have no idea. I suspect that there may have been criteria...personnel or companies/associations/countries who participated. I could assume that a similar dynamic might be evident with bilateral trade agreements – some initial success criteria but no disciplined tracking – perhaps other than gross economic indicators.
R 2	From what I remember the media reported number of trade deals/contracts/memorandums of understanding and total dollar value of these.
R 3	It appears to me that the real success was for a concentrated effort by Canada, its departments and the private sector to go out and sell the products of the company. While what was reported in Canada was the value of the contracts, it was probably more important to be seen as Canada being open for business. I know for example that many contracts and contacts really happened after the missions were finished.
R 4	Criteria for success: contracts signed, contacts made, potential contracts
R 5	My only comment is that to identify a clear role for trade missions and the role of government in trade, you would have to see an externality or information failure so that the private traders miss opportunities for trade that are created with the intervention of government. My guess is that this is not the norm. Most private entrepreneurs are quite good at identifying foreign sources for purchases and foreign opportunities for sales. So my guess is most government to industry trade is about capturing rents or getting the taxpayer to absorb risks that the private company does not want to absorb – for example the Export Development Corporation.
R 6	I think when CEOs join the Prime Minister on trade missions, it bestows an aura of credibility. It opens doors more quickly, since you get quickly acquainted with many people in the foreign country. The rest – is political stuff. Prime Ministers bragging how many contracts were signed, etc., which is silly. Obviously those contracts were negotiated a long time. It's fluff and the numbers irrelevant.
R 7	I don't know

R 8	The criteria of success for the trade missions would have been twofold: First, building linkages between the countries in order to enhance country to country trade relations; secondly, supporting specific trade deals between Canadian businesses and overseas government/businesses.
R 9	The prime minister, Jean Chrétien, was a strong supporter of the initial trade missions to China. In addition to leading the missions personally which gave great prestige to them, he also set both Industry Canada and External Affairs Commercial strong goals to support the trade mission objectives. I was involved with the industry Canada side primarily. Industry Canada commissioned researchers knowledgeable, for example re China, to write materials for practitioners explaining the cultural differences and how to deal with them practically. In addition, Prime Minister Chrétien worked cooperatively with the Canada China Business Council which functioned essentially as a trade association for Canadian companies entering or considering entering the China market. At one point, Prime Minister Chrétien and President Jiang both attended a CCBC meeting in Toronto that I attended. All of this support helped Canadian companies feel more secure about trying to build trade relationships with Chinese counterparts. CIDA and the Canada Export Development Corporation provided mechanisms for securing the financing of deals as well. So I hope this shows that there was a strong collaborative and cooperative effort between government, trade associations, and private enterprise supported at the highest levels of government. Everything was done to facilitate the building of trade relationships between private companies and foreign counterparts. Now, a weakness of this approach was that from time to time the geographical focus shifted. One year the focus was on China. Another year it was on Latin America. Likely it would have been more effective to have continued with Chia, and perhaps India.
R10	# contracts signed and $value
R11	- raising Canadian profile in China - increase/enhance trade - overall trade makes splash - long term/exporting emphasis on trade missions → where to consummate documents (e.g. signing ceremonies) presence of leaders encouraged deals with greater impetus on ……

	Question 2: Why do you think the Team Canada Trade Missions were curtailed in 2005?
R 1	There was no demonstrable political benefit after the change in government and yet there was a visible cost that could be presented to the public as an expense that could be cut. There may also be affinities with senior public servants who were supportive but whose allegiances were with the previous government. Thus a change in elected government, to a group who had no real knowledge of the longer-term values and with no verifiable benefits, cancelled the program in favour of visible public support for cutting what were perceived and unnecessary costs.
R 2	The Conservative party took power in 2006 and has remained in power ever since. Trade missions do not appear to be on their political agenda.
R 3	I'm not sure why they were curtailed. I believe it may have been the cost and the view of the public that companies were being subsidised by the government. I personally don't believe that.
R 4	Curtailed in 2005: change of government, benefits not justifying the costs
R 5	
R 6	
R 7	I don't know
R 8	The Trade Missions were curtailed because of the amount of effort and costs that were involved. I suspect there was a general decline in interest in the business community for launching these endeavours.
R 9	This date approximately coincides with the defeat of the Liberal administration and the commencement of the Conservative. I think it was clear that the Conservative government supported stronger trade relationships with the United States and were less committed to Asia and Prime Minister Harper seemed to develop a cool relationship on the subject of China. Here it was speculated that he was trying to gain favour with Chinese ethnic voters who were not supporters of the PRC government. And there were legal/extradition issues between the two countries with Canada refusing to extradite individuals considered criminals in China and vice versa.
R10	Liberal government ran into political trouble and subsequently lost power. Conservative government had other priorities.

R11	Reason – Prime Minister Jean Chrétien was the originator of the concept there was an impression that the trade missions were associated with Jean Chrétien / Successor did not see it as helping to establish his own new imprint / Dissatisfaction by participants / Novelty wore off (not seen as productive) / Weariness on the part of provincial premiers and business (lots of time and effort) / Dates for trade missions often announced without consultation with premiers / Involved massive logistics (burdensome)

	Question 3: In your view, of what value, if any, are trade missions?
1R 1	The biggest value may be in providing common experience in simultaneously educating civil servants, industry leaders and elected officials in what various other countries are doing and where there might be mutual opportunities and challenges. The, (sic) in designing and developing subsequent government-sponsored programs to support and stimulate industry sectors/products, at least the three decision-making groups would have had some common exposure and experience on which to base their program design decisions. (They don't need to argue as much about who has the right perspective.)
2R 2	- Political→looks as though the government is 'doing something' - Helps to establish a social and economic network between Canada and countries that are or are potential strategic trading partners - the dollar value of trade deals is a 'selling point' however, I have not seen any reports that conclusively demonstrate the long-term value - in a recent paper entitled Do Trade Missions Increase Trade? (Heady and Riesz, (sic) 2009) the authors found no long-term impact on Canada's trade after trade missions
3R 3	The biggest value is showing outsiders that Canada as a whole is open for business and allowing potential trading partners to see the many options here.
R 4	Value of missions: focus on exports, encouraging Canadians to think of exports, high profile of visits to foreign countries both in Canada and in the countries visited
R 5	
R 6	I think when CEOs join the Prime Minister on trade missions, it bestows an aura of credibility. It opens doors more quickly, since you get quickly acquainted with many people in the foreign country. The rest – is political stuff: Prime Ministers bragging how many contracts were signed etc., which is silly. Obviously those contracts were negotiated for a long time. It's fluff and the numbers irrelevant.
R 7	They are of very limited value, to the best of my knowledge
R 8	The trade missions provided a platform for provincial and private sector firms to engage with overseas interests
R 9	The bulk of Canadian trade is with the United States. I assume this is the case because it is considered easier, less risky, and there is less cultural distance. The problem is that this makes Canada very depended on American economic realities and American political influence. A major politic value of trade missions is to reduce Canadian trade dependence on the US.

	A second value is that when missions are supported at a high level, as Mr. Chrétien used to do, it attracts the attention of the foreign government and corporations because it is evident that this is not just a passing fancy and that the Canadians are serious about building real trade relationships, the Canadian corporations attending missions are more likely to find serious counterparts with whom business may be discussed. Thirdly, a (sic) when the government's agencies support the process, there is a strong effort to help relatively risk averse Canadian companies to build the knowledge needed to reduce the uncertainty of venturing into a relatively unfamiliar market.
R10	Limited unless political agreements are in place ahead of time. Then trade mission can provide an opportunity for grandstanding. Not much use otherwise.
R11	- Effective where government involvement is seen as having value - Business with government is unfavourable/unnecessary to have government as partner - Others might say there is a cachet associated with trade with official involvement - Effective in cases where businesses are new to export - Lots of team work needed to be done - Lots of ground work needed - TCTM cumbersome/should be more targeted/identify a particular jurisdiction/requires spending time to identify right sectors, companies, audiences

	Question 4: In your view, should Team Canada Trade Missions be reinstated?
1R 1	Not unless there is some agree management/governance framework for determining the value received – in a circumspect way. This would include direct benefits to both industry and government (financial return over time), social benefits (better understanding/appreciation of Canada's role in international development), and longer-term international relationship benefits (educational, cultural, social programs like health and poverty management, etc., and the potential risks like exposure to intellectual property abuses, unreasonable erosion of our natural resources, etc. As a country, we do need to appreciate that the investment of time, money and expertise is worth it.
R 2	It is difficult to measure the value of the enhanced 'network' owing to a trade mission. Presumably, the effects would be felt within about 5 years (hopefully it would show up in the trade statistics) But this has not been supported) (see Heady and Riesz (sic) 2009). So in light of the evidence, I would say 'no'
3R 3	I believe that they should be reinstated. If people forget about you they don't deal with you. Again optics and perception matter.
R 4	Reinstatement: if benefits justify the costs
R 5	
R 6	
R 7	In the absence of a compelling business case, I would say no. Before going on one, I thick a compelling business should be complete and made public.
R 8	I am unsure about the need to re-instate the missions. Have you given any thought about the term 'Team Canada'? Among those who are in the baby-boom generation, this was the name of the Hockey Team that defeated the Soviets in the early 1970s, and continues to be the name of our hockey reams. It resonates strongly in the political culture here.
R 9	Yes, but only if it is taken on as a political/economic priority by the Prime Minister's Office. And trade missions should be established on an ongoing basis mainly with major trading partners, or potential partners in the emerging markets. So that would include the United States and the EU. It would also include China, India, Brazil, and Russia.
R 10	Gov't needs to do its homework with China, India, and South America. Once this is done, trade missions might become worthwhile
R 11	- No, not the model that existed

	-	A modified version
	-	Learn from it and use it to form a new model
	-	Large multisectoral trade mission does not make sense

About the Author

Everett Ofori teaches Marketing, Management, Negotiation, and English for Specific Purposes (English Conversation, Medical English, Public Speaking, Business Writing, Medical Writing, etc.). Everett has conducted lessons or designed curricula for the following organizations.

- Accenture
- Actelion
- Ageo Central Medical College, Saitama, Japan
- Amazon Web Services (AWS)
- Asahi Kasei
- Asahi Soft Drink Research, Moriya
- AXA
- Bandai
- Barclays
- Becton Dickinson
- Boston Consulting
- Chugai
- Coca Cola
- Deutsche Bank
- Disney Japan
- ExxonMobil
- Fujitsu
- Goldman Sachs
- Gore
- Gyao
- Hitachi Automotive
- Hitachi Design
- IIJ (Internet Initiative Japan)
- ING
- Johnson & Johnson (Janssen)
- JP Morgan
- JVC Kenwood
- Kistler
- Marubun
- McKinsey Japan
- Mitsubishi (Shoji)
- Mizuho Bank
- Moody's
- National Institute of Land and Infrastructure Management, Tsukuba, Japan (NILIM)
- Nomura
- Orix
- PriceWaterhouseCoopers
- Quest
- Rakuten
- Recruit
- Reinsurance Group of America (RGA - Japan)
- Sekizenkai Nursing School, Shimosoga, Kanagawa • Sumitomo
- Summit Agro International
- Suntory
- Tokyo International Business College, Asakusabashi, Tokyo
- Toyohashi University of Science and Technology
- Yokogawa Meters and Instruments
- Yokohama Child Welfare Vocational College (Hoiku Fukushi), Higashi Totsuka, Kanagawa

Notes

Notes

Notes

Notes

Notes

www.ingramcontent.com/pod-product-compliance
Lightning Source LLC
Chambersburg PA
CBHW081345080526
44588CB00016B/2378